# AS Drama and Theatre Studies
# Study Guide

*Edexcel*

## Max Harvey and Nigel Williams

D1103371

# R·

Rhinegold Education

239–241 Shaftesbury Avenue
London WC2H 8TF
Telephone: 020 7333 1720
Fax: 020 7333 1765
www.rhinegold.co.uk

**Rhinegold Drama and Theatre Studies Study Guides**

AS and A2 Drama and Theatre Studies Study Guides (AQA and Edexcel)

**Rhinegold Performance Studies Study Guides**

AS and A2 Performance Studies Study Guides (OCR)

**Other Rhinegold Study Guides**

GCSE, AS and A2 Music Study Guides (AQA, Edexcel and OCR)
GCSE, AS and A2 Music Listening Tests (AQA, Edexcel and OCR)
AS and A2 Music Technology Study Guide (Edexcel)

Rhinegold Publishing also publishes Classical Music, Classroom Music, Early Music Today, Music Teacher, Opera Now, Piano, Teaching Drama, The Singer, British and International Music Yearbook, British Performing Arts Yearbook, Rhinegold Guide to Music Education, Rhinegold Dictionary of Music in Sound.

First published 2004. Second edition published 2008 in Great Britain by
Rhinegold Publishing Ltd
241 Shaftesbury Avenue
London WC2H 8TF
Telephone: 020 7333 1720
Fax: 020 7333 1765
www.rhinegold.co.uk
© Rhinegold Publishing Ltd 2008

You should always check the current requirements of the examination, since these may change. Copies of the Edexcel Specification may be obtained from Edexcel Publications, Adamsway, Mansfield, Notts, NG18 4FN.

Telephone: 01623 467 467, Fax: 01623 450 481, Email: publications@linneydirect.com

See also the Edexcel website at www.edexcel.org.uk

**Edexcel AS Drama and Theatre Studies Study Guide**

British Library Cataloguing in Publication Data.
*A catalogue record for this book is available from the British Library.*

ISBN 978-1-906178-37-6

Printed in Great Britain by Headley Brothers Ltd

# Contents

## The authors

**Max Harvey** was head of drama at Wellsway School for nine years before becoming director of sixth form. He has been responsible for establishing drama within the school's curriculum and developing schemes of work and assessment structures for all key stages. He studied drama at Exeter University before completing his teacher training at Bretton Hall. Max has worked in an advisory capacity for the education department of the Theatre Royal Bath and is on the board of directors. More recently, he has contributed to books on the role of citizenship within the school curriculum and has acted as a consultant for *Teaching Drama* magazine.

**Nigel Williams** has been director of drama at Gordonstoun School for seven years. He has been teaching drama and theatre for 20 years in a variety of schools ranging from an inner-city comprehensive to a rural upper school. Nigel trained at Bristol University and St Paul's teacher-training college in Cheltenham, and he studied drama in education at Leicester University. He also trained in mime and physical theatre at the London City Institute. He has directed numerous school productions and as director of Bedfordshire Youth Theatre between 1986 and 1996, he commissioned and produced new plays as well as traditional, contemporary and musical texts. He was an Associated Examining Board examiner for A-level Theatre Studies for eight years and was a team leader for Edexcel on AS Drama and Theatre Studies. He has also been responsible for the in-service training of drama teachers in Bedfordshire.

## Acknowledgements

In the writing of a guide such as this many people have contributed. The authors and publishers are grateful to the following people for their specific advice, support and expert contributions: Nicola Harvey, Laura Hobbs, Lucien Jenkins, Sarah Jones, John Nicol, Alan Perks, Harriet Power, Andrew Psirides, Ben Robbins, Ginny Spooner and Rose Vickridge. The authors are also conscious of having drawn on a lifetime's reading. More recently, the growth in use of the internet has made an unparalleled amount of exciting information and challenging opinion widely available. Although every attempt has been made to acknowledge both the primary and secondary sources drawn on, it is impossible to do justice to the full range of material that has shaped the creation of this book. The authors would therefore like to apologise if anyone's work has not been properly acknowledged. They would be happy to hear from authors and publishers so that any such errors or omissions may be rectified in future editions.

# Introduction

**Personal response**

You will have chosen to study Drama and Theatre Studies at AS level because you have a keen interest in certain elements of the theatrical process. Whether you have been involved as an actor, designer, director or audience member, you will have started to form opinions on what you like and dislike. This **personal response** is vital if you are going to succeed. You need to learn to trust your instinct while developing your understanding of theatre through performance, observation and research.

This guide offers extra help with your Edexcel AS Drama and Theatre Studies course; it is not a substitute for what your teachers have to offer. It will take you through the various elements of the course and explain the requirements of each unit, identifying what the examiners are looking for, while offering advice and suggestions for practical activities.

**Teamwork**

The majority of the work will rely on you working closely with other members of your class. You will need to be open and honest, while recognising the importance of compromising your individual ideas in order to ensure group success. Throughout the book, we shall be offering ideas for practical work for you to experiment with in lessons. These exercises will enable you to recognise each person's strengths and allow you to learn from one another. In drama and theatre studies, the end result is dependent on the work of the whole group. In order to be successful you will need to work well as a team. All theatres rely on this philosophy.

**The theatrical process**

As you study drama, you will gain an improved understanding of the potential of the written text. You will encounter several different plays which may be from a range of genres, and you will learn how to interpret the words in performance and evaluate their possible impact on an audience. In this guide, there is advice on how to approach specific plays, but many of these ideas can be applied to any text from any period. By drawing comparisons to other theatrical practitioners you will develop a command of production techniques. By using the suggested tasks as a starting point for your own work, pursuing some of the ideas for wider reading and getting excited by the possibilities of live theatre, you will gain an excellent foundation for tackling all aspects of the course.

## The AS modules

### Unit 1: Exploration of Drama and Theatre (40%)

This unit has three methods of assessment. For the first two, you will be required to study **two different plays**. You will be taught about the original performance conditions and the concepts that influenced the playwrights. You will look closely at the structure of each play and the different techniques that are used to create meaning. By finding other plays, directors or theatre companies that have influenced or been influenced by the plays you are studying you will gain a wider understanding of their social, cultural, historical and political context.

Your understanding of the texts should be reinforced through **workshops**, which will enable you to understand their dramatic potential. You will record your investigations in a portfolio, called your **exploration notes**. These notes may include drawings and diagrams, as well as written work. Your teacher will be assessing your contribution throughout the workshops and you will be given a separate mark for your practical and written responses.

> Your exploration notes should be no longer than 3,000 words. See page 51.

The third aspect will be in the form of a **written evaluation of live theatre**. The production you see could be one of the texts you have already studied or a different play. Your response will look at the play in performance. Your thoughts on the performers, designers and directors need to be organised with appropriate examples to illustrate your ideas. In addition to this, you should consider the context in which the play was originally performed and its effectiveness as a contemporary production.

> Your evaluation should be no longer than 1,000 words. See page 97.

## Unit 2: Theatre Text in Performance (60%)

During this unit you will be assessed in two different aspects of production:

> **Section A** focuses on the performance or design skills needed for a **monologue or duologue** that you have chosen

> **Section B** also focuses on performance or design skills but this time the text will be an entire **play**.

> The play will be chosen by your teacher.

The scripts may be similar in style to those studied in Unit 1, or they may be from another genre. If you opt for **performing**, you will be marked on your acting ability. You will need to think about how you can create a role that will reflect your dramatic skill and understanding. Section A requires you to communicate your own interpretation of the text whereas in Section B you will be directed by your teacher. While they will give you advice on how to develop your character successfully, the responsibility for both performances lies with you. You will need to document your understanding in a 500-word written concept.

Alternatively, you could focus on **design** skills, opting for one or more of the following areas: lighting, set and props, costume, mask, make-up and sound. Each skill should be supported by a portfolio of evidence and a final design linked to the play being performed.

> An external examiner will visit your school or college and assess your contribution. They are not able to make comments or give any feedback while they are with you.

The two separate sections in Unit 2 mean that it is possible for you to focus on performance in one section and design in the other.

# Understanding Theatre

## What is this chapter for?

One of the many exciting aspects of theatre is its variety. The evolution of formal performance during the last 2,500 years has led to an incredible array of performance styles. The joy of this AS-level course is that you are free to explore as many of these styles as you wish. Of course, there are guidelines that will be set by both the examination board and your teacher, but within these there is real freedom for exploration.

The main focus of the course is on practical understanding. You will be assessed either on your performance or design skills, and your ability to analyse and reflect on the work of others. Therefore, it is important that you have a sound understanding of different theatre styles and the work of key practitioners.

It would be impossible to outline or even attempt to define each of the dramatic styles that have ever existed within the context of this book, nor will you be expected to refer to them all in any of the assessment tasks. The aim of this chapter is to encourage you to develop an interest in theatre, and to consider how any performance has been influenced by other plays, practitioners or events in the world.

You will not be examined directly on the information in this chapter concerning the early history of theatre, key practitioners and design ideas; rather, you should use it as a way in to the course and as a point of reference as you progress through the modules. Experiment with the ideas practically and spend time researching those that you find most interesting; this will enable you to create your own understanding of theatre which will help you to respond to tasks in a confident and informed way.

## A brief history of early theatre

### Theatre in ancient Greece

**Origins in festival**

The religious festivals of the ancient Greeks featured dramatic performances, which were intended as worshipful acts to gods, and in which western theatre as we know it originated. Many Greek plays have survived and some of the most famous playwrights of that time are still performed today, such as Aeschylus, Sophocles, Euripides and Aristophanes. Their plays were performed during the Dionysia, a festival held in Athens in honour of Dionysus, the god of wine, agriculture and theatre. Each playwright put on four performances; the first three were serious in content, while the fourth was a comic satyr play.

Satyr plays should not be confused with satires: they were lighthearted performances which foregrounded themes of merriment, drinking and sexuality, and featured a chorus of satyrs (deities of the woods and mountains).

Most ancient Greek plays were based on mythology or history and dealt with individuals' search for the meaning of life and the true nature of the gods. The plays were predominantly tragic in nature. The word 'tragedy' probably originates from the Greek words *tragos* ('goat') and *aeidein* ('to sing') – 'goatsong' – which is thought to be a reference to the sacrificial goats offered to Dionysus at the festivals. Most surviving plays from the period begin with a prologue which gives the audience an exposition to the following action. The chorus then typically introduces a section called the parados, a dialogue between the chorus and the solo actor, during which introductions to characters are made, exposition given and mood established. The final scene is known as the exodus, when all the characters, as well as the chorus, depart. This structure influenced much subsequent dramatic writing, including that of Shakespeare.

**Plays**

Parados was originally the corridor or gangway through which the chorus entered.

In early Greek theatre, the roles of director and writer in each play were fulfilled by the same person. As the plays developed, however, more actors were allowed on stage and three actors became the normal cast size. Because of the limited number of actors allowed on stage, the chorus evolved into a very active part of Greek theatre. Although it is unclear how many actors there would have been in the chorus, it was given as much as half the total lines of the play. The chorus was used as a mirror to the action of the play and reacted to it as the playwright hoped the audience would. Words, sound, movement and music were used to set the mood and heighten the drama, and the chorus even interacted with the characters and action of the play. This established the convention of the narrator and commentator which is used in some modern theatre, such as *Blood Brothers* (1983) and *Road* (1987).

**Chorus**

No women appeared on stage, female roles being played by men, and violence was very rarely directly dramatised. Murders, suicides, self-harm, executions and fatal accidents took place off stage, and the dead body was then brought on stage, the death being described, rather than shown to the audience. Shakespeare uses this technique when dramatising the deaths of characters such as Duncan in *Macbeth* and Ophelia in *Hamlet*.

According to legend, Greek tragedy was created by a man named Thespis (from whom the term 'thespian' derives). It was claimed that Thespis was the first person to act on stage in a play (or to appear separately from the chorus) and that he introduced a new dramatic style, in which one singer or actor performs the words of individual characters in a story, distinguishing between the various characters by use of masks.

**Thespis**

**Aeschylus** wrote some of the oldest tragedies in the world and the introduction of the second actor to the stage is attributed to him. His plays include *The Persians* and the *Oresteia* trilogy.

**Dramatists**

**Sophocles** introduced the third actor to the stage, fixed the number of chorus members to 15 and was the first to use scene painting. His plays include *Antigone*, *Electra* and *Oedipus Rex*.

**Euripides** explored the psychological motivations of his characters' actions, which had not been done by other playwrights. His plays include *Medea*, *Hercules* and *The Trojan Women*.

**Aristophanes** was responsible for developing comedy within Greek theatres, including the controversial *Lysistrata*, a humorous tale about a strong female character who leads a group of women to end the war in Greece.

**Performance spaces**

While the Greeks gave us the term 'theatre', Greek performance spaces were very different from the majority of our modern theatres, which are more influenced by the playhouses of Shakespeare's time and Victorian theatres.

Greek performance spaces were carefully designed to create effective acoustics and to amplify the spoken word. They were large, simple, half-circular spaces which were normally carved from the lower slopes of hills. This allowed the creation of a raked area for the audience to sit and watch the action of the play without being blocked by the person sitting in front of them. This was especially important as many of the spaces were built to accommodate audiences of up to 14,000 people. The notion of creating comfortable seating with good sight lines has remained the basis of theatre design to this day, and has also influenced sporting and entertainment stadiums.

Peter Hall directed a seminal production of Aeschylus' trilogy, the *Oresteia*, in 1981, in a new translation by Tony Harrison with the National Theatre. The production tried to capture the theatre space, set, costumes and masks of an ancient Greek production.

**Web link**

The Olivier Theatre at the National Theatre in London is a rare example of a modern performance space built in the tradition of Greek theatre. It can be seen at: www.nationaltheatre. org.uk/?lid=1541

**Web link**

Peter Hall returned to the National Theatre in 2001 to direct *The Bacchae* by Euripides. See the following link for interviews and images from the production: www.nationaltheatre.org. uk/?lid=1191&dspl=images

 Consider the following aspects of Greek plays:

➤ Violence and death normally occurred off stage

➤ The play was usually set in a single location

➤ The actors usually played more than one role

➤ The action was highly stylised, using masks and choral work.

Consider also that the chorus:

➤ Reacted in the same way as the playwright hoped the audience would

➤ Set the mood and heightened the drama

➤ Added spectacle, song and dance

➤ Often gave advice and interacted with the action of the play.

Choose a recent newsworthy event that had tragic consequences. This could be as epic and large-scale as an international conflict or something more intimate that you've read in the local paper recently. Use a chorus to describe location, time and sequence of events and choose one actor to play the various parts in the tragedy. The actor could use simple masks to represent the different characters involved. The chorus should remain on stage throughout, reacting, judging and passing comment upon events. Perform your piece in front of a small audience. What was the impact of the action being reported, rather than directly seen? How does concealing an actor's face behind a mask affect the relationship between character and audience?

## Theatre in ancient Rome

While theatre in Rome was influenced by the dramatic tradition of ancient Greece, unlike its Greek counterpart it was less influenced by religion than by culture and contemporary events. While in Greek theatre violent events took place off stage, in Roman theatre they tended to be depicted on stage, in full view of the audience.

**Differences from Greek theatre**

Roman theatre was less philosophical than Greek theatre; it focused more on comedy and featured acrobatics, music and dance. The Romans had a wide array of different forms of entertainment available to them, such as chariot racing, horse racing, foot racing, wrestling, fights between wild animals and fights between gladiators. This had an influence on theatre, which was characteristically spectacular and sentimental, and was intended to act as a diversion from people's everyday lives.

The Romans did not build their theatres on hillsides like the Greeks, but instead erected standing structures on level ground, with stadium-type seating and awnings which could cover the stage and the majority of the seats. The first permanent theatres in Rome were dedicated to Venus, the Roman goddess of love and beauty. Theatre design was elaborate; theatres contained stage houses with dressing rooms and side wings, and corridors that provided access to the auditorium. The **pulpitum** (stage) was large and raised about five feet above the ground and had a back curtain.

**Performance spaces**

Many design characteristics of the pulpitum influenced theatres built in western Europe in the 16th century.

In early Roman theatre, actors were slaves, owned by the theatre managers. Later, citizens began acting in the theatres, often becoming famous and wealthy as a result. Actors had plenty of opportunity to work most of the year round.

**Actors**

Roman audiences tended to be loud and freely shouted insults at the actors if they disliked a play. Actors developed a system of coded costumes, to denote certain character types. For instance, a black wig was used to show that a character was an old man, whereas a red wig indicated that the character was a slave. A purple robe indicated a young, male character and a yellow robe denoted a female character.

Female characters were played by men in early Roman theatre, so a coded costume to represent women was necessary. As Roman theatre developed, women slaves began to take on female roles.

Stock characters were those characters who the audience were familiar with and who were easily recognisable. The various stock characters were identifiable by different costumes. Over time the outfits worn by the stock characters became more realistic. Masks were used – at first, this was to help distinguish different characters, as actors played more than one role, but over time they became more exaggerated. This is thought to have been one source

**Stock characters**

of the larger-than-life masks of **commedia dell'arte**.

The most common stock characters found in Roman comedy are:

➤ **Adulescens**: the hero, young and rich, but not particularly brave or bright

➤ **Virgo:** a young woman, the love interest of the adulescens

➤ **Senex**: an old man, foolish and overprotective, sometimes a father or an old lover

➤ **Miles gloriosus**: a boastful soldier, vain and proud, he thinks he is brave, but in reality he is stupid and cowardly

➤ **Servi:** slaves, loyal

➤ **Ancilla:** a maid or nurse

➤ **Matrona/Uxor:** a mother/wife, shrewd and temperamental

➤ **Meretrix:** a prostitute, either mercenary or devoted.

**Dramatists** **Plautus** was one of the most popular Roman dramatists. He specialised in comic plays such as *Pot of Gold*. His plays tend to deal with everyday domestic affairs and the action is normally located in the street. He abandoned the notion of a chorus and included act and scene divisions. Plautus used jokes and witty, fast-paced, short-lined dialogue with slapstick humour and songs.

**Terence** was another popular playwright, specialising in comedy. However, his plays, such as *The Brothers*, are less boisterous than Plautus' and have more complex plots.

**Seneca** was one of the few Roman playwrights who dealt with tragedy, with plays such as *The Trojan Women*, *Medea*, *Oedipus* and *Agamemnon*. His plays follow a five-episode, or five-act structure. The writing displays elaborate speeches with use of soliloquy and asides, and foregrounds the theme of morality. It includes violence and horror which is often shown on stage. The characters are sophisticated and dominated by a single driving passion, such as revenge, which often leads them to their deaths.

Watch *A Funny Thing Happened on the Way to the Forum* (1966), a film version of the musical with music and lyrics by Stephen Sondheim. It was inspired by the farces of Plautus and tells the story of a slave who, in an attempt to win his freedom, assists his young master in wooing the girl who lives next door.

**Web link**

See images of the National Theatre's 2004 production of *A Funny Thing Happened on the Way to the Forum* at: www.nationaltheatre.org. uk/?lid=8469&dspl=images

 Consider the following characteristics of Roman theatre:

➤ Fast-paced comic acting

➤ Conversational language

➤ Easily identifiable stock characters

➤ Large, over-exaggerated movements and gestures.

Write the names of Roman stock characters on pieces of paper and place them in a hat. In a second hat, place the names of all the students in your group, as well as your teacher, written on pieces of paper. Now write out the names of various locations – such as bedroom, brothel, street and so on – and place these in a third hat. Pull out two names, two characters and a location from the hats. Those students called are given a stock character and create a comic freeze, imagining what their characters would be doing in the particular location. These freezes should be exaggerated.

> Try this with a piece of music, such as a Scott Joplin rag, to heighten the comic impact.

## Medieval theatre

Once the Roman Empire began to disintegrate, the large entertainment industry which it had built up also went into decline. During the early part of the Medieval period, often referred to as the 'dark ages', there was a great deal of political unrest and the church existed as the only stable form of government. There is very little documentation relating to theatre during this period, due to a number of factors: a lack of surviving records, low literacy rates and the church's opposition to certain forms of performance. There are, however, references in documents of the period to travelling actors, jugglers, mimes, minstrels, bards and storytellers, who would cross the country in search of new audiences.

**Rebirth of theatre**

Although the Church banned certain kinds of dramatic performances in the early Middle Ages, ironically, in the 10th century, it was within the Church that theatre experienced a revival. The ceremonies and rituals of the Christian year were performed according to local custom. They were often based on biblical themes and performed by altar boys in Latin.

**Performance spaces**

Liturgical drama was staged on **mansions** – small scenic structures used to represent places (a throne might be used to denote the palace of Pilate) – or **platea** – more general acting areas next to the mansions. Structural elements of the church were often used as mansions; for instance, the choir loft might serve as heaven, while the altar might be used to represent Christ's tomb. Costumes were drawn from ordinary church vestments and simple machinery was sometimes used to lift players upwards, symbolising the ascent to heaven.

Towards the end of the 13th century, plays moved from church interiors to churchyards and other open spaces, such as town squares, streets and even fields. As a result of this increased geographical distance, the church exercised less control over the plays themselves. More plays began to be presented in the local vernacular language, rather than Latin, making their content more readily accessible to a lay audience.

**Guilds**

Control of the plays gradually passed into the hands of secular groups known as guilds (organised groups of tradesmen). However, scripts still needed to be granted approval by the Church, before being performed. The plays were known as **mystery plays** ('mystery' is an archaic term for craft or guild). All of the plays were based in

**Further viewing**

The film *The Reckoning* (2003), directed by Paul McGuigan and based on the novel *Morality Play* (Penguin 1996) by Barry Unsworth, is set in the 14th century and centres on a travelling group of medieval players. It provides a useful insight into the staging of medieval plays.

some way on the Bible or religious teachings, and different guilds gained control over particular plays and stories. For instance, the bakers' guild might be given plays about Noah to perform, whereas the shipwrights' guild might perform plays about the Last Supper.

From the mystery plays, a new style of play developed: **morality plays**, such as **Everyman**. These aimed to impart a moral to the audience, to improve their behavior and to reinforce Church doctrine. They were often larger than life, containing exaggerated characters, actions and events. God was seen to be the driving force behind the events of the play rather than the characters themselves.

### Staging

Once removed from churches, Medieval theatre used two principle kinds of stage: **fixed** and **moveable**.

Those plays performed on fixed stages tended to be more intricate and ambitious in terms of their staging. They often made use of trapdoors, allowing characters to appear or disappear suddenly, as well as machinery to create the impression of flying (used particularly with angels and devils, and to depict the resurrection). All of these technical tricks drew from staging principles established by the mansions and platea in liturgical drama.

The fixed stages also allowed the display of several different locations at once: they could be set up in courtyards and town squares to depict contrasting places, such as heaven and hell. Moveable stages were often created on wagons; they progressed through the streets, while the audience remained in one location – much in the same way as modern parades.

### Decline of Medieval theatre

In the later Middle Ages, Latin comedies and tragedies were studied in schools and universities, and this led to revived interest in ancient Roman and Greek culture. Greek and Roman plays began to be performed and new plays were written that were influenced by classical styles.

Dissension within the Church led to prohibition of religious plays in Europe. In England in the 16th century, the monarch and the nobility began to support professional theatre troupes, such as Shakespeare's Lord Chamberlain's Men, which catered to their upper-class patron's tastes. These patrons wanted to be entertained by the theatre they watched, rather than observe a religious teaching.

### Medieval plays in action

Medieval plays are still acted each year in certain cities in Britain and across the world. They can be seen, as they would have been performed, in places such as Chester, Wakefield and York. Perhaps the most internationally famous of all the mystery play performances is the Oberammergau Passion Play, which is performed in Oberammergau, Bavaria, every ten years, its first performance being 1634.

**Web link**

Follow this link to see some images from the Oberammergau Passion Play performed in 2000:
www.oberammergau.de/ot_e/passionplay/

 In a group, choose a story from the Old Testament which you all have some knowledge of, such as the story of Adam and Eve, Cain and Abel or Noah's Ark. Find two or three sturdy tables that you can use as moveable stages. Retell the story through drama, using the tables as raised areas to act on. You might also want to use them as scenic elements.

Find a song that you think represents the story: for instance *I Got You Babe* for Adam and Eve, *He Ain't Heavy He's My Brother* for Cain and Abel or *Raindrops Keep Falling on My Head* for Noah's Ark. Use a recording of the song or sing it yourselves at a particularly poignant or significant moment, to bring added pathos and meaning to your depiction. Be brave and take your drama into the playground or dining room and act it out before an audience, in the style of travelling Medieval players!

Bear in mind when doing this exercise that Medieval plays contained a strange mix of comedy, exaggeration, poignancy and morality, and therefore may seem quite alien to modern audiences.

In Unit 4: Theatre Text in Context, which you will study as part of your A2 course, you will be given the opportunity to explore the history of theatre in greater depth.

During the following pages we will explore the ideas of three key practitioners – Stanislavski, Brecht and Artaud – through a practical format. The aim is to provide you with a series of tools that you can use during the workshop and rehearsal process in your course.

## Rehearsing theatre: Stanislavski

Konstantin Sergeyevich Stanislavski (1863–1938) is often considered to be the father of modern theatre, as he provided a rehearsal system that allowed actors to create characters in which they – and an audience – could believe. He was born in Russia and took part in his first performance when he was just seven. His privileged upbringing enabled him to experience a variety of theatre forms, and when he was 14 his father converted an outbuilding on their estate into a well-equipped performance space.

His surname was actually Alekseyev; he adopted Stanislavski as a stage name.

The dominant forms at the time were opera, farce and melodrama, in which the entertainment relied on stock characters. The acting was almost mechanical, with physical movements superficially repeated in order to convey clichéd emotion (for example, a hand placed on the heart represented love). Rehearsals – when they occurred – were formulaic in style and rigidly structured to save time and expense. There was hardly any exploration of character. Characters communicated directly with the audience, rather than with the other characters: actors would face the front for the most part and the set would be arranged around such action. Costumes were based on what was available, with certain actors preferring to keep the same outfit from one performance to the next.

**Stock characters**

Despite this, Stanislavski quickly became fascinated by the art of acting. On rare occasions he encountered people who had real presence. They were able to convey a physical truth that allowed him to truly believe in the character. This was something that he admired and sought to emulate. He tried copying their mannerisms in an attempt to recreate their power on stage. Initially he was extremely unsuccessful but ironically this became his real strength. His passion for acting perfection and his search for a sense of realism helped him to develop a system which is commonly used today.

One of Stanislavski's key influences was the actor Mikhail Shchepkin (1788–1863), who believed the actor should 'crawl under the skin of the character'.

In 1897, Stanislavski co-founded the Moscow Art Theatre and established a clear set of ideals that needed to be maintained in all

**Moscow Art Theatre**

productions. The company's work was based on ensemble acting: actors would be expected to alternate between large and small roles. The style of performance had to be clear and sensitive, detailed and truthful. The set and costume needed to be intricate and had to be redesigned for every production. The highest standards were expected at all times.

**Key texts**

*An Actor Prepares* (Methuen Drama 1989), *Building a Character* (Methuen Drama 1979) and *Creating a Role* (Methuen Drama 1998).

Stanislavski's search for a new style of acting is extremely well documented. He wrote three books as a guide to his system: *An Actor Prepares*, *Building a Character* and *Creating a Role*. Each of these is clearly structured and easy to read. They are written from the perspective of a young actor, Kostya, who is desperately trying to improve his skill. He attends classes with the fictitious director Tortsov, who leads him through a range of experiences that help him to understand the art of acting. This master-student format is extremely effective and allows Stanislavski a medium for presenting common mistakes or obsessions without sounding patronising or judgemental.

## Stimulating the desire to create

Unlike his contemporaries, Stanislavski placed real emphasis on the importance of the rehearsal. The actors needed to examine each text, and explore the characters and the performances needed to be organic, adapting to the unique circumstances of each night.

However, in order to create, he realised that there was a need to ensure actors were focused and committed to the work, without any of the baggage of the outside world. Exercises became an essential element of an actor's training. Some were general, appropriate for anyone at any time. Others were more specific off-text work, where the improvisation or discussion might directly feedback into the creation of a particular role.

Try some of the following exercises:

Students begin by walking around the room touching different objects and calling out their names, for example: chair, wall, clock. Now, walking again, try calling out the name of the object that you previously touched. So, as you touch the wall shout 'chair', as you touch the clock shout 'wall'. If you are feeling confident, try naming the object touched two turns before (when you touch the clock shout 'chair'). This exercise warms up your mind and helps you to forget about other thoughts. It also helps to settle nerves as students laugh at their inability to remember the names of simple objects.

Get into pairs. Stand opposite your partner. Stare at each other and take it in turns to say a number in the following sequence: 1, 2, 3, 1, 2, 3, 1 … and so on. Try to say the numbers as fast as possible. This task sounds easy but try it: it's amazing how hard it is to count like this! If you feel comfortable with this exercise, try the following variations:

> ➤ Whenever you say 1, tap your head with your left hand

> ➤ Whenever you say 3, stamp your right foot

> ➤ Alternate your movement so both hands and feet are used

> ➤ Try removing the number 1 but maintain the action

> ➤ Remove the number 3 and maintain the action.

This is an excellent way of stimulating your concentration. The concept appears so easy but your brain finds it difficult. This is similar to acting. What could appear simpler than being yourself on stage? This apparent contradiction is something that obsessed Stanislavski during his life.

Ask four members of your group to leave the rehearsal space then hide an object in the room (Stanislavski used a pin in a curtain). Send one person outside to explain to the volunteers what they need to find. and that the first person to find it will win a prize. They are free to talk and even distract others. Once they enter, watch how they search and monitor any use of sound. When the object is found, the volunteers repeat the exercise, exactly as they have just performed it.

This exercise is based on a section of *An Actor Prepares*.

Usually, the second version will be a lot less convincing. The object should still be hidden in the same place and therefore it is extremely difficult to act the search as convincingly. This is why Stanislavski's system is so useful, as it gives you practical solutions to these problems. Try repeating the exercise when you have finished reading through the ideas in this chapter. Hopefully, you should find it a lot easier to recreate the scene.

## Given circumstances

As a way of preventing his actors from relying on stock characters, Stanislavski emphasised the specific nature of each play. He expected his company to explore what he called the 'given circumstances' of each text in an attempt to find the subtle nuances in the script. The given circumstances can be defined most simply as the facts that cannot be changed by the actor, anything over which they have no control. Rather than discarding an action by saying 'my character wouldn't do this', performers were told to base their role on the specific information the playwright has given them. Examples of such given circumstances include the story of the play, the events within it, the period and place in which it's set, and the director's and designer's interpretations. These would be the starting points for any work done on the text.

66 The investigation of the script, the clear understanding of its nature and its relation to an actor's own experience is the primary process in rehearsal from which all else follows. 99

*Stanislavski: An Introduction* by Jean Benedetti (Methuen Drama, an imprint of A&C Black Publishers 1982).

Choose a play with which you are familiar, and identify and list the given circumstances. If you saw it as a production, try to distinguish between the facts provided by the playwright and the interpretation of the director. Compare your list with another member of your group or with discussions of the play on the internet.

### Magic IF

❝ IF acts as a lever to lift us out of the world of actuality into the realm of imagination. ❞

Stanislavski, *An Actor Prepares*, trans. E. Hapgood (Methuen Drama, an imprint of A&C Black Publishers 1989).

### Imagination

*Stanislavski: An Introduction* by Jean Benedetti (Methuen Drama, an imprint of A&C Black Publishers 1982).

As a way of exploring the play, Stanislavski applied the concept of the magic IF – in which the actors were encouraged to believe in the given circumstances no matter how fantastic they may have been. The actor needs to ask himself the question, 'If I were this person, how would I feel?' This ensures each role is deeply rooted in the facts of the play. In the later stages of his work, Stanislavski changed this concept to 'What would I do?' as he developed a new emphasis on physical action (see page 23).

However, it would be wrong to assume that all essential information is supplied by the playwright. In fact, in some plays, a lot of questions are left unanswered. Therefore, the actor needs to supplement the information with their imagination in order to 'create the moments between the scenes – the flow and continuity between the character's life'.

When a character leaves the stage, where do they go? If an off-stage conversation is referred to in the script, improvise what happened. This will help to create the complete picture. Magic IF acts as a key here: by asking themselves what they would do in a particular situation, the actor unlocks their own imagination, creating actions that are true to themselves and thus believable to an audience.

Find a partner and act out the following: A is a friend who has agreed to meet B at the bus stop before going on to the cinema. B is late because they have just witnessed an accident in which a car and a young cyclist collided. Improvise the scene with A being quite frustrated and B reluctant to talk.

Once you have come to a natural end, try running the scene again but this time think about the circumstances. A needs to consider how often B has been late in the past. Do they often go to the cinema? What else was A considering doing that evening? B needs to imagine the specifics of the accident and how they felt at the scene. Did they come directly from the accident or did something else happen? Each of these facts should help to create a more complete picture and consequently a more believable scene.

## Units and objectives

When acting, have you ever been daunted by the length of a scene? Have you ever been conscious of making mistakes because you were thinking about what was approaching rather than the section you were working on?

Realistic scenes are often extremely complex. Characters' emotions can vary tremendously and yet tension within a scene can be reliant on the briefest of exchanges within the heart of some lengthy dialogue. Stanislavski believed that in order to create a successful performance, each scene should be subdivided into units, with a new unit beginning whenever there is a change in the psychological state of the character. These breaks could be as short as a word or encompass the whole scene, depending on the play. They are identified by the actor and director and used as temporary divisions while working on the text.

Each character in each unit is given an objective. This is always in the form of an active verb and the phrase 'I want …', expressing an action that will drive the scene forwards. Quite simply, the objective is the character's intention for the extract and should be the dominant force behind all thought and movement.

Eventually the actor should be able to connect all the units together in order to decide what the character's main objective is for the whole play. This is the **superobjective** – an overall focus that motivates the character throughout the play.

**Tip**

Objectives should always be positive. Phrases such as 'I don't want to be here' don't help the actor. The focus needs to be on what the character wants to do.

---

 Ask one member of your group to decide on an objective and sit on a chair facing the audience. They could try one of the following:

➢ I want to control my feelings

➢ I want to forget what I've just done

➢ I want to be alone.

Decide on a location for the scene, perhaps the lounge of their parents' house. Add another character to the scene and give them a conflicting objective. This will act as an obstacle within the scene and create tension.

The actions of other characters can hinder an objective. These are referred to as **obstacles**.

---

Arrange your group in a circle and put one chair in the middle. Ask a volunteer to sit on it. The aim is simple. Someone from the circle (A) has to improvise a scene with the person sat in the centre (B). A's objective is 'I want the person in the middle to get off the chair'. B needs to accept the given circumstances of any scene they are given and they must be careful not to block the action. Behaviour must be as realistic as possible.

---

The best way of understanding how the technique works is by applying the ideas directly to a text. Look at the unit overleaf from *The Cherry Orchard* by Anton Chekhov and apply objectives to it based on the given circumstances.

Chekhov, *The Cherry Orchard*, trans. Michael Frayn (Methuen Drama, an imprint of A&C Black Publishers 1978).

**Given circumstances**

Dunyasha is a chambermaid who romanticises her life and fancies herself. She is in her late teens and has airs above her station. Yasha is in his twenties. He has just come back from Paris, is arrogant and affected with an extremely high opinion of himself. He is a womaniser.

The unit is set in the nursery of a country mansion. The occasion is a family gathering to greet returning relatives. There is much coming and going.

| Comments | Text |
|---|---|
| | *Enter Yasha with a rug and travelling bag* |
| How much of the stage space does Yasha cross? | **Yasha**: (*crosses with delicacy*) All right to come through? |
| At what point does she recognise him? | **Dunyasha**: I shouldn't even recognise you, Yasha. You've changed so abroad! |
| | **Yasha**: Mm… And who are you? |
| | **Dunyasha**: When you left I was so high… (*Indicates from the floor.*) Dunyasha. Fyodor Kozoyedov's daughter. You don't remember! |
| Is she surprised? Offended? | **Yasha**: Mm… Quite a pippin, aren't you? (*Looks round and embraces her. She screams and breaks a saucer.*) |
| Is Yasha's comment a compliment or is it patronising? | |
| Is the dropping of the saucer an accident or does she do it for attention? | *Exit Yasha swiftly* |

> 66 The printed words do not contain the full meaning, as in purely literary forms. They depend on what lies beneath them. 99

*Stanislavski: An Introduction* by Jean Benedetti (Methuen Drama, an imprint of A&C Black Publishers 1982).

## Subtext

In most realistic plays, the spoken dialogue contains a subtext – a meaning beneath the text. Awareness of this was crucial to the development of Stanislavski's theatre and prevented his actors from drifting into the two-dimensional performances of the past. It was no longer possible simply to copy the physical actions of other actors or attempt to recreate their vocal tones. The external portrayal needed to be backed up with an internal, intellectual response. The performance became a personal interpretation based on an actor's own experience and instinct.

This concept needs to be remembered when tackling all scripts, since there is a tendency to play scenes at their face value. However, the script has been carefully written by the playwright, with words chosen for maximum impact and it is vital that you consider alternative interpretations, reading between the lines.

 With a partner, act the following dialogue at face value:

**A**: I'm sorry.
**B**: Really?
**A**: You know you can trust me.
**B**: Thanks.

Repeat the scene experimenting each time with more complex characterisation. What could the given circumstances be here? Perhaps B is a husband who has recently cheated on A, his wife. Or is it the other way around? Imagine all the possible subtexts that could be hidden underneath this simple extract.

In a group of three, improvise the following scene.

It is lunch time and three friends are discussing their food. All of their dialogue must be related to the food they are eating but one member of the group has a crush on one of the others, and must reveal this subtext through their vocal and physical work. If acted well, the scene will be funny but the dialogue in itself will appear quite basic. This should bring out the value of subtext.

## Emotion memory

If an actor is to engage intellectually with their role, then they should also look to connect emotionally. Personal experience is essential when attempting to convey a truthful performance and all actors should strive to learn how to harness past events in order to feed into the detail of their role.

The key to these feelings is in the senses, since they have the power to stimulate the past. Imagining the smell of home cooking can create a sense of calm. The sound of the sea might stimulate romantic thoughts. The sight and feel of a busy street could create anxiety. Using your own memory bank to create truthful actions on stage is not an exercise to be treated lightly: it is an intensely personal experience and may take time. In this sense, it is more a private rehearsal technique.

> " Since you are still capable of blushing or growing pale at the recollection of an experience, since you still fear to recall a certain tragic happening, we can conclude that you possess an emotion memory. "
>
> Stanislavski, *An Actor Prepares*, trans. E. Hapgood (Methuen Drama, an imprint of A&C Black Publishers 1989).

? Think of a moment when you were clearly embarrassed. Try to recreate that emotion by considering the circumstances and how they affected your senses.

Stanislavski acknowledged that emotions were a difficult tool to harness and could at times result in imposing an incorrect intensity of feeling onto a script. As he modified his ideas, he realised the emphasis needed to come from action. The actor is looking for the correct physical reaction to the emotion conjured up. To find this physical action, you need to conjure up the emotion through remembering the small details of the moment. For example, remembering the first time you fell in love is unlikely to provide you with much physical information. But by remembering the details (the smells, where you were, the music that might have been playing) you should be able to build up the overall memory and remember your physical reaction at that time.

## Circle of attention and public solitude

In the Russian theatre of Stanislavski's time, gestures were bold, voices were loud and characterisation was unsubtle. The performance was aimed directly at the audience, who could sit back and be entertained by the spectacle. Stanislavski was

> " In such a small space you can use your concentrated attention to examine various objects in most intricate details, and also to carry on more complicated activities such as defining shades of feeling and thought. "

Stanislavski, *An Actor Prepares*, trans. E. Hapgood (Methuen Drama, an imprint of A&C Black Publishers 1980).

appalled by the false nature of such work and insisted that his actors should not be distracted by the 'black hole' of the audience. They needed to create an imaginary **fourth wall**, a barrier between themselves and the auditorium, with their point of focus always on the stage. This would help to embody the philosophy of ensemble acting, where the focus was not on one star actor, but the company as a whole.

As a way of emphasising this idea, each actor was asked to imagine himself or herself within a small pool of light. This was referred to as a 'circle of attention' and had the effect of focusing the performer's mind on the smallest of details and drawing the audience into the action. The effect is similar to the image of a solitary child playing with a toy. Their focus on their own world of play is intense and as an onlooker you can often become hypnotised by their actions. Stanislavski referred to this effect as 'public solitude': despite sharing a space and being observed by a large group of people, you are able to convey a sense of true isolation.

In a small group, ask for one volunteer to act in front of the others. The performer should have a small object to focus on, such as a box of matches, a bunch of keys or a ring. Without talking they need to improvise a scene that suggests an emotional reaction to the object. As an audience, try to pinpoint what skills are used in order to convey the mood of the scene. Are you interested in the action? Which elements of the performance are most successful?

This intense level of concentration is essential in developing a well-rounded character. Think about yourself for a moment and where you focus your attention. Essentially, you focus on three different areas – another person, an object or yourself. This may appear quite obvious, but in terms of creating a believable character on stage, your concentration can often wander to other things: When do I move? Why isn't the audience laughing? What's my next line?

**Communion**

> " Exterior action, movement, gesture were reduced to almost nothing. The actors were required to 'radiate' their feelings, to do everything through their eyes, by tiny changes in tone and inflection. To 'commune' with each other. "

*Stanislavski: an Introduction* by Jean Benedetti (Methuen Drama, an imprint of A&C Black Publishers 1982).

From this, Stanislavski developed the notion of communion, which is an unspoken language on stage. He said that actors must at all times have communion with something or someone: it is only by maintaining an uninterrupted exchange of feelings and actions between the characters on stage that an audience's attention can be held. He explained how this was to work by asking his actors to visualise rays coming out from their eyes and fingertips that must always be in constant connection with someone or something. Stanislavski searched for an intimate performance and used small rehearsal spaces to help him create the desired effect.

The concept of intense concentration and discipline in performance is easy to grasp but it is a lot more difficult to maintain practically.

In a group of three, recreate the following situation in stages, focusing on another character, an object or yourself:

A enters and sees an envelope under a chair. They look inside, see there is a letter and read it silently to themselves. It is addressed to B and is written by C. C writes how they hate B's attitude, how B appears to victimise C viciously at every opportunity. A, having read the note, puts it back in the envelope. Pause at this point. Ask A how easy it was to maintain their focus. Were the audience drawn into the performance?

Repeat the scene but this time carry it on with A trying to replace the letter under the chair as B enters and wonders what A is doing. B's reaction should indicate that they haven't read the letter themselves. Improvise the dialogue, making the letter a focus for both characters at certain points. Discuss whether it became more difficult to retain the focus with two actors on stage.

Play the scene again; this time lead up to B insisting on reading the letter. At this point C should enter, looking for the letter that has dropped from their pocket. C sees the letter in B's hand. Improvise. When the scene comes to a natural conclusion, discuss the action and the use of communion.

## The method of physical action

Stanislavski's early concern with recreating truthful emotions through intellectual exercises was modified as he matured and developed as an actor and director. He became concerned that some aspects of his system, such as emotion memory, were not only complex but perhaps even emotionally dangerous for an actor to undergo. He realised that there was a need for balance between internal and external action. After all, physical activity is inextricably linked to mental thought. Many of us learn better when we are active. If you have lost your iPod or your homework, you may have tried pacing round the house as a way of reminding yourself where you left them. So, as an actor, it is vital to use both of these elements to generate a truthful performance.

Stanislavski became interested in the unique pace of movement as related to emotion, and came to stress the importance of finding an inner rhythm for a character. If you can find the correct rhythm for an action, you are likely to generate an emotional response as believable as those discovered through emotion memory.

**Tempo-rhythm**

 Get into pairs. Person A should walk around the room as they naturally would, while person B observes. After a minute, B walks behind A, copying their walk exactly. B should note the positioning of the arms, how the head is held and the change in weight and balance when A turns corners. After a minute, A moves away while B tries to maintain A's walk. Repeat the exercise with B being observed. You should note the uniqueness of each person's walk and how different it can make you feel.

---

This link between the physical and the mental is quite difficult to grasp but is an extremely useful acting tool. Benedetti manages to summarise the theory in a succinct way:

> Within the action of the play events, emotions have a particular pulse and pattern to them. Tempo, as in music, denotes the speed of an action or feeling – fast, slow, medium. Rhythm internally indicates the intensity with which an emotion is experienced; externally it indicates the patterns of gesture, moves and actions which express the emotion.

The simplest way of imagining this concept is by placing yourself in a position in which you do not want your physicality to portray how you are feeling emotionally. If you are going for a job, your inner nerves might be hidden by an external calm. Consequently your internal rhythm would be high but your external gestures might be small. This intricate detail helps to ensure an extremely complex understanding of character and hopefully develop a more sophisticated portrayal.

*Stanislavski: An Introduction* by Jean Benedetti (Methuen Drama, an imprint of A&C Black Publishers 1982).

## Rehearsing theatre: Brecht

Bertolt Brecht (1898–1956) played a huge part in influencing modern theatre as we know it today, and you will be employing many of his ideas, theories and practices in the way you work on this course without realising it. He was a playwright, a director (of his own plays and those of other people) and author of a good deal of commentary on how theatre should be created. His theories changed during his lifetime, and were not fully realised in all the plays he wrote, but many of them support much of what he was trying to communicate.

### Life and background

Brecht was born in Augsburg, Germany in 1898 and lived there until the early 1920s. He was born into a fairly affluent family and studied medicine at the University of Munich before returning to Augsburg and serving in an army hospital during the First World War.

During this time, he developed an anti-war sentiment in response to the horrors he observed in the hospitals. Married to this was an anti-bourgeois attitude that reflected his anger and frustration at the way society had experienced war and dealt with its aftermath, as well as an interest in **Marxism** as a progressive model for the financially and politically unstable Germany. He also developed an interest in the **Expressionist** movement in art and literature.

See opposite for more on Expressionism.

In order to escape the parochial society of Augsburg, Brecht moved to Munich, and soon after that to Berlin. Here he began the second phase of his writing, his *Lehrstücke*, or 'learning plays', in which he started to explore the ideas of epic theatre and the notion of instruction through plays. During this time he became a fully-fledged Marxist and spoke out against the Nazi party.

In 1933, he was forced to go into exile to escape the Nazis, and he fled to Switzerland and then Denmark before eventually travelling to the USA. He did some film work in Hollywood but always felt uncomfortable there because of his communist roots. In Nazi Germany his work was reviled, his books destroyed and his citizenship withdrawn. It was during this time in exile that he wrote most of his great plays, further developing the idea of epic theatre.

In 1949 Brecht returned to a divided Germany and formed his own company, the Berliner Ensemble. He was looked on with suspicion in capitalist West Germany because of his political stance, and also in communist East Germany due to his unorthodox theories. His contributions to theatre and his significance as a theatre practitioner were eventually recognised in the 1950s. Brecht died of a heart attack in 1956.

## Influences

Brecht dedicated himself to creating a new way of thinking about and using theatre. In his quest for the new, however, he took much from the past and present to help shape his ideas.

Expressionism was a movement in literature, music and art that originated in Germany before the First World War and ended in the 1920s. It tried to destroy superficial ideas of reality and explore the deeper meanings underneath. It stood for all things erratic and explosive over the smooth and linear. The resulting works of art appear distorted, and sometimes even tortured and grotesque.

Playwrights of the time writing in this style were affected by feelings of anger and despair at the state of society, particularly since the war, and the content of their plays reflected their attitude towards the values of society and the idea of capitalism. Many of the characters within the plays were reduced to titles to represent these concepts.

Brecht ultimately rejected Expressionism because he felt it relied too heavily on the irrational. However, Expressionism certainly influenced the way he tried to get audiences thinking about stories and theatre with a new perspective in the way he fragmented the line of his stories, making them episodes, and the way he treated the characters of his plays (in that they were often **archetypes** and represented types of people).

Brecht took much from the communist writing of Karl Marx (1818–1883), in terms of his hatred of capitalism, his anti-militarist views, his sense of justice and injustice, and his understanding of the importance of history. These ideas and principles became very apparent within the content of his plays.

Brecht was accused of plagiarism during his life, as many of his ideas for stories were taken from other writers such as Maxim Gorky, Christopher Marlowe, Sophocles and Shakespeare. But Brecht borrowed to reinvent and not merely to replicate. It wasn't

### Further study

Using the internet, an encyclopedia or the resources of your school's history department, find out more about what happened to Germany after the conclusion of the First World War.

### Further study

To understand Brecht's political development, his reasons for exile and the context surrounding his work, you will need a basic grasp on world developments 1933–1955, including the politics of Nazi Germany and the Cold War.

**Expressionism**

### Further viewing

There were also Expressionist films made during this period, most famously Fritz Lang's *Metropolis* (1926). Try to get hold of a copy of the film. See how it uses camera angles and editing to fragment the linear nature of the film and distort the reality of the story.

In the play *Gas* (1918) by Georg Kaiser, for example, the characters include: the Engineer, the Girl, the Gentleman in White.

**Marxism**

Although always sympathetic to communism, Brecht never became a member of the Communist Party.

**Influences**

just narrative and content that he used – he also borrowed form and structure ideas. The play *Woyzeck* by Georg Büchner influenced Brecht in terms of themes, but more importantly showed Brecht how to use unconnected scenes, which was the beginning of his idea of montage. The way in which Shakespeare used characters to comment on the action through use of prologue and epilogue, and the way in which the characters used the conventions of theatre language, such as the aside and soliloquy, also showed Brecht the potential for controlling the audience's response.

### Other theatre forms

Brecht also became aware of Japanese noh theatre, where plays are often morality stories that require a response or judgement from the audience.

Brecht was also very interested in non-western theatre forms. Watching the famous Chinese actor Mei La Fang perform in Moscow in 1935 without make-up, costume or lighting made Brecht realise that an audience would accept the fiction of theatre without a production having to cause them to 'suspend their disbelief'. This had a tremendous influence on the way he presented his work to the audience, the way he worked with his actors and the way that he staged his and others' plays.

### Sporting events

His concern for the theatre's relationship with the audience also led to his interest in sporting events, particularly boxing. Brecht wanted theatre to have the same universal appeal and be equally popular. He wanted theatre to learn from the relationship that the audience had with the action in sport, and the spontaneous and impulsive responses that were elicited by the action.

### Erwin Piscator

Brecht later felt much more at ease with the ideas of the designer Caspar Neher, who worked closely with Brecht to create stage pictures with sets and staging that complemented the action and supported the actors.

Brecht's career was very closely linked to his fellow German theatre director Erwin Piscator. Piscator was most interested in political theatre and the idea of agitation propaganda or 'agit prop' theatre, in which theatre was a vehicle for protest and social change. Piscator was also concerned with the spectacle of theatre and would often use large casts, technically sophisticated staging and projection. Brecht learnt much from Piscator in these terms. However, he wanted to create a simpler storytelling technique, where the audience were challenged into thought and judgment – he did not want them to be overwhelmed by theatricality or the message.

### Theatre before Brecht

Brecht should not necessarily be cast in opposition to Stanislavski – this is too simplistic. Brecht was a huge admirer of Stanislavski's work, and much of Brecht's work was only possible as a consequence of the Russian's thoughts and theories.

For a real understanding of how Brecht changed and redefined theatre, we need to understand what had gone on before him in terms of theatre history. Brecht was reacting against the form and content of plays. Stanislavski's system, and the advent and consolidation of 'realism' within European theatre, had made Brecht determined to change the place of theatre within society. He also wanted to change the attitude of the audience towards plays. German audiences were mainly bourgeois and took theatre very seriously, viewing it as art with their role as passive onlookers. He wanted to make theatre popular, relevant and accessible.

### Further reading

See Brecht's comparison of dramatic and epic theatre in *Brecht on Theatre*, ed. and trans. John Willet (Methuen Drama, an imprint of A&C Black Publishers 1978).

## Key concepts

If Stanislavski's work was concerned with empathy, feelings and the heart, then Brecht could be considered as someone concerned with distance, thinking and reason. These basic principles were the foundation for what Brecht called **epic theatre**. Let's break this down into some key areas.

Brecht wanted to create a new relationship between the play and the audience. He argued that the invisible **fourth wall** created by Stanislavski made the audience much more passive. They were drawn into the fiction of the drama, but could do nothing to change the situations, characters or the ending. They became emotionally involved with the situations and characters, but did not think about why the situations had occurred and what that might mean.

In order to get the audience more mentally engaged with the play Brecht developed the notion of the **Verfremdungseffekt**, which is now referred to in English as the **alienation effect**. This is not an easy word to translate, and has often been misinterpreted or misunderstood – it is not concerned with literally 'alienating' the audience from the play.

What Brecht was trying to achieve was a set of theatrical devices to make the play seem strange (alien) to the audience, so that they would be forced to think about the events, action and characters in a new and unfamiliar way. Brecht wanted the audience to become more involved, to be both emotionally engaged in a scene and then immediately stand outside it to think about it, and to make a judgment on it. He was not afraid of emotion and understood the power of it in performance, but he wanted his audience to be able to stand back from it at times, to analyse it.

The role of the actor in this process was vital. Whereas Stanislavski required his actors to identify with their roles and embody them on stage, Brecht wanted his actors to distance themselves from the characters they were playing. He created many devices to help his actors achieve this distance. He felt his actors should demonstrate, rather than become, a role. He saw them as storytellers, who could play many parts and have a view of the characters they were playing. Within his plays and performances he allowed his actors to multi-role and allowed the audience to see the actor changing parts. He allowed them to step out of their emotional engagement with a character to look critically at what they represented.

An actor might do the following things to ensure they are 'demonstrating' in this way:

➤ Play more than one role and change from role to role in plain view of the audience

➤ Speak in the third person

➤ Transpose the dialogue into the past tense

➤ Speak the stage instructions

➤ Use very clear, stylised body language, facial expression, tone of voice and movement to reflect the social status and outlook of that character

➤ Use costume (or tokens of costume) to help clearly define characters

## The audience

> See pages 22 and 39 for more on the fourth wall.

## Alienation

66 The theatre-goer in conventional theatre says: Yes, I've felt that way too… I am made to cry with those who cry, and laugh with those who laugh. But the theatre-goer in the epic theatre says: I would never have thought that… I am made to laugh about those who cry and cry about those who laugh. 99

*Brecht on Theatre*, ed. and trans. John Willett (Methuen Drama, an imprint of A&C Black Publishers 1978).

## The actor

66 Whereas Stanislavski, in Brecht's view, can only offer us artificial reconstructions of reality, Brecht is determined to 'show things as they are'. The premium is still on 'truth' but the definitions have altered. 99

Shomit Mitter, *Systems of Rehearsal: Stanislavsky, Brecht, Grotowski and Brook* (Routledge 1993).

> This is referred to as **gest** or **gestus**.

> ➤ Use song to introduce or comment on the action of a scene, so that the audience can step back and be objective, and begin to analyse why certain events have happened.

**The playtext**

In the period before Brecht, plays were concerned with a clear narrative that flowed from one scene to another. Within these stories issues would be raised by characters and their interaction with one another, but resolved by the end. Brecht was also concerned with storytelling and narrative, but he felt this did not necessarily have to be linear in style – the story could begin, stop and travel anywhere. The story itself could also be fragmented and made up of self-contained scenes or episodes. This episodic work was known as montage.

**Montage**

**Further viewing**

*Battleship Potemkin* (1925) by the Soviet filmmaker Sergei Eisenstein, uses montage to show Tsarist troops quelling a civilian riot. The juxtaposition of images creates a disturbing sequence: exactly the effect that Brecht was trying to achieve in theatre.

Brecht thought that another way to make the audience look strangely at the play would be to break the unities of action, time and place, and fragment the chronology and linear nature of the story. He thus broke his plays down into episodes to show that theatre could be like a piece of Expressionist art or a film. By placing together scenes of unequal length, seemingly unrelated and presented in differing styles, he forced the audience to think about their relevance and relationship to the story, the characters and themselves.

The episodes themselves could be in a variety of styles, and could shift modes from a multi-character scene to a monologue or even narration to keep the audience engaged – but also to help them refocus and remain objective.

**Staging**

**Further viewing**

Good examples of recent films which use montage are *Pulp Fiction* (1994) and *Memento* (2000).

Brecht was clear that he wanted the mechanics of theatre shown to his audiences. He did not want them to try to suspend their disbelief, but rather always to know that they were in a theatre and watching a fiction. With this in mind, the set could be simple or suggested using staging or props that represented locations. If there was a change in time or location, it could be shown to the audience in the way that the set was changed or moved.

He also thought that placards and projections could swiftly communicate to the audience changes in action, time and place. Lighting was used only to illuminate the action of the story, and was not to be used to create subliminal effects or moods in support of the action. If colours or effects were employed then Brecht insisted that their use was explained to the audience, so that they were not deceived into feeling but were led into thinking.

**Web link**

Andrew Moore's teaching resource site at www.universalteacher.org.uk is very clear and helpful in its description of the stages of Brecht's plays and thinking.

All these ideas served to emphasise the anti-illusionary approach to theatre, forcing the audience to recognise that they were in a theatre, and that the all-important element was the meaning of the story, not the spectacle.

## Phases of Brecht's thinking

| Period | Important works | Commentary |
|---|---|---|
| The early period | *Trommeln in der Nacht* (*Drums in the Night*, 1918–1920)<br><br>*Mann ist Mann* (*Man is Man*, 1924–1926)<br><br>*Die Dreigroschenoper* (*The Threepenny Opera*, 1928)<br><br>*Aufstieg und Fall der Stadt Mahagonny* (*The Rise and Fall of the Town of Mahagonny*, 1927–1929) | The plays were humorous in a rather bleak and cynical way, and presented social and political questions attacking bourgeois values. |
| The learning plays | *Der Flug des Lindberghs [Der Ozeanflug] (The Flight of Lindbergh [The Ocean Flight]*, 1928–1929)<br><br>*Das Badener Lehrstück vom Einverständnis (The Baden-Baden Lesson on Consent*, 1929)<br><br>*Der Jasager (The Yes-Sayer*, 1929–1930)<br><br>*Der Neinsager (The No-Sayer*, 1929–1930)<br><br>*Die Massnahme (The Measures Taken*, 1930)<br><br>*Die Ausnahme und die Regel (The Exception and the Rule*, 1930) | The *Lehrstücke* (teaching plays) were short, parabolic pieces, written between 1928 and 1930. These plays, which were written to instruct children, were not attractive to audiences. They warned Brecht against being too obviously **didactic** – trying to use his plays to teach lessons and make points. This led the playwright Ionesco to call him 'the Postman', as he only wanted to deliver messages.<br><br>*Der Ozeanflug*, broadcast as a radio play, was produced without the reading of the main part, which was to be spoken by the audience, who were supplied with scripts. There were also three longer propaganda plays: *Die Heilige Johanna der Schlachthöfe (St Joan of the Stockyards* [slaughterhouses]), which parodied Shakespeare, Schiller and Goethe (and Shaw's *Major Barbara*), and contained many devices of what became epic theatre, such as a loudspeaker announcing political events of the time, or projection of captions commenting on the drama; *Die Mutter (The Mother)*, which dealt explicitly and didactically with political revolution; and *Die Rundköpfe und die Spitzköpfe (The Round-heads and the Pointy-heads)*, a play that took its plot from Shakespeare's *Measure for Measure* but also dealt with the Nazi emphasis on what they deemed inferior and superior races. |
| The later years | *Mutter Courage und ihre Kinder (Mother Courage and Her Children*, 1938–1939)<br><br>*Das Leben des Galilei (Life of Galileo*, 1937–1939)<br><br>*Der gute Mensch von Sezuan (The Good Person of Szechuan*, 1939–1942)<br><br>*Der kaukasische Kreidekreis (The Caucasian Chalk Circle*, 1943–1945) | The first two of these plays contained episodic narrative theatre – each scene prefaced by a caption indicating what happened. In the third play the scenes presenting the action were followed by interludes, in which the actors stood back from their roles and commented on the actions of their characters. In *The Caucasian Chalk-Circle*, Brecht used a play within the play: in order to resolve the conflict of two groups of peasants who wished to farm a valley, a play is presented by the singer, musicians and actors. The singer and musicians stood outside the drama of Grusche, Azdak, Simon and Natella, and provided both narrative and commentary. These plays are very much a part of the **dialectic** style – whereby Brecht wanted to use scenes and situations to create an argument with all sides shown, and with the audience incited to play an active role in making their own mind up during the play, and when they leave the theatre. |

> " Art is not a mirror held up to reality, but a hammer with which to shape it. "
>
> Ascribed to Brecht.

## Brecht in practice

In order to understand Brecht's concepts fully you need to try to apply them practically. Rather than give you small exercises to work on each concept, as with the Stanislavski material above, here you will find a large three-step approach to practical work that tests your understanding of Brecht's epic theatre as a whole.

### Stage 1: the accident

There has been a road accident, and as a passerby you have witnessed it.

Imagine you are telling the story to a group of people who did not see the accident. Tell the story and include all the characters that were in it. Feel free to impersonate or even caricature them. Try to use gest, narration, dialogue, third person, descriptions and even token costume to bring the story to life.

This exercise allows the actor to demonstrate the characters within the story and use devices to make the story fresh and strange to the audience. It also supports the anti-illusionary aspect of theatre, in that the audience is aware that the passerby is just telling the story and is not really any of the characters within it. However, it also gives the audience an insight into the attitude and judgement of the storyteller.

Choose someone else who was involved in the accident and retell the story from their point of view. If you are working in a group, agree on the facts of the accident and then each of you work out your version of events. Show these versions to each other to see how different they can be from varying perspectives.

### Stage 2: a well-known story

This is an excellent exercise to try in a small group. Remember that Brecht wanted theatre to be fun and exciting, like spectator sport. Have fun with this by doing it with pace and real wit.

Choose a story that all of your group knows. A good example would be *The Three Little Pigs*.

Decide what set, staging items or props you will use in advance. You may use a table to represent the houses in the story. You may choose to use no props at all but create and indicate the locations with members of your group forming shapes.

1. **The story.** Improvise the story using dialogue and action only, with each member of your group playing a different character

2. **The narrator.** Build on your initial improvisation by adding narration. Each of your group must add a narrative speech to introduce their characters and describe some element of the action.

3. **The monologue.** Give each of your characters an opportunity to present their thoughts and views with a short monologue.

4. **The attitude.** You must now build on step 3 by allowing each of your characters an opportunity to speak in the third person, to indicate the attitudes and feelings of the character they are beginning to demonstrate. You could perhaps introduce and/or close their monologue with this.

5. **The placard.** Create a number of placards with pens and card that do a number of things. Use some placards to introduce location, time and/or character. Use other placards to indicate the attitude and internal thoughts of the characters.

6. **The gest.** Choose a moment, a scene or even a character and create a movement/body language sequence that demonstrates who they are and how they are feeling. This can be as simple as the wolf arriving at each of the houses with the expectation of a meal.

7. **The music.** Choose a song or a piece of music that you think could introduce or comment on some action of the play. Be as topical or as traditional as you want – a piece of current music from the charts or a film, or something older, such as jazz, folk or classical music. Think about what you want the music to say when it is juxtaposed against a particular scene or moment.

8. **Shifting modes.** You must now build on step 7 by rearranging the chronology and structure of the story. You must create a series of episodes that are no longer in chronological order. You could perhaps begin with the ending. The episodes must also shift between different modes of presentation, such as scenes of monologue, extended narration, dialogue, action, song and gestus. Try to surprise your audience.

9. **Alienation.** Perform your piece, and discuss whether you have found a way of making the story strange and fresh to an audience. If so, in what way?

---

Stage 3: a news story

This can be quite a disturbing exercise but it really helps you get to grips with the *Verfremdungseffekt*. You could work by yourself or in a group on this exercise.

Take a recent news story that deals with a serious crime. If it is a well-documented crime, such as the Yorkshire Moors murders, then there will be lots of material available through internet sites. If you feel uncomfortable with exploring a recent crime then you could perhaps look at a more historical or fictitious crime such as Jack the Ripper or Sweeney Todd.

After a period of research, your task is straightforward. Create a piece of epic theatre that uses montage and episodic scenes to retell the story of the crime, making it strange to the audience so that they can view it with a fresh perspective. Use the steps from Stage 2 to

See the table on phases of Brecht's thinking (page 29) for more on dialectic and didactic.

**Further study**

The following concepts can be explored in more detail in the collection of Artaud's essays *The Theatre and Its Double* (Calder Publications 1998) and *Antonin Artaud: Blows and Bombs* by Stephen Barber (Faber and Faber 1994).

**Surrealism**

**Balinese dance-drama**

66 Dialogue does not specifically belong to the stage but to books. I maintain the stage is a tangible, physical place that needs to be filled, and it ought to be allowed to speak its own language. 99

Artaud, 'Production and Metaphysics' in *The Theatre and Its Double*, trans. Victor Corti (Calder Publications 1998).

help you approach the task. Try to make the piece dialectic and not didactic. Try not to suggest or impose answers and judgements, but set out problems and questions for the audience to think about and decide upon.

## Rehearsing theatre: Artaud

The theatrical legacy of Antonin Artaud (1896–1948) does not provide a structured series of exercises or a method for actors to follow. Instead, Artaud's work provides a vision that stems from his violent hatred of realism. He represents the other end of the performance scale from Stanislavski: he didn't want to portray realism in his productions but to transcend it – a theatre that challenged the audience, forcing them to see new ideas and values. His ideas may initially appear fragmented and at times incoherent, but through his writings, sketches, recordings and photographs one is able to create a sense of a man whose passion for change was coupled with extreme frustration and mental torture.

### Life and background

Artaud was born in Marseilles into a strict religious family which he found suffocating. He had a troubled childhood, suffering from meningitis and depression, the symptoms of which led to him being isolated at school. He was extremely strong willed and reluctant to conform to the conventions of society; as a consequence of this, his parents arranged for him to be incarcerated in a sanatorium in 1915, where he remained for a period of five years. During this time, he was prescribed opium and this was the start of a long-standing addiction to drugs.

Once released, Artaud embarked on a fascinating series of experiences that helped him to formulate his extreme views on both society and theatre. He was a prolific poet and became angry when his work was rejected by the magazine *La Nouvelle Revue Française*. In 1924, he became an active and influential member of the **Surrealist** movement. They shared a political viewpoint based around anarchy and free-thinking, and a vision of the theatre as a place not for bourgeois entertainment but for emotional discovery. However, the relationship between Artaud and the group was often strained and two years later he was expelled. He acted in many films and was celebrated for his non-realist style.

In 1931, Artaud witnessed a performance by Balinese dancers in Paris that acted as a catalyst for the development of his theatre. Balinese dance-drama is religious in nature and involves the acting out of Hindu legends in a stylised way, with the use of deeply unrealistic make-up, symbolic masks and hand gestures. The performances are given in local tongues, accompanied by percussion.

Artaud was struck by the magical quality of the work. The dancers' dependence on gestures, facial expressions and visuals created a physical language that appealed to the unconscious. The focus was not on the distant words of a playwright but on the direct relationship between director, actor and audience. Artaud was impressed by the fact that his experience of the performance was (since he understood no Balinese) independent of a verbal language. This, he argued, was the true purpose of theatre: to offer something that could not be offered by a novel or poem, or any other medium. Without language or a familiarity with the story, drama is more effective, more visceral, more engaging. He wanted to devise drama that appeared to his audiences as the Balinese dance-drama appeared to him.

Two other influences affected the development of his ideas. The first was the painting *The Daughters of Lot* by Leyden, which he saw at the Louvre. He frequently took friends to see it and monitored their response. The violent images in the painting had a theatrical quality to them and he considered the impact that such a still image could have on stage. The second influence was film and in particular the work of the Marx Brothers. Artaud was fascinated by the manner in which they juxtaposed images to create humour. Their non-realist style was liberating and he quickly realised the potential power of laughter within his theatre.

## Theatre of Cruelty

Artaud organised his ideas into a manifesto, called the **Theatre of Cruelty**. He used the word cruelty in the broadest sense, implying that theatre should go to the very extreme of all that a director can exert on the actor and the spectator. His aim was to reinvent the theatrical experience, abolishing the traditions of realism, and allowing design and performance skills to work together to maximise the sensory experience of the audience.

Before we can experiment with practical ideas it is important to understand the essence of Artaud's theatre. It was revolutionary, which partly explains why he was unable to achieve a production that did justice to all of his aims.

His desire to break from the restrictions of psychological theatre started with the nature of the performance space. The stage building should be a single, undivided locale, probably a barn or a hanger, which would allow direct communication between the actors and audience. All decoration needed to be removed from the space so that every area could be used. The audience would be in the middle on swivel chairs, while a walkway would be built around the edges of the auditorium to enable certain action to take place above the spectators. The show, as Artaud called his performance, would fill the space, using different areas and levels to engulf the audience and assault their senses.

Artaud believed that traditional theatre was a slave to dialogue, so he tried to redefine the aural experience. He believed language prevented the actor from fulfilling their vocal potential, and instead focused on sounds rather than words. Screams were important to him since they represented the most primitive emotion.

He considered musical instruments to be important, both through their ritualistic associations and their ability to create mood. He demanded experimentation in order to generate a new scale that

**Other influences**

### Practical exercise

Try experimenting with recreating visually striking paintings or images from magazines. Experiment with using the whole of the performance space. Try animating these pictures using bold gestures and sounds rather than words.

### Web link

See the site www.theatrelinks. com/?page_id=6 for a selection of Theatre of Cruelty links.

**Performance space**

**Sound**

66 In Europe, nobody knows how to scream anymore. 99

Artaud, *The Theatre and Its Double*, trans. Victor Corti (Calder Publications 1998).

could vibrate through the body, and oversized instruments that could become a visual part of the performance. The notes would be accompanied by recorded sounds of church bells or footsteps, which could be played at a high volume.

### Costume and design

All costume should be devoid of any contemporary relevance and should be specifically designed for each show. However, he felt it might be appropriate to look at images from the past and designs that might take their influences from certain cultural rituals. Artaud believed that the performance could be enriched by traditional outfits which have a certain mystical beauty. Masks and even puppets were encouraged as a way of moving away from realism and discovering a new physical expression that added a dream-like quality to the performance.

### Lighting

As Artaud was forming his ideas, technical equipment was limited. Although he was able to isolate key areas of the stage or flood the performance space with light, he envisaged that more sophisticated equipment was necessary in order to release the power of his show. He demanded the discovery of oscillating light effects, new ways of diffusing light in waves, sheet lighting 'like a flight of arrows'. Colour was to be used with subtlety and finesse in order to communicate complex images. Recent advances in lighting technology such as lasers, strobes and computer-controlled effects are excellent examples of Artaud's vision being fulfilled.

> If you are unfamiliar with the play, look at the plot summary on page 64.

Using the principles of Artaud's theatre, create a design for a performance of *Oedipus Rex* by Sophocles. Sit the audience in the centre and consider how each of the elements above could be used to increase the impact of a production.

## Other important concepts

### The plague

> 66 A real stage play upsets our tranquillity, releases our repressed subconscious, drives us to a kind of rebellion. 99
>
> Artaud, *The Theatre and Its Double*, trans. Victor Corti (Calder Publications 1998).

When formulating his ideas, Artaud struggled to find a notion that could encapsulate everything he was thinking and imagining. He settled on the metaphor of the plague and became so inspired by it that he explored it in the opening chapter of his collected writings. He considered how the plague attacked the lungs and the brain of the body but also affected the heart of society. It had the ability to disrupt order, to release individuals from social conventions and drive them to extremes. This was how his theatre would affect his audience; they would be shaken and irritated by the inner dynamism of the spectacle. After the performance, however, the audience would be purified. He concludes his essay with a passionate declaration of his theatre's power:

> Artaud, *The Theatre and Its Double*, trans. Victor Corti (Calder Publications 1998).

Theatre action is as beneficial as the plague, impelling us to see ourselves as we are, making the masks fall and divulging our world's lies, aimlessness, meanness and even two-facedness. It shakes off stifling material dullness which even overcomes the senses' clearest testimony, and collectively reveals their dark powers and hidden strength to men, urging them to take a nobler, more heroic stand in the face of destiny.

Artaud's writings are filled with references to the religions of different cultures. He was clearly fascinated by their mystical quality and their ability to generate a heightened level of engagement from those who participated. This concept was essential if Artaud's theatre was going to bring about change in his audience.

The easiest way of understanding this idea is thinking in terms of personal experience. What rituals do you participate in? A religious service clearly serves as an excellent example if you feel emotionally engaged with the ceremony, but it is possible to consider ritual in a broader sense. For example, your routine of getting ready in the morning may be so well structured that at the end of the process you feel your mental state has changed. This process of change is central to understanding the power of ritual. Artaud proposed the use of rhythms, chants, choral speaking and choreographed movement as a way of emulating the experience of more formal ceremonies.

**Ritual**

Artaud, through his associations with the Surrealist movement, became fascinated by the concept of both dream and reality working together to produce a heightened reality or 'surreality'. Realistic theatre was preoccupied with mirroring life on stage, but Artaud felt it was unable to show the darker thoughts that can sometimes fill our minds. Imagine how much more intense your experience of the world would be if you knew the dreams of everyone you met. Their unconscious thoughts would no longer be suppressed and would have to be confronted.

**The double**

See page 32 for more on Surrealism.

The 'double' idea was linked to the concept of the **dopplegänger**, most clearly identifiable in the story of Jekyll and Hyde, in which Hyde represents the hidden side of Jekyll's character. Presenting both of these characters on stage would undermine any tendency to revert back to realistic acting.

---

Improvise a scene in which a teacher is lecturing a student about their behaviour. The student is outwardly polite and apologetic. Now repeat the scene, introducing a third character, the dopplegänger of the student, who should physically and vocally express their frustration.

---

## Artaud and the Cenci

Unlike Stanislavski and Brecht, Artaud never managed to achieve a successful production. Much of his life was spent exploring and reacting to different stimuli and consequently his ideas lack order and have a limited practical awareness. However, he did manage to produce one of his scenarios called *The Cenci*, which was based on Shelley's verse tragedy and a document by the French author Stendhal.

The plot is violent and contains images of rape, torture and murder. The protagonist Cenci (the role Artaud played) is killed by his two servants when they plunge nails into his throat and one of his eyes.

Artaud believed that each scenario should only be performed once: 'Let's recognise that what has been said does not need to be said again; that an expression is worth nothing second time, and does not live twice.' Artaud, *Collected Works*, trans. Victor Corti (Calder Publications 1970–1976).

The graphic and disturbing nature of the stimulus was important to Artaud. He believed that such images had the power to release the audience from their current mental state and make them confront their dreams and primitive instincts. This journey would have a **cathartic** quality, liberating and cleansing the spectator.

Unfortunately, his show was full of compromise. It was performed in the round, breaking the theatrical convention of the time and did contain some of the images and sound collages he had strived to achieve. However, it was heavily reliant on text and fell short of many of his ideals. After 17 performances and a series of damning reviews, the production closed.

One of Artaud's difficulties was trying to make his cast understand his vision. His constant references to different literary works left them confused. He became quickly frustrated and exhausted by the whole experience.

## Exploring Artaud

**Practical experimentation**

In order to understand Artaud's philosophy, it is important to try to realise his ideas practically. To attempt simply to intellectualise his Theatre of Cruelty is to misunderstand its power. Some of the ideas for experimentation presented here will appear strange and perhaps embarrassing, but by committing to the exercise you will gain an overview of his approach.

> " I am well aware that a language of gestures and postures, dance and music is less able to define a character. But whoever said theatre was made to define a character? "
>
> Artaud, *The Theatre and Its Double*, trans. Victor Corti (Calder Publications 1998).

Get into groups of six. Number each other 1 to 6. Number 1 begins by creating an image in the space. Freeze. 2 enters and forms another image that must react to 1's position in some way while making contact with them. 3 enters and forms another freeze, making sure they touch one of the people on stage. Repeat the process until all six actors are on stage. 1 should now move from their initial position and form a new image in reaction to the other five while keeping physical contact with someone. Repeat the process with all the other numbers and allow the shape to evolve continually.

Ask a group of people to watch and give feedback. Some will impose characters onto the scene and attempt to find a narrative order to the work. For example, they may identify a victim who is bullied or a group who are travelling on a journey. Others will perceive it from an emotional perspective so that they associate with the fear or anger (or whatever emotion) at a given moment. The latter is closer to Artaud's vision, in which images communicated directly with the audience's unconscious.

In his essay 'An Affective Athleticism', Artaud stressed the importance of physical training for the actor. Not only should the actor learn to understand the body but also harness its power in order to achieve maximum impact. In society, it is smothered by rules, unable to express itself properly. In the Theatre of Cruelty, it would be released.

Clear parallels can be drawn between Artaud's theatrical aims and his personal experiences of mental institutions. He was often held in a straight jacket, restricting his physical freedom, and despite constantly battling with an addiction to drugs, he feared moments in sleep or drunkenness when he was out of control.

His main focus was on breathing and its relationship with the state of the soul. In a concept similar to Stanislavski's emotion memory, he advocates a precise command of breathing, since he believed it was inversely proportional to external expression. The more restrained the emotion, the more intense the breathing becomes. However, in moments of extreme anger, breath is used in short controlled bursts.

Experiment with improvising two scenes looking at two contrasting states. First, imagine a scene between an employer and employee in which the latter is publicly and viciously embarrassed and then sacked in front of their colleagues. Initially, experiment with the worker as unable to talk, focusing on the intensity of the breathing. Make each breath audible and intense. Repeat the scene with the employee now able to answer back. Use bursts of dialogue and breath control.

Just as an athlete uses certain muscle groups to increase performance, Artaud felt his actors should become familiar with certain localised points as a way of exploring emotion. Many of his ideas stemmed from the Chinese concept of acupuncture. He believed fright and sorrow originated in the small of the back, anger and attack came from the solar plexus and heroism derived from the chest. By focusing on these areas and moving between them, shades of emotion could be explored in their truest form.

> The solar plexus is between the chest and the navel.

The body was the foundation for the Theatre of Cruelty, and the regular rhythm of the heart, the power of breath control and the immediacy of the scream were tools in achieving his goals.

Lie on your back, put your hands by your side and bend your knees so the soles of your feet are flat on the floor. Breathe in through your nose and out through your mouth. Monitor your breathing and try to slow it down. Every time you exhale, turn the breath into a hum. Maintain it for as long as possible. Continue to do this while focusing on your body. How do your feet feel: comfortable, tired, tense? Work your way up through your body. Focus on your stomach. Is it full? Bloated? Hungry? Instead of humming, try to express how your stomach feels through abstract noise. Now focus on the heart. Is it fit and healthy? Does it feel like blood is flowing freely or is it a real effort to send it through the body? Vocalise this feeling. Using the rhythm of your heart, convert this feeling into a combination of vocal and physical work.

> It may be useful to try this exercise in pairs with one person reading the instructions while the other follows.

> If several people have tried this exercise, ask them all to perform at the same time, so that you have a collage of hearts. This all may appear strange on the page or even embarrassing to perform but the key is the potential impact it has on an audience.

> " Actors should be like torture victims who are being burned and making signs from the stake. "
>
> Artaud, *Collected Works*, trans. Victor Corti (Calder Publications 1970–1976).

## Acting Artaud

Artaud's theatre relied on a form of spatial expression. It focused on image rather than language and the combination of actor and design skills helped to ensure a total theatrical experience. We have already looked at his theatre as being against the traditions of psychological realism but, ironically, realism is a useful tool in accessing some of Artaud's ideas.

Consider a scene in which an actor is smoking a cigarette. Stanislavski might ask an actor to focus on their motivation for smoking, how the cigarette is held, what this might reveal about the character. Artaud would begin by focusing on the body and in particular the lungs as the smoke is inhaled, the gathering of tar and the emotional kick of the nicotine. Rather than simply using this as an internal reference for the actor he might encourage the actor to express this sensation externally through a series of physical gestures and abstract sounds which have no link to the reality of the action. He saw this as being true to the essence of the act, rather than asking an audience to read the impact of such an event on the face of a character.

Experiment with the following ideas, moving from realistic to more symbolic acting. Although the exercises are suitable for pairs, it is often useful to try the activity at the same time as others, which will allow you to experience a variety of interpretations and look at the impact of performing several images at the same time.

---

Consider the story of Oedipus and his wife Jocasta. Unbeknown to them both, Jocasta is also Oedipus' mother. When she discovers the truth, Jocasta goes to her room and hangs herself. When Oedipus discovers her, he removes two brooches from her dress and stabs out his eyes. Try performing this in a semi-realistic style, miming the hanging and blinding. Repeat the exercise to a count of 20, 10 for Jocasta's actions, 10 for Oedipus'. Now consider how an Artaudian actor might perform the section. At this stage no words are permitted, neither can there be a realistic mime of hanging or stabbing of eyes. The focus should be on the internal feeling and how it might be expressed externally. It doesn't matter if people watching aren't able to identify what you are doing. Remember, Artaud's theatre is not driven by character. Perform the entrance of Jocasta and Oedipus over a count of 20. Experiment with other pairs performing their scenes at the same time as yours. What is the impact of such work? Does Artaud's style dilute or concentrate the experience?

> In Sophocles' *Oedipus Rex*, this all takes place off stage and is reported in a vivid messenger's speech.

---

Try the nursery rhyme Little Miss Muffet. Consider it first from a Stanislavskian perspective. Why did Miss Muffet sit on her tuffet? Was it a calm act on a summer's day or a moment of defiance from a young girl who had been sent to her room? Why did the spider approach her? Was he trying to intimidate, was he lonely or did he have a liking for curds and whey?

Perform the scene in a realistic style. Repeat to a count of 20, exaggerating the characterisation by emphasising the emotion. Now repeat the exercise in the style of Artaud. Focus on the emotions experienced in the scene and express these physically through physical tension and abstract sound. This second version is clearly more comical but remember humour was considered to be a powerful force and it is important that you experiment with it in different forms.

---

**Involving an audience**

There is no doubt that a true Artaudian performance would be an assault on the senses of any spectator. The staging itself was designed to make them feel trapped and before his performance of *The Cenci*, Artaud indicated his desire for his audience to be plunged into a bath of fire participating with their souls and nerves. Although he was never able to achieve this onslaught, it is easy to imagine how his performance style could be threatening.

The concept of swivelling seats adds an interesting dynamic, undermining the more formal rows of the traditional proscenium-arch theatres. It allows the audience to participate actively, choosing where to look and when to turn. His staging removed the reliance on the imaginary **fourth wall** between actor and audience. This barrier would have prevented the direct communication that Artaud felt was necessary in engaging the inner sense of all who experienced his show.

In order to understand the power of his theatre fully, one has to experience it from an audience's perspective. During the next few exercises it is important that you experiment with both performing and watching the work. By understanding how it feels to be surrounded by performers, you will gain a greater insight into the potential power of the performance.

---

Get into a group of at least five people, one of whom will need to leave the room while the performance is prepared. When they re-enter, they will be blindfolded and will experience the work through their other senses. Find a photograph in a newspaper or magazine of a scene from life that creates a specific mood or emotion. For example, consider the image of a slightly jaded-looking cottage with an old person asleep in a worn armchair. Discuss the feel of the scene and how you might convey that through sound, touch and movement. You can use realistic sound effects like the breathing of the old person, but also experiment with conveying the atmosphere of the scene. Try to organise your ideas into an order and rehearse the scene. When you are ready, invite the volunteer back into the room and actively involve them in your environment as you perform the work. Lead them around the space and encourage them to explore key areas through touch.

Once the exercise is complete, ask the volunteer to feed back what they understood by the experience. The level of response will vary tremendously and could range from phrases like 'I could sense death in the room' to 'there was a coal fire in the corner'. Repeat the exercise with different images and volunteers to see if the group can hone their technique.

---

Get into groups of four or five. Recreate a nursery rhyme in the style of Artaud. Remember your audience will be sat in the middle. Don't feel limited by character – experiment with how choreographed sound and synchronised movement could be used to convey the scene. Avoid using traditional speech. Try switching the action from one end of the room to the other and invading the audience space in the middle.

After the piece has been rehearsed, perform it to an audience. How did they react? Were they able to identify the nursery rhyme? Did this affect their experience? How did sitting in the centre intensify the experience?

---

> 66 The overlapping of images and movements will, by the conspiracies of objects, of silences, of cries and of rhythms, arrive at the creation of a true physical language based on signs and not words. 99
>
> Artaud, *Collected Works*, trans. Victor Corti (Calder Publications 1970–1976).

It could be argued that dipping into Artaud's ideas and using them to reinvent the theatre form is a betrayal of his vision. However, as actors, you will need to experiment with a range of styles that not only demonstrate a knowledge and understanding of other practitioners, but also a command of different techniques which will enable you to communicate your ideas successfully. Experimentation is the key to success. Be brave in your approach and select those ideas which best suit your needs.

## Contemporary theatrical practitioners

### Kneehigh

**Key productions**

*Tristan and Yseult, The Bacchae, The Wooden Frock, The Red Shoes, Pandora's Box, Cry Wolf, A Very Old Man with Enormous Wings, Wagstaffe the Wind-up Boy, Nights at the Circus, Journey to the Centre of the Earth, Cymbeline, Rapunzel, A Matter of Life and Death, Blast!, Brief Encounter.*

**Brief history**    Originating from very humble beginnings in 1980, Kneehigh has quickly established itself as one of the most innovative theatre companies in the country. Founded on a desire to create live theatre, passionate but untrained individuals created a series of workshops for the surrounding community. These sessions quickly evolved into productions and their reputation grew. The lack of formal performance spaces in Cornwall meant that the company were forced to present much of its early work outdoors. Rather than hindering their development, it actually strengthened it and many of the grander, more ambitious productions still contain the spirit of an open-air piece, celebrating the impact of the natural world on the people who inhabit it. In their own words: 'We create vigorous, popular theatre for a broad spectrum of audiences, using a multi-talented group of performers, directors, designers, sculptors, engineers, musicians and writers. We use a wide range of art forms and media as our "toolkit" to make new and accessible forms of theatre.'

The initial idea or 'itch', as Emma Rice, the artistic director, describes it, evolves through research into a more defined concept which is then linked to music. Writers create an initial script but are present during the whole process to help adapt the text as it evolves. Rehearsals takes place in a National Trust barn in Mevagissy. This isolated venue, without mobile phone reception, helps to foster the community feel of their work. A collaborative approach is considered to be essential to the devising process and actors are continually reminded to 'hold your nerve' when improvising.

Their productions focus on universal and at times complex themes in a relatively innocent and childlike manner. Traditional barriers between actor and audience are broken down to ensure that everyone is engaged in the journey. Their performances are magical celebrations of storytelling, making use of music and subversive comedy to underscore often tragic tales of human weakness. Expect oversized props, strong physical images and occasional use of song to activate the audience's imagination and stimulate childhood memories.

## DV8

> **Key productions**
>
> *To Be Straight With You, Just for Show, The Cost of Living, Can We Afford This, The Happiest Day of My Life, Enter Achilles, Bound to Please, MSM, Strange Fish, If Only…, Dead Dreams of Monochrome Men, My Body Your Body, eLeMeN t(h)ree Sex, Deep End, My Sex Our Dance, Bein' A Part Lonely Art.*

DV8 was formed in 1986 by Lloyd Newson. Trained in Melbourne and London, Newson established the company as a celebration of **physical theatre**, a term first used by Grotowski. Since then he has won international acclaim for both live performances and filmed versions of his work. In their own words: 'DV8 Physical Theatre's work is about taking risks, aesthetically and physically, about breaking down the barriers between dance, theatre and personal politics and, above all, communicating ideas and feelings clearly and unpretentiously. It is determined to be radical yet accessible, and to take its work to as wide an audience as possible.'

The company sees research as a vital stage in the choreography of any dance and fought hard to maintain funding to support this aspect of their work. Performers are often asked to observe, discuss and explore a reality that they have experienced rather than simply relying on what Lloyd Newson describes as the 'sterile environment' of the rehearsal studio. This preparatory work helps to define the performance vocabulary for each piece. A scenario is written and a set is built before rehearsals begin, which allows the dancers to use and feel comfortable with all aspects of the space. Performers are encouraged to drop all inhibitions during rehearsal

**How do they work?**

" If theatre were a box of chocolates, then this would be the champagne truffle in a dark chocolate robe. "

Lyn Gardner, *Guardian*.

**What is their style?**

> **Further study**
>
> Visit their website at: www.kneehigh.co.uk. Search for reviews of *Tristan and Yseult*, *The Bacchae* and *Rapunzel* on the internet. Look at images from their past productions; this will give you an immediate flavour of their style.

**Brief history**

**How do they work?**

" … dramatic coherence, human integrity, irresistable visual power, were all there in the most outstanding work I have seen all year. "

Ismene Brown, *The Daily Telegraph*.

and to lose themselves in the improvisations. All work is filmed to remind them of what they created.

### What is their style?

Unlike most contemporary dance, the focus of their work is on content rather than the aesthetic beauty of a movement. Their aim is to communicate through movement issues that are relevant to contemporary society. While this is their foundation they are eager to ensure productions have their own identity and they try to find the most appropriate forms for their work. Newson affirms that he is not a dance purist; set, lighting and music are integral to the process and if movement cannot communicate meaning then he is happy to use words.

### Further study

Visit their website: www.dv8.co.uk. Read reviews of *To Be Straight With You, Can We Afford This / The Cost of Living, The Happiest Day of My Life, Bound To Please*. Watch the DVD of *Enter Achilles* – a striking comment on the alcohol-fuelled male world.

## Complicite

### Key productions

*Shun-kin, A Disappearing Number, Measure for Measure, Vanishing Points, The Noise of Time, A Minute Too Late, Pet Shop Boys Meet Eisenstein, The Elephant Vanishes, Strange Poetry, Mnemonic, The Resistible Rise of Arturo Ui, Genoa 01, The Noise of Time, Light, The Vertical Line, The Street of Crocodiles, The Chairs, The Caucasian Chalk Circle.*

### Brief history

Established in 1983, Complicite is a company renowned for both its exploration of classic texts and innovative devising work. Artistic director Simon McBurney's training at Jaques Lecoq broadened his understanding of the endless forms theatre can take. The multicultural environment in which he trained emphasised for him the unpredictable and fluid nature of theatre, a theme which is evident in all of his work. As Complicite's website states:

> Always changing and moving forward to incorporate new stimuli, the principles of the work have remained close to the original impulses: seeking what is most alive, integrating text, music, image and action to create surprising, disruptive theatre.

"
Complicite is more than a theatre company: it is a state of mind. When each collaborative adventure into the unknown starts off, anything is possible. The result is an astonishingly broad and continually evolving spectrum of work.
"

Roger Graef, Complicite website.

### How do they work?

The rehearsal space itself is key to the devising process. Complicite's focus is on a playful environment which is filled with objects, words, research, images – anything that helps stimulate the imagination. They focus on creating conditions for invention, a joint vision for all performers, which they then use as a basis for any exploration. The language of movement is a fundamental aspect of any performance and rehearsals often look at what can be communicated through the positioning of the performers.

### What is their style?

### Further study

Visit their website: www.complicite.org. Read reviews of *Measure for Measure, Mnemonic* and *The Chairs*. Look at the short videos on the website which recount stages of the rehearsal process for *The Dis.*

Fundamentally, all of Complicite's performances are based on image in the most complex sense of that word. The production experience stems from a crafted collage of movement, language, sounds, rhythms and props. It is storytelling in all of its surprising beauty; yet their work also frequently has political undercurrents which challenge the ideas that dominate contemporary living.

## Designing theatre

## Staging

Every theatrical practitioner has a preferred style of performance. Some will enjoy the intimacy of small studio theatres, others will be excited by grand theatres that allow for spectacular effects. The nature of the staging will ultimately influence the style of acting and the demands placed on set, costume, lighting and sound.

The first theatres in ancient Greece were semi-circular in nature and often cut into a hillside. Thousands of people sat on the curved raised seats looking down on the central performance area. However, it wasn't until the Elizabethan period that the first theatres were built in this country. Although these did utilise some of the Greek traditions, the characteristic Elizabethan stage was the thrust stage, which brought the actors out into the audience. This was an important element of the performance style and ensured a direct relationship between the cast and the public.

> 'Elizabethan' refers to the reign of Elizabeth I, 1558–1603.

**Thrust stage**

**Web link**

Shakespeare's Globe Theatre in London is a faithful recreation of an Elizabethan theatre. Visit www. shakespeares-globe.org

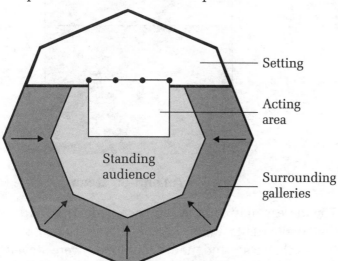

Setting

Acting area

Standing audience

Surrounding galleries

**An Elizabethan public theatre**

> The arrows, here as in the diagrams that follow, indicate the direction of the audience's gaze when watching the action.

This structure has been reinterpreted over time and has taken on many different guises, particularly in modern theatres such as the Swan Theatre in Stratford.

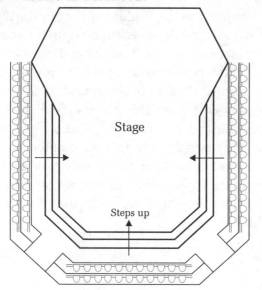

Stage

Steps up

**A thrust stage**

## End-on and proscenium-arch

During the Elizabethan period, private performances of plays were often commissioned by the rich to take place in existing venues such as great halls. These were on a smaller scale and involved an audience sitting in rows, all facing one direction. This became known as end-on staging, since all of the action took place at one end of the room.

As the popularity of such performances increased, specially designed theatres were built in order to accommodate the demand. The size of the auditorium meant that the performance space needed to be more clearly defined, so the stage was framed with what has since become known as a proscenium arch, which added a certain formality to the performance.

> The arch would be closed with a curtain for scene changes and at the end of acts.

### Web link

The Lyttelton Theatre in London is an example of an end-on, proscenium-arch theatre: see www.nationaltheatre.org.uk/?lid=1543/

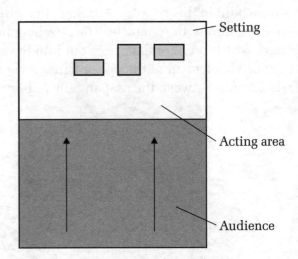

An end-on stage

The increasingly complex and detailed nature of the staging meant that playwrights wrote longer, more detailed scenes (for fewer scene changes), and new techniques were developed in order to create different locations in the large performance area. This became the predominant performance style, although by the turn of the 20th century certain practitioners had become frustrated with the formality of this method of staging.

## Theatre in the round

> See pages 32–40 for more on Artaud and his concept of theatre.

In a reaction against realism, Antonin Artaud wanted his audience to be trapped in the middle of the auditorium, with the actors performing around them. A more popular concept that has evolved is the exact reversal of this: the audience are positioned on all four sides of the performance space, surrounding the actors. This is usually termed **theatre in the round**. It can be difficult to direct, as the actors will invariably always block the view of some of the audience and set has to be kept to a minimum. Having said this, it is an extremely intimate experience, which enables the audience to remain focused on the action while being aware of the reaction of other audience members. Street theatre often works on this principle, since the performer has to define their space in a public area.

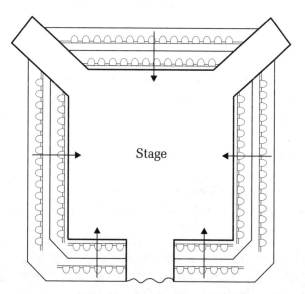

**A theatre in the round**

While theatre in the round is a fascinating experience, the very nature of the audience's position means that it can often be limiting in terms of design. A traverse stage has the audience on two sides facing each other while allowing for two clear areas at either end for fixed set or group images. The audience can at times feel they are watching a tennis match as their heads follow the action back and forth across the space. The style is particularly suited for comedy, as it enables members of the audience to feed off the reactions of one another.

**Traverse staging**

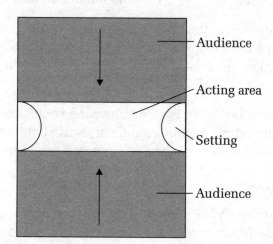

**A traverse stage**

A promenade performance can be one of the most exciting staging methods, and although it is often used in modern productions, it links back to some of the most early drama work. The concept is extremely simple. The audience is encouraged to walk around the venue following the action. The performance could be located in the ruins of an old church or in a large hall or barn. Their movement is led by the stage action and there is a certain amount of skill thus needed to control the audience's focus. The style does allow for elements of surprise, however, since characters or pieces of set can be introduced behind the audience while their focus is held elsewhere.

**Promenade performance**

## Set design

The nature of the set is clearly influenced by the audience position and the style of the piece. Certain performances may require an accurate recreation of a room in a certain period. Other plays may allow total freedom for the designer, where the only limit is their own imagination. If you have little experience of design then it is important that you start by visualising key images. This may be based on one of the locations implied in the script or it could stem from the mood of the piece. Try to sketch these ideas on paper and then use the starting points below to create your design formally.

**Size.** What are the dimensions of your performance space (width, depth and height)? Draw an outline of the stage to scale on your set plan. Will tabs (curtains) or flats (wooden scenery) be used to frame the space? Is there a need for a painted backdrop?

**Scale.** Will your design fill the stage space? Will it be in proportion with the actors using it? For example, a large sweeping staircase or a small crooked door may reflect some of the themes of the play.

**Period.** Will your set need to transport your audience to a different moment in time, past or future? If the play is set in the present, which aspects of the modern world does it reflect?

**Colour.** How could you use colour to create an appropriate atmosphere? Black and white can symbolise a cold environment, whereas bold colours on a table might emphasise its significance.

**Texture.** Should the floor of the stage be rough or smooth? Will the audience have to cross the performance space to get to their seats? What might the texture of the set say about the location or even the world of the play?

**Entrances and exits.** How do characters enter and leave the space? Does one exit have more significance than another? Are levels used to distance these moments from the main action?

## Costume

The nature of your costume will rely heavily on your performance style. Costumes true to the original period of the piece will need to be well researched. It is important to recognise the social context of the play since a character's social class may restrict what an actor can wear.

**Style and genre.** The grandness of design might be a very important aspect of your piece. Certain plays contain set pieces which rely on the impact of the costume. Hats and handbags may become bold reflections of characters. Conversely, your piece may be quite physical with neutral costumes supported by simple signers, for example a briefcase symbolising a businessman.

**Themes.** How will the issues explored in the play be represented in the manner in which the characters are dressed? Tightly buttoned jackets may represent the formality of the piece, although if they are slightly ill-fitting it may imply that a character is uncomfortable with this element of society. More abstract pieces may require you

**Web link**

An impressive directory of set, lighting, costume and sound can be found at http://dmoz.org/Arts/Performing_Arts/Theatre/Stagecraft. There are many examples which will help both new and experienced designers.

to make fantastical designs which represent animals, emotions or even states of mind.

**Colour.** Consider how colour can reflect both the mood and the status of the character. Hair and make-up could be used to accentuate any personality traits.

## Lighting

Some students become intimidated by lighting since it can be the subtlest of all design elements. In a realistic performance, for example, you may be totally unaware of any lighting changes, with the exception of blackouts. Having said this, if it is used creatively it can be an incredibly powerful tool, manipulating audience response without them realising it.

Essentially, there are three main types of lantern: a **profile** (sometimes known as a spotlight), a **fresnel** and a **flood**. They each have slightly different uses and are categorised based on the number of lenses used to control the light output, which is two, one and none respectively. A profile is a sharp, narrow beam of light, whereas a flood produces wide, unfocused light. A fresnel uses a special type of lens to create a spotlight effect.

When designing a lighting rig, you should consider the following:

**Colour.** Coloured gels are used to create different moods, with a straw-like colour frequently used for a warm environment and steel blue used for a cold atmosphere. Lights shone on a white cyclorama will change its colour and ultimately manipulate the mood of the scene. Lanterns without gels create a harsh white light.

**Position.** In a realistic performance, areas of the stage will be lit by a group of lanterns that cancel out any shadows and create a general cover of light, but certain moments within your play may require particular effects. Floor lights at the front of the stage will cast long shadows behind the actors. Lighting directly from above will isolate an actor, often making them look vulnerable. Using a torch held in different positions will help you to discover the best location for your lantern.

**Intensity and fade times.** Once the rig is complete, you will need to consider which lanterns you want on, how bright you want them and the speed of the changes between each of these states.

**Gobos.** These are metal discs that are placed inside profile lanterns to cast a shadow that represents an image. Realistic images like window frames are often used, and rotating gobos can be used to create a swirling hypnotic effect.

## Sound

There are very few technical terms to grasp when discussing sound. The skill is mainly in selecting the appropriate effects for the piece. Essentially, your sound will be created either off stage or on stage, or it will be prerecorded. It could involve a live band, microphones to amplify and distort sounds, or a specific noise that creates an image in the audience's mind. The BBC produces

**Lanterns**

**Further study**

Find out about parcan, birdie and strobe lanterns, and how gauze can be used to create lighting effects.

A cyclorama is a large backdrop, usually white, which helps to frame the stage. It is frequently used to represent the sky.

a comprehensive range of sound effects on CD that are readily available, and there is a vast range of effects to download from the internet.

When designing your play, consider how music – live or recorded – can manipulate mood. Audiences are used to this technique in both television and cinema, and there are many soundtracks to films that would create an extremely powerful opening to certain plays. Sound may be the first design element experienced by an audience, so think carefully about the position of speakers, the volume of each track and the style of music or effect used.

# Exploration of Drama and Theatre

## Introduction

In Unit 1: Exploration of Drama and Theatre you are required to interpret two plays through practical exploration, wider reading and research. The plays are chosen by your teacher and should be from two different periods of history and cover different theatrical genres. The lessons that you have with your teacher should involve practical work, discussion and research. We will discuss four plays here, but don't worry if your chosen play isn't one of them. All the approaches that are suggested could be applied to any playtext that you are studying, especially if it is written in a similar style or genre. Use the sections on each of the plays to create questions on and approaches to the texts you are studying.

In addition, you will be required to write an evaluation of a live theatre performance. This could be a version of one of the texts you are focusing on in lessons or an entirely different play. Either way, it will inform your practical understanding and it may challenge your perceptions of successful theatre.

Throughout your work, remember that the purpose of this unit is to get you to think about drama and theatre in a way that will help you later on in the course when you begin realising other plays. Through practical work, this unit aims to bring you into contact with different approaches to writing, rehearsing and performing as well as directing, designing and acting.

You will be assessed on **three** areas:

➤ Practical work

➤ Exploration notes

➤ Evaluation of live theatre.

## Practical work

Since you will be assessed throughout your practical work, the contributions that you make to your class lessons – through responses, group work, rehearsal work and performing work – are very important. Be positive throughout this unit and bring enthusiasm to the sessions, contributing as much as you can.

It should be no surprise to learn that throughout this unit, the divide between practical exploration and theoretical discussion will often become blurred. Discussion and research are an intrinsic part of a successful performance just as an understanding of a

### Further study

As a starting point, try exploring the ideas and practice of important theatre practitioners and see if their approaches could be applied to your chosen plays in rehearsal and performance. See the Understanding Theatre chapter for information on Stanislavski, Brecht and Artaud (pages 15–40). You could also research Brook and Grotowski.

Evaluation of live theatre will be dealt with in greater detail on pages 97–121 and requires a slightly different approach, although it is important not to see it in isolation from the other two areas.

Mark schemes are an essential tool when trying to understand what exactly is expected of you. The details for all units can be downloaded from the Edexcel website at www.edexcel.org.uk.

playwright's use of language can only be fully appreciated through delivery of the lines.

The exam board stipulates the practical exercises that could be covered in this unit and identifies the skills that should be demonstrated and will be assessed:

**'Off the text' exercises.** These require you to move away from the restrictions of the text and explore its themes through parallel situations. For example, the emotions experienced by the characters in a Greek tragedy could be linked to difficulties faced by families today. Such exercises help you to understand the issues that are present within the world of the play without being restricted by the script.

**Improvisation.** This is another method of exploring the text through practical work, focusing more closely on the world of the play. What might the characters say once they leave the stage? How did they behave when they first met? Improvising such scenes allow actors to understand what Stanislavski referred to as the 'total life of the character'.

**Discussion.** This should be active exploration of the text rather than theoretical argument. Use discussion as a tool to debate different interpretations by showing and evaluating the work.

**Rehearsal.** The process of developing a scene is intrinsic to script work and it relies on the actors revisiting the text and reflecting on their work. Although you will feel pressured to get through the material as quickly as possible, the benefits of detailed rehearsal of certain scenes will challenge and deepen your understanding of the text.

Examples of contemporary practitioners are detailed on pages 40–42.

**Practitioner technique and style.** At least one of your plays should be linked to a practitioner. Demonstrate a command of this practitioner's approach, using their terminology in an appropriate situation.

**Vocal technique.** As a performer you need to be aware of the specific demands of the play and the different characters within it. Experiment with accent, tone, projection, pace, pitch and pause in order to demonstrate an understanding of the most appropriate vocal skills needed to communicate the play's themes.

**Movement skills.** A full awareness of the different physical demands made by both plays is needed. Consider carefully how you should use gesture, posture and movement to highlight your understanding of character and performance style.

The mark scheme is broken into bands which allow your teacher to identify which description best suits you. The highest three bands equate to grade E or above at AS with the highest band for A-grade students. To achieve the highest band, you will need to be 'outstanding' with a 'comprehensive' understanding of both plays.

## Exploration notes

Your exploration notes are a very important series of notes that you will complete once your practical sessions are over. It's a good idea to keep a log of all of the practical sessions you take part in; you can then use this to help you put together your final notes. Remember that your response should always be in note form – it is not supposed to be an essay. Your notes could take the form of bullet points, bubble charts, flow diagrams, research material, personal observations, annotated sections of the text or any other clear way of giving your response to the eight areas which Edexcel specifies. These areas are, as follows:

1. Social, cultural, historical and political context

2. Response to a practitioner

3. Characterisation

4. Language

5. Vocal awareness

6. Non-verbal action

7. Visual, aural and spatial elements

8. Interpretation.

> These eight areas, which should be covered in your exploration notes, are described in more detail on pages 52–53.

Here are some guidelines for completing your exploration notes:

**Guidelines**

➤ The maximum length of your notes is 3,000 words. It is extremely important to adhere to this.

➤ Your notes should always be clear. Make sure that even if they are based around diagrams, they are still easy to read and to follow. They can be handwritten or word-processed.

➤ Plan your notes well before you start putting them down on your final sheets of paper.

➤ Use the log that you have created during the course of all your practical work.

➤ Divide the sheet up into sections so that you know where you are going to write the responses for each of the eight areas.

➤ Ask yourself questions about the play, and about how you tackled certain problems in rehearsal and performance. This will help you to shape your answers.

**Structuring your notes**

When considering how best to structure your response it is important to bear in mind the word limit of 3,000 words. If you deal with each of the eight areas within each play separately, this gives you fewer than 200 words to demonstrate your knowledge of each.

Alternatively, you could integrate your discussion of the different areas for each play, referring to several different factors when focusing on one aspect of the text, while drawing comparisons with the other play. While this potentially reduces the number of words needed, you need to make sure that all areas are covered

> Although there is a word limit, there is no page limit. You might like to complete your notes on A3 paper. Remember that while images and diagrams will help to demonstrate your understanding, it is always important to explain their relevance.

sufficiently and that your ideas are clear. If you are planning to integrate the different sections, it may be useful to conclude each section of text with an abbreviation highlighting which aspects of the specification you have addressed within it, for example SCHP ('social, cultural, historical and political context').

Ultimately, you will need to decide which of these two methods of writing your notes will be most successful for you.

## Areas to cover in your exploration notes

Whichever method of structuring your notes you choose, you will need to ensure that you address the following aspects of the text:

**Social, cultural, historical and political context**

Give each play a context. Find out about the playwright, when the play was written and why it was written. It would also be helpful to find out about other plays which were being performed at the same time it was written and what was going on in society at the time, so that you can establish what political or historical significance the play has. You should also demonstrate an understanding of what the play would have meant to a contemporary audience.

**Response to a practitioner**

Some plays will be typical of a genre which has been strongly influenced by a theatre practitioner, for example Stanislavski or Brecht. If this is the case for your text then it is important that you demonstrate a command of the way it has been influenced. However, you may also choose to link your ideas to contemporary practitioners who have a distinctive style to their work. Examples of these are explored on pages 40–42. Alternatively, you may wish to use other companies which are not listed in this book.

**Characterisation**

What information does the text provide about the protagonists? Consider the factual circumstances of each role and also look at the more subtle indicators of character, such as the comments and reactions of other characters. This should not be a plain character study; it needs to be a creative vision of the character's role in the performance as a whole.

**Language**

Identify the different types of language used in the play: who uses them and when do they use them? Why has the playwright chosen to use different registers of language? This area is concerned with how the play's meaning is communicated to the audience through the characters. A dialogue might be used or a monologue delivered to the audience, or one character might communicate their thoughts as a soliloquy. The style of the language might be naturalistic, stylised, representative, poetic and so on.

**Vocal awareness**

Document your practical experiences of experimenting with different vocal techniques. Look at specific sections of the text where varying your vocal tone is essential in communicating meaning. Try to identify the intended impact on the audience.

**Non-verbal action**

Show that you understand the effect any movement may have, whether it be the smallest hand gesture or a bold stride across the stage. Some of these actions may be explicit in the stage directions but others will be more subtle. What are the most appropriate physical actions for the text?

How does the play look and sound, and how is the space used by the performers? This area concerns the function and the symbolic effect of these elements, as well as the decisions that can be made by a director when staging the play. In general:

➤ **Visual** refers to the set, lighting and costumes

➤ **Aural** refers to the sound and music

➤ **Spatial** refers to the staging.

> Don't confuse set and staging: the set is the design of the fixed space; staging is how the director moves the actors within this space.

You will need to discuss all of these and consider in depth some specific key moments or examples. You will need to consider how the play can be directed to allow blocking of the actors and movement.

This is an opportunity for you to demonstrate a fully integrated approach to the text in performance and should be a combination of all the other elements. You should demonstrate a unified vision which shows a complete understanding of how your text could work successfully in performance.

In order to achieve a mark within the highest band of the assessment criteria for your exploration notes, you need to demonstrate 'an outstanding knowledge and understanding' of both plays, with your comments closely linked to your practical experiences. All notes that you make need to be 'accurate, concise, analytical and well researched'.

## Equus

*Equus* was written in 1973 by Peter Shaffer and focuses on the disturbed mind of Alan Strang and a psychiatrist's attempts to treat him.

### Social, cultural, historical and political context

Peter Shaffer and his twin brother, Anthony, were born in Liverpool in 1926. After he finished his schooling, Peter Shaffer was conscripted to work in a coal mine as many of the country's adult population were fighting in World War Two. He loathed the experience and it gave him a long-lasting appreciation of what many individuals are forced to endure to earn a livelihood.

> Anthony Shaffer is also a playwright, like his brother, and is perhaps most famous for his screen plays, *Sleuth* (1972) (adapted from his play of the same name) and *The Wicker Man* (1973).

After graduating from Cambridge in 1950, he moved to New York, undertaking various jobs while he wrote a series of detective novels. His first play, *Five Finger Exercise*, was directed by John Gielgud in 1958 and proved to be very successful. His reputation continued to build in the years that followed but was cemented with his first full-length play, *The Royal Hunt of the Sun* (1964). The play received great critical acclaim and during the next 20 years he wrote many more celebrated texts, including *Amadeus* (1979) and the comedy *Lettice and Lovage* (1987).

A common theme in his plays is the battle between two central characters. The early drafts of *Equus* focused on Alan's act of violence. However, Shaffer gradually came to realise that the interest in the piece stems from the clash between the boy and his psychiatrist, Dysart.

Shaffer also regularly explores the theme of worship in his work. His characters are often grappling with the notion of celebrating or destroying someone's faith and Alan's commitment to his pagan horse rituals is something that Dysart admires. His patient's behaviour is by no means normal and yet Dysart's marriage can not be described as normal either. At least Alan has passion and by 'curing' him, Dysart is afraid he will also suppress this: 'Without worship you shrink, it's as brutal as that' (scene 25).

There are many references to religion in *Equus*. Some of these stem from the obvious conflict between Frank and Dora's differing views on Christianity, but others are more subtly raised throughout the narrative. Alan quotes his father when he declares 'Religion is the opium of the people' (scene 6). This references an argument of the 19th-century philosopher, Karl Marx. Research Marx and his views and see how these might provide further insight into the conflict between Frank and Dora's middle-class upbringing.

In scene 11, Dora explains that Alan used to have a picture on his wall of 'Our Lord on his way to Calvary'. Carry out an image search on the internet to find appropriate examples of this picture. Now improvise a scene between Alan and his mother at bedtime. He should be staring at the image while his mother reads from the Bible, Job 39:18. How might performing such an improvisation alter an actor's performance in scene 14?

Shaffer has been strongly influenced by the theories of Carl Jung whom he described as 'one of the greatest minds of the 20th century'. He became interested in the discussion of mythical figures and the concept of 'neurosis as an escape from legitimate pain'. Research Jung's theories and then discuss in small groups whether or not Dysart applies Jung's approach. Find examples from the text which support your ideas.

In 2007, the revival of *Equus* at the Gielgud Theatre received great critical acclaim, suggesting that the play still has contemporary relevance. Consider how a modern audience might respond to the following issues and questions which the play raises:

➢ Alan's violent attack on the horses is considered shocking and socially unacceptable and his behaviour deemed abnormal. Is it the fact that his attack is carried out on a horse which an audience finds singularly disturbing?

➢ Are there any ways in which animals are treated which might be considered cruel, yet are still socially acceptable?

➢ What behaviour does Alan consider to be cruel?

➤ Alan has an obsession with television which his father detests. What behaviour might Frank find frustrating in a 21st-century teenager?

## Response to a practitioner

Shaffer's style in his early plays was often naturalistic and experimented with farce. However, as he developed as a writer, he became frustrated with realistic acting and its obsessive focus, as he saw it, on the 'minute fragment, minutely observed'.

**Artaud**

Instead, he advocated a form of 'total theatre' which involved combining the words of the text with 'rites, mimes, masks and magic'. He realised that in order to sustain interest in contemporary theatre, he needed to create performances which had the power to 'perturb and make gasp: to please and make laugh: to surprise'. In many ways, this may make you reflect on the work of Artaud and his similar love of the ritualistic spectacle. In fact, *The Royal Hunt of the Sun* resembles some of the lavish scenarios that Artaud documented. However, while an Artaudian style of presentation is definitely evident in his work, Shaffer's reliance on language suggests that he is not quite so strongly influenced by Artaud as we might initially suspect.

**Brecht**

It is when we compare his work to the practitioner Bertolt Brecht, that we find most similarities. Shaffer's work is truly epic in style. He relies heavily on narrative, distancing the audience from becoming too involved in the action of the play. The nature of Alan's violent act is disclosed from the very start and so dramatic interest stems from the motivation behind his behaviour, rather than an unfolding plot. The playwright explores the social influences on Alan through a series of structural devices which recreate past action. The direct address of Dysart encourages the audience to think and reason their way through the events, raising questions without providing easy answers.

The staging of *Equus* is clearly Brechtian. The mechanics of theatre are on display at all times and all the actors remain on stage, in full view of the audience, the latter surrounding the action as if they were a jury judging the behaviour of the protagonist. The boxing ring-like area serves to create a multitude of settings, always representing a location rather than becoming it. But it is the horses which constitute the boldest acknowledgement of Brecht's style. Minimalist in design and ritualistically adorned, the animal masks are resolutely human, and the actor is always evident.

---

 In order to understand the power of narration, try the following two exercises.

**Yes, and...** Divide your group into pairs. You and your partner are going to improvise and narrate a story one sentence at a time. The content is not particularly important at this stage, the focus is on beginning each new sentence with the phrase 'Yes, and...' On a simplistic level, this phrase should reinforce the importance of accepting and adding to your partner's ideas. However, in terms of

Brecht, it also focuses attention on the role of the two narrators, who should use eye contact with the audience to communicate their story. The narration might go along the following lines:

**A**: We were walking home from a party at one in the morning.
**B**: Yes, and it was dark, cold and I was starting to feel unwell.
**A**: Yes, and I suggested that we should take a shortcut.

After five minutes of rehearsal, perform your improvised narrative to the rest of the group.

**Question and answer.** Working in the same pairs, try a slightly different approach to narration. This time, only one of you has walked home from the party. The other is a parent who wishes to know why you arrived home so late. The parent should do most of the narrating of the story, with the son or daughter answering, for the most part, 'Yes' to the questioning narrative. The response, 'No', should be used sparingly, to occasionally elaborate on an aspect of behaviour. As the story is being told by the parent, their partner (playing the son/daughter) performs the action. After improvising the scene, show your work to the rest of the group. Now read through scene 19 and look at how Shaffer uses Alan's hypnosis as a device to reveal the past. What other devices are used throughout the play to keep the action in the past tense? Identify these in your notes.

> 66 Tragedy obviously does not lie in a conflict of Right and Wrong but in a collision of two different forms of Right; in this case, surely, between Dysart's professional obligation to treat a terrified boy who has committed a dreadful crime and Alan's capacity for worship. 99
>
> Peter Shaffer, a personal essay, *Equus* ed. T. S Pearce (Longman 1983).

## Characterisation

Shaffer's decision to focus on the conflict between two protagonists in many of his plays has resulted in his style of characterisation gaining some criticism. His central characters form the crux of his intellectual debates while the others are often in danger of being perceived as social stereotypes whose role is simply to aid the debate. When working on the text, it is important that you consider this argument and analyse to what extent you believe it to be true.

 Assign each member of your group one of the following characters to focus on: Alan, Dysart, Frank, Dora, Jill and Hesther. You should each write a 200-word monologue using your character's dialogue. You can only use the words your character speaks in the text, although you may wish to consider whether it would be better to speak the lines directly to the audience or try to create a scene in which you encourage the audience to imagine the other characters on stage with whom you are interacting. Focus specifically on voice. Think about how changes in accent, tone, projection, pace, pitch and pause can successfully communicate the character's state of mind. Prepare your piece outside of lessons and perform it without the use of a script. Although movement is obviously important in the creation of character, you should focus specifically on your delivery of the words. Perform each of the pieces to the rest of the group and through discussion, identify which of the lines particularly epitomise the character's attitude. You may find it appropriate to identify these within your notes, demonstrating an understanding of each character's perspective on the world of the play.

The conflict that exists between Alan and Dysart is paralleled by conflicts in many of the play's other relationships. Begin by focusing on Dora and Frank. Discuss the inherent conflicts in their relationship. Then look at the other disagreements that exist between Dysart and Hesther, Alan and Jill or indeed any of the more subtle battles in the play. Document the key elements of this discussion in your notes.

Shaffer's action often takes place against the backdrop of a stagnant society, where excitement and ecstasy are absent. Alan, according to Shaffer, has a 'rather dreary and colourless provincial life ... working with not much to look forward to in an electrical and kitchenware shop with an unimaginative but kindly father and ... mother'. In groups of four or five, create the physical image of this shop. Consider how you would position Alan in the scene. Try creating a further **four** images which suggest how his physicality alters during a day's work. What might the physicality of the other characters imply about their social class?

The interest in the relationship between Dysart and Hesther stems from their familiarity and mutual respect for one another. In pairs, improvise the scene when they first meet. Where might this scene take place? Is it at a time when Dysart's relationship with his wife has already become stale? How might this affect Dysart and Hesther's discussion?

## Language

The language of Shaffer's characters is an extremely important aspect of the world of the play. Each character has a different quality and rhythm of speech. If you take lines of the text at random, you will often be able to attribute them to the correct character, such is the distinctive nature of the language. Note, for instance, Dysart's use of third-person poetic narrative and his monologues of self-doubt; characteristics of Alan's speech include his vivid descriptions of the horses, use of ceremonial language and occasional use of expletives.

In addition to the distinctive qualities of individual characters' speech, there are certain styles of language which can be recognised in the play, as a whole:

➢ Naturalistic dialogue

➢ Religious quotations

➢ Frequent use of questioning to aid plot development

➢ The language of commercials and electrical products.

In general terms, most of the language used by any character other than Alan is relatively mundane. The world in which the adults live is bland and part of the play's contemporary appeal lies in the fact that their behaviour is deeply rooted in the past. Dora's adherence to religious doctrine and Frank's criticism of television reinforce the image of suffocating parents. Even Dysart, the psychiatrist trying to understand Alan's crime through persistent questions, can appear unrelenting in his style. It is only when he describes Alan that his language becomes more vivid. One of the play's great ironies lies in the fact that Alan is the most interesting character. He should be someone whom we detest but we cannot help admiring his passion, which is evident in all aspects of his language.

Look at Dysart's opening monologue. Identify the words which celebrate the relationship between Alan and the horse. Now look at the words or phrases which Dysart uses to describe himself. This opening passage is the audience's introduction to the world of the play. What does it reveal about the play they are going to watch? How might the actor playing Dysart emphasise the key phrases you have identified through either movement or voice? Make notes on your observations.

Alan occasionally uses expletives to change the tone of a scene. Find examples of Alan's swearing and suggest why Schaffer has chosen to use them at each point. How are the audience expected to react to their delivery?

Apart from his sessions with Dysart, Alan rarely has any moments of naturalistic dialogue with another character. The main example of this is in scene 32. Most of the language in the play takes the form of intense questioning between characters which could be performed at quite a fast pace. However, in this scene, the ellipses suggest a greater awkwardness in the delivery. Working in groups of three, with one person as a director, stage scene 32, finishing at the point at which Dysart interrupts. Consider how you could communicate Alan's inner turmoil. Perform the work to the rest of the group and discuss the most successful interpretations. Make notes on the points that were raised.

## Vocal awareness

The style of *Equus* provides many opportunities for experimentation with sound which should allow you to demonstrate a strong awareness of the vocal techniques required. Stage directions and text should be referenced in your notes with clear annotations explaining what you have learnt.

Stand in a tight circle with all the members of the group (or lie on your backs on the floor with your heads pointing towards the middle). Starting with a hum, experiment with sounds to create the mood during scene 21, when Alan describes entering the field late at night. No words should be used and you should avoid creating sound effects which are too literal.

There is no need to justify the sounds you are making but do make sure you are listening carefully to the contributions of others. If your group is large, you may want to divide into two or more groups and then perform your work to others. Make notes on the sounds that worked most successfully.

Look at the choral work in scene 15 when most of the actors help to create the essence of Alan's workplace. Shaffer's stage directions are quite explicit here: 'There is a constant background mumbling made up of trade names, out of which can be clearly distinguished the italicised words, which are shouted out.' With the actor playing Alan standing, and all other actors at the sides of the stage, contributing only with their voices, try to create Shaffer's vision.

Undertake research into how each of the advertising slogans in scene 2 should be sung. The 1977 film adaptation of *Equus* is useful for learning the different melodies, although you may also be able to find them by searching on the internet. Apply them practically to the scene. How should the actor playing Alan sing the lyrics? Should it be a dispassionate mimicking of the advert or a more aggressive defence against Dysart's persistent questioning?

Shaffer disliked the film adaptation of *Equus*: see page 61.

Despite the criticism which has been levelled at Shaffer's simplistic characterisation, during the course of the play each character undertakes a journey of self discovery and, as a result of this, their movement and voice should significantly alter. The skill you need to exhibit in your notes is to demonstrate an understanding of this progression in a clear, succinct and sophisticated manner. Select **three** short excerpts of text from different parts of the play which highlight the developing relationship between Dysart and Alan. Photocopy these sections and place them in your notes. Annotate the script to show how the actors' vocal delivery could reflect this evolving relationship.

It can be difficult as an actor to break up the text into its component monologues. They can appear such a daunting challenge that an actor might end up delivering lines at a fast pace without appreciating the shape and development of the character's thoughts. Using Dora's monologue in scene 23 as a

See pages 128–134.

guide, apply some of the exercises outlined in the section on monologues. Identify what you have learned about the changes in vocal technique and document this in your notes.

## Non-verbal action

Despite Shaffer's tightly written prose, it is the physical imagery that brings the world of the play to life. It is the key to Alan's world, his excitement and fear, and occurs in a sufficiently abstract way for the audience to impose their own interpretation on events. As Shaffer observes, 'visual action is to me as much a part of the play as dialogue'. Even without masks to represent the horses' heads, there is plenty to experiment with physically.

Look at scene 10: the young horseman arrives in slow motion, rides around at normal speed before allowing Alan to touch his imaginary horse and climb onto his shoulders. This sequence might be difficult to imagine but it needs to be carefully structured in order to dispel any comic images which might arise of pantomime-style horses or Monty Python knights. Rehearse this scene with a partner, ignoring the dialogue and focusing on the physical images. In your notes, you could present your ideas through a series of stick men rather than written description.

In order for the key moments of action to be successfully communicated through mime, it would help to be familiar with the shape and dimensions of a horse. Arrange a visit to a local stables and ask to groom one of the horses. Note how its neck and head moves. How does the movement of its legs convey how it's feeling? Take photographs of your visit and annotate the images in your notes.

The National Theatre's 2007 production of *War Horse* (adapted by Nick Stafford from a Michael Morpurgo novel of the same name) used life-size horse puppets. Visit www.nationaltheatre.org.uk/warhorse to view images from the production.

The power of some of the extreme visual images in the play is often juxtaposed with more subtle changes in physicality. Scene 14 is a classic example of this: Frank's embarrassment is highlighted in the stage directions and as the scene develops Alan's extreme, disturbing mime contrasts with Frank's controlled discomfort. In groups of three, rehearse this scene up until the point when Frank coughs, looking closely at the movements of father and son.

## Visual, aural and spatial elements

Shaffer is quite explicit in his introduction to the play about how the original production was staged. He does this to help the reader understand the style of the performance rather than being prescriptive and suggesting that this is the only possible interpretation. It is fair to assume, however, that your version should reflect the Brechtian staging with minimal use of set and the theatrical devices and actors in full view of the audience. You may find it useful to watch the 1977 film version to gain an understanding of the period. However, be aware that this is quite a literal production of the text and although Shaffer wrote the screenplay, he was clearly disappointed with the final result: 'What depressed me about the film is that it didn't have any of the images I wanted to see in it.'

Your response to this section should show a comprehensive understanding of how the whole text could work in performance. It is important that you don't design a stage which would work effectively for one scene but be totally impractical for others.

Look at Shaffer's description of the setting in the introduction to the text. He identifies several key elements:

➤ A square of wood (like a boxing ring) set on a circle of wood

➤ Wooden rails and three gaps

➤ The revolving nature of the square

➤ Olive-green benches in the square and the circle

➤ A metal pole

➤ The audience on the stage

➤ Two ladders from which the horse masks hang

➤ The visible lighting grid.

Using these key elements, design your version of the set considering the size of the stage space and auditorium. Indicate clearly where your audience are positioned, and the nature and colour of the materials you will be using.

---

The design of the horse masks is key to conveying Alan's fascination with the animal. The original design was made of 'alternating bands of silver wire and leather'. In your staging designs you should include your vision of how the masks will look. Begin by finding images of a horse's head which you could use as a starting point. Trace over this image, although remember that you are designing the mask: only use lines which are essential for representing the contours of the face. Decide which materials you will use and identify these on your plan.

---

Characters' costumes not only help to create the period of the piece, they can also convey details about their individual personalities. Be wary of inadvertently creating a modern version by clothing Alan in a hoodie and jeans. This would imply a naive understanding of the text. You could choose costumes which are from no distinct period, giving the play a timeless element, which would be reinforced by the Strangs' old-fashioned nature. You might

**Further viewing**

The 1977 film of *Equus* was directed by Sidney Lumet and starred Richard Burton as Dysart and Peter Firth as Alan. Watch some of Shaffer's other plays which have been adapted into films: *Five Finger Exercise* (1962), *The Royal Hunt of the Sun* (1969) and *Amadeus* (1984).

**Key elements**

**Further study**

Use the internet to find images from different productions of the play. Avoid being confused by some of the images of the 2007 West End production starring Daniel Radcliffe: although a white horse was used in the promotional photographs it did not feature in the production itself.

decide instead to set it firmly in the 1970s. A further option would be to have all the characters in neutral colours with the style and material of the costume reinforcing their roles. For example, Dora could be wearing a tight-fitting blouse, firmly buttoned up to the neck, representing a need to protect and hide herself.

> Amon Tobin's music evokes a particularly moving and disturbing collection of moods which might be effective in reflecting some of the key moments of action.
> Listen to his album, *Supermodified* (Ninja Tune 2000).

The use of sound in the piece needs to be as abstract as the set. Very little reference is made to sound in the script and, taken literally, this might suggest that only a few additional noises should be added to those created by the chorus of horses. However, you might consider adding some instrumental tracks to provide an underscore to certain moments of action.

The lighting of the relatively simplistic set will enable you to convey both mood and location. The warm, exhilarating nature of Alan's ride on the beach should provide a stark contrast to the darkened stables at night. You don't need to be thoroughly proficient at all aspects of lighting, although you can gain a good overview of some of the key areas for consideration by visiting: http://en.wikipedia.org/wiki/Theatre_lighting. There may also be examples of successful designs and accompanying photographs on the internet. Try searching for 'Equus lighting design' and check for any helpful images.

## Interpretation

Whatever form your exploration notes have taken, it would be helpful to prove your comprehensive understanding of the play by selecting a section of the text and linking together the different theatre skills you have explored. This should be a distillation of your ideas for the whole play, which you have explored through research, discussion and practice. By making notes on the different activities explored in this section, you will have demonstrated an awareness of the play's potential in performance. However, the interpretation gives you a chance to organise all of the different elements into one coherent vision.

**Sample interpretation**

The example shown opposite focuses on scene 29. Remember that the exam board expects you to have your notes firmly embedded in practical exploration so be careful not to become overly focused on theoretical detail. You will not be able to identify each point in every line; the aim is to show an insightful awareness of the different production elements in the extract.

# Interpretation: Equus by Peter Shaffer

Intended impact of scene: to present Alan and Frank Strang's embarrassment about sex.

I experimented in rehearsal with how to use the hat to convey Frank's nervousness: held tightly in right hand, occasionally loosening grip to imply moments of doubt.

Dysart's voice needs to be quiet and unobtrusive, almost monotone. He is a passive observer of the scene.

The use of the word 'God' is important. In front of Dysart his language is stronger but here there is an innocence (and of course it's a reminder of the theme of religion). He should face forward, staring blankly, frozen by fear.

*(Frank steps into the square furtively from the back, hat in hand, and stands looking about for a place.)*

**Dysart:** Was that the first time you'd seen a girl naked?

**Alan** *(to Dysart):* Yes! You couldn't see everything, though … *(looking about him.)* All round me they were all looking. All the men – staring up like they were in church. Like they were a sort of congregation. And then – *(He sees his father.)* Ah! *(At the same time Frank sees him.)*

**Frank:** Alan!

**Alan:** God!

**Jill:** What is it?

**Alan:** Dad!

**Jill:** Where?

**Alan:** At the back! He saw me!

**Jill:** You sure?

**Alan:** Yes.

**Frank** *(calling):* Alan!

**Alan:** Oh God!

As Shaffer intended, the scene takes place on the central square, with the audience positioned on all four sides, judging the action like a jury.

The actor playing Alan should alter his physicality as he moves from narrator to character. His embarrassment is shown through poor posture, shoulders hunched and head low: a clear contrast to his fascination with the film and its audience.

The scene should be well lit, although the actors should create the sense of a dark cinema. When working on this scene, we rehearsed in virtual blackout, with the light from a projector providing the only illumination. The rest of the group played other people in the busy cinema. We repeated the scene first with the lights on and then with fewer people on stage. This helped the actor playing Frank to create the location with stumbling movement and overuse of his arms to steady himself in the implied darkness.

## Oedipus Rex

Thebes is gripped by a devastating plague. Oedipus, the king of Thebes, has already rid the city of the sphinx, a monster with the head of a woman on the body of a lion who sat at the gate of Thebes and asked riddles of those trying to pass, killing all who failed to answer correctly. He now insists he will find the cause of the plague. He consults the oracle of the god Apollo and is told that he must find the killer of Laius, the former king of Thebes. Oedipus publicly curses the murderer and proclaims that he will stop at nothing until the truth about Laius' murder is known. As the action unfolds, segments of the past are slowly revealed, allowing Oedipus to finally realise that he is '…The unclean thing/The dirt that breeds disease' – the murderer of Laius. Furthermore, the previous king was his father. It becomes clear that his wife is also his mother, and she kills herself in shame. Horrified, Oedipus blinds himself and Creon, his brother-in-law, banishes him from the city.

*Oedipus Rex* by Sophocles is a Greek tragedy written in approximately 427–426 BCE. Today, Sophocles is probably the most famous and successful of all Greek playwrights. He was born near Athens in 496 BCE into a wealthy family. At the age of 28, he competed for the first time in the City Dionysia and by his death in 406 BCE at the age of 90, he had won at this festival an incredible 24 times.

During his life, Sophocles wrote at least 123 plays but only seven have survived. He is credited with being the first Greek playwright to use three actors, which enabled him to explore his ideas in a more complex form. This meant that the role of the chorus was slightly less pronounced and allowed for more interaction, engagement and tension between characters.

When you read through the play for the first time, make sure you read the introduction and the stage directions, as these will provide you with a more complete understanding of it. After the first reading of this, or any, text you should consider the following issues:

➤ What happens in the story? List the events in the order they happen.

➤ How is the story told? Think about the structure and the form – the devices and conventions used.

➤ Are there any stage directions? Do they help when considering the form of the play?

➤ What immediate problems do you find when thinking about taking the words off the page and putting action on the stage?

### Social, cultural, historical and political context

Sophocles was a well-respected social figure in Athens with military experience. He was passionately religious and had strong moral values. He was a loyal citizen, although as he grew older he became cynical about the new democratic government that was being developed. One of his many strengths was his ability to explore complex human thoughts, emotions and desires through

---

### Plot summary

According to legend, the sphinx asked Oedipus: 'What walks on four legs in the morning, two legs at noon, and three legs in the evening?' He correctly answered that it is man, who as a baby crawls on all fours and in old age uses a stick as a third leg. In frustration that he had solved her riddle, the sphinx threw herself from the city walls.

### Further reading

The translation used in this section is by Don Taylor in *Sophocles Plays volume 1* (Methuen Drama, an imprint of A&C Black Publishers 1986).

*Oedipus Rex* is the Latin translation of the Greek name for the play. You may also see it referred to as *Oedipus Tyrannus* and *Oedipus the King*.

For more on the Athens Dionysia see pages 8–11.

Be careful when discussing stage directions for plays that are not modern. No ancient manuscripts of Sophocles' plays included stage directions and those you find in your text have been added by later editors and translators. Try comparing different translations of *Oedipus Rex* to see how they vary.

### Web link

Many websites offer plot summaries and theme analyses that can help to clarify any grey areas. Try www.gradesaver.com/ClassicNotes/Titles/oedipus as a starting point and then work from the links provided.

drama. Characters in his plays were thought to illustrate universal truths, demonstrating patterns of behaviour that audiences could recognise in themselves. His central characters are known for being strong-willed individuals who, against the backdrop of a glorious past, are confronted with great personal disaster.

The infamy of Oedipus' tale means that there is a wide range of sources over many different periods to explore. Think of your notes as a scrapbook of ideas about the play and the story. Cut and paste different source materials and then add your own annotations. Look at images as well as text and be careful not to let one source dominate. Remember that personal analysis is essential.

The relatively simple structure of *Oedipus Rex* combined with its formal tone may initially suggest that it is a piece of historic theatre with little significance for the modern world. However, the style of leadership demonstrated by Oedipus in his opening speech is similar to the rhetoric used by many political figures today. The references to religion may have less relevance, although comparisons can be drawn with contemporary beliefs relating to fate and destiny.

**Further study**

Sigmund Freud developed the theory of the Oedipus complex as a way of explaining the love a child might feel towards one parent while experiencing hate for the other. Look at this theory in more detail, tracking its relevance and influence. See, for example, www.freudfile.org.

---

**?** Look at the role of religion in *Oedipus Rex*. Which gods are mentioned in the play? Would their significance be lost in a contemporary production? How might modern western views on religion alter the perception of certain characters and scenes? Focus on the concept of fate and destiny versus choice and free will. Theoretically, Oedipus was doomed from birth, yet was there any chance he could have survived once the murky details of his life are exposed? What similar concepts exist today?

---

**?** Oedipus' **hubris**, or extreme self-belief, is ultimately his downfall. Modern-day politicians often tread a fine line between being strong leaders and appearing arrogant. Look at how George W. Bush and Tony Blair reacted to the 9/11 attack on New York, and the subsequent wars in Afghanistan and Iraq. Is too much self-belief a weakness? Consider what comments a performance of *Oedipus* could make to today's society about someone falling from a position of greatness. Does society derive pleasure from watching people fall in this way?

Hubris means more than just pride: it means having so much belief in yourself that you overstep, often violently, the limits that as a human being you should remain within, thus offending the gods.

---

Steven Berkoff adapted *Oedipus*, renaming it *Greek*. He set it in London, using cockney caricatures, and translated the original plague into images of acid rain, deforestation, football hooliganism and AIDS. The central character, Eddy, is warned of his fate by a fortune teller but he seems to have a lot more control over his destiny than Oedipus. Berkoff criticises the inertia that he sees in society, and the language he uses is violent and designed to shock. Read the play and note the choices Berkoff has made in adapting *Oedipus*. Is such an adaptation necessary for contemporary society?

**Web link**

A useful website showing reviews and photographs of the 1988 production of *Greek* can be found at www.agirlwholovesbrucepayne.com/greekjune2002.html. *Greek* was later turned into an opera by Mark Antony Turnage. What is it about the story that invites this treatment?

More information on Kneehigh can be found on pages 40–41.

More information on Kneehigh can be found on pages 40–41.

## Web link

You can find the text of Aristotle's Poetics at www.authorama.com/the-poetics-1.html.

66 Tragedy tries as far as possible to keep within a single revolution of the sun. 99

Aristotle, *Poetics*, in *Classical Literary Criticism* trans. Penelope Murray and T. S. Dorsch (Penguin Classics 2000).

The exception to this is the choral odes, during which much time could elapse off-stage.

These 'three unities' are so frequently attributed to Aristotle himself that almost everyone in the theatre now believes them to be his idea. It is important that you demonstrate a knowledge of these unities in your exploration notes since they are a standard critical way of summing up how Sophocles built his play, and have been very influential on generations of playwrights.

## Response to a practitioner

There have been many modern-day productions of Greek theatre which have attempted to make the genre accessible for a contemporary audience. The Actors of Dionysus create relatively faithful versions of the texts, albeit in a 21st-century setting. Kneehigh Theatre tends to take a more liberal approach to the traditions of Greek theatre. Their 2004 production of *The Bacchae* by Euripides featured an all-male chorus dressed in tutus.

However, Sophocles' style is best summarised by the writings of **Aristotle**. Aristotle (384–322 BCE) is one of the most influential of all Greek philosophers. His writings covered all major areas of thought, including science, ethics, politics and art, and his views on drama were particularly influential on later scholars. In his opinion, Sophocles' *Oedipus Rex* was the finest example of a tragedy.

He argued that most plays followed certain principles, which he outlined in his *Poetics*; however, it was the structure of *Oedipus Rex* in particular that impressed him and his ideas are largely based on this play. Although the thought of reading Aristotle may sound daunting, *Poetics* is actually a clear, insightful and short introduction to the rules of theatre and his ideas have been echoed in Shakespeare as well as in the work of many modern playwrights. Essentially he stressed the importance of the dramatic unity of action, so that the play is properly focused and avoids distractions. Later writers elaborated on Aristotle's ideas and offered a rule that plays ought to possess **three** dramatic unities – time, place and action:

1. **Time.** All events must take place in chronological order. The running time of the performance must mirror the time we spend in the world of the play. *Oedipus Rex* happens in real time.

2. **Place.** The play should be set in one location, putting the focus on plot and character development. *Oedipus Rex* is set in the royal courtyard, outside the palace of Oedipus in Thebes.

3. **Action.** The action in the play must be consequential and rational. Aristotle criticised episodic plays, which consist of a series of episodes that do not follow rationally from one to another, requiring the audience to believe in an unlikely turn of events or coincidence.

Aristotle identified key moments in the text as:

➤ **Reversal of situation**, when a character bringing what seems like good news or information actually finds themselves delivering bad news and adding to the suffering of the central character, as with the messenger who reveals to Oedipus that the parents he has avoided for so long were not in fact his mother and father.

➤ **Recognition**, when a character realises the full extent of their role in the tragedy, following all the detective work. Both Jocasta and Oedipus have moments of recognition.

➤ **Suffering**, which usually happens in the last episode where the protagonist is publicly humiliated for their actions. At this point, an audience should experience a form of **catharsis**.

> Catharsis is the release or cleansing of emotional tensions. Such scenes were thought to help the audience become better citizens through the play, since they could experience extreme emotions in a controlled way. The idea was Aristotle's answer to Plato's hostility to tragedy, which he considered to encourage the wrong emotions and behaviour in its audience.

In pairs, identify short extracts of the text which illustrate moments of reversal, recognition and suffering for Oedipus' character. Rehearse these as a series of short scenes thinking carefully about how his behaviour might alter over time. Perform your work and make notes on the most successful practical examples demonstrated.

Greek rhetorician, Gorgias (483–378 BCE) stated that tragedy is about the emotional experience of the audience. Aristotle attempted to define this experience by focusing on the emotions of fear and pity. He believed that any performance should awaken 'pity for the undeserving sufferer and fear for the man like ourselves' in order to have the greatest impact on an audience. Reread the section of *Oedipus Rex* from the messenger's speech to the end. Make a list of moments which elicit our pity for Oedipus and moments where we might fear for ourselves. Which list is longer? Would it be possible to evoke this response from an audience in a contemporary production?

## Characterisation

The action within the play centres on its eponymous character. Other roles are there to facilitate or comment on his downfall. Oedipus begins as a strong individual. He is a king, a man we respect, and his initial speech increases his status. However, from the moment of Tiresias' entrance he loses power and his downfall begins, since his pride prevents him from accepting the words of the blind seer. Each new action serves to accelerate his descent. It is only when he emerges as a blind man, aware of his crimes that he begins to regain our sympathy and some of his initial status.

> 66 Comedy aims at representing men as worse than they are nowadays, tragedy as better. 99
>
> Aristotle, *Poetics*, in *Classical Literary Criticism* trans. Penelope Murray and T. S. Dorsch (Penguin Classics 2000).

It's important to understand the qualities that would have given the people of Thebes confidence in their leader. Select four members of your group to write a motivational speech for the student body in a maximum of 100 words each. They should imagine that their friends are quite negative and need inspiration from a well-respected friend. Perform the four speeches and identify which of them was the most successful. What qualities did this student demonstrate? How did they gain your confidence? Link these points to the advice you would give the actor playing Oedipus at the beginning of the play.

 Chart Oedipus' downfall on a graph, noting how his high status falls over time. Label key moments of the action within the play, indicating the characters involved and quoting lines of dialogue which are particularly important. Copy this graph into your notes identifying moments of reversal, recognition and suffering.

---

How does Creon in the last scene of the play compare with Oedipus at the start? What information is implied about each character's style of leadership? How might this be reflected through accent, tone, projection, pace, pitch and pause?

---

**Rehearsal**

The role of the chorus is vital in the play and its presence will clearly add to any production. It is possible to use it as a stylised image of humanity, where individual identities are ignored. However, there is more dramatic potential if you consider it as a group of 12 to 15 individuals who represent a cross-section of the citizens of Thebes. They can speak or sing the text individually, in unison or in canon and their movement could be realistic or choreographed. Their role is to question, reject, reinforce and explore the behaviour of the protagonist. Their reactions to the actions and words of the protagonists are important in guiding the response of the audience. Look at their speech beginning 'Like a shadow thrown in the dust', immediately after the scene with Oedipus, the shepherd and the Corinthian. How might the performance of this first stanza make the audience re-evaluate the words and actions of characters? Rehearse this section as a whole group and make notes on your decisions.

> Sophocles is said to have increased the chorus in Greek theatre from 12 to 15 members.

## Language

The majority of the action in *Oedipus Rex* takes place before the play begins. The language of the text focuses on how Oedipus discovers the truth about who he is and what he has done. Think of it as a detective story where the clues gradually reveal the murderer.

> Heightened language is more formal speech which can, on occasions, appear unrealistic. The words are carefully chosen by the playwright to ensure maximum impact.

The style of the language within the play will depend on the translation you use. However, there are immediate features that should transcend all editions. Much of the language will be heightened and poetic, written in verse. There should be a clear difference between the strength of Oedipus' royal declamations at the start of the play and the words of the shepherd. Try to focus on the differences between the characters as this will provide a starting point for your analysis.

---

*Oedipus Rex* works on two levels: the words spoken by the characters and the images created on stage. At the beginning these work in unison. Oedipus enters through the palace doors. He speaks like a great orator and his movement should be confident in order to reflect his obvious power.

Individually, rehearse the opening 11 lines, finishing on 'Everyone knows my name'. Consider how vocal and physical work could ensure Oedipus' character has maximum impact at the start of the play. Now, in groups of four or five, perform this section to one another, identifying specific moments where the communication of his greatness is most successful. Write these down in your exploration notes.

---

**Movement**

As the play progresses, the power in Oedipus' voice should be betrayed by the lack of control in his movement. Consider how physical and vocal language could be used to ensure the blind prophet Tiresias has more status then the king. Tiresias speaks in riddles and uses his vision to prophesy. Look closely at how his language baffles and threatens the powerful king, for example: 'I know, but you do not / That the woman you love is not the woman you love.' In pairs, try positioning Tiresias centre stage and consider how his stillness could be contrasted with the over-confident and arrogant movement of the king.

The language of the chorus is much more evocative and poetic than that of the main characters and is essential in creating the world outside the play: the dying city, the influence of the gods and a sense of personal suffering. Think about how the chorus can work in a modern production. There is a danger in supporting their spoken words with literal gestures since these could appear trite and superficial. Instead focus on more abstract movements in order to create mood and atmosphere.

In groups of about six to eight, look at the first chorus section. Begin with 'Our agonies are beyond telling', and finish on 'Will you not answer our cry?'. Nominate someone to be the chorus leader. Everyone else should individually underline eight short phrases from this section that they feel carry impact. The chorus leader should read the entire section while everyone else will only speak their chosen lines. This creates a variety of textures and emphasises the individual and collective suffering of the people of Thebes.

Experiment with simple movements that aid the communication of this section of the text. The group should begin with their backs to the audience and only turn slowly to face them when they say their first line. Try rocking, swaying, standing in a tight group, in small groups or even individually. Record what you have learned in your notes. In order for the audience to imagine fully the horrors of the off-stage action, the messenger's language is brutal and activates powerful images in the mind. If delivered well, the language of the messenger's speech can have an even greater impact on the audience than such events would if depicted on stage, as it plays on the resources of the audience's imagination. Photocopy a section of the speech and stick it in your notes. Imagine you are directing the section. Annotate the text to show how you would want it to be performed. Try to identify changes of pace (including pause), tone, volume and emotion. Consider how vocal delivery might reinforce the power of key phrases.

## Vocal awareness

The structure of Greek tragedies means that there are certain stylised ways of presenting action. The fact that there was a maximum of only three characters on stage at once means that the playwright needed to use different forms of writing to convey the tension. In a contemporary performance, these restrictions may feel artificial and it is vital that actors demonstrate the full range of vocal techniques in order to engage the audience.

 **Stichomythia** is a series of one-line exchanges that would often be spoken quickly in order to increase tension. The technique is used when Oedipus challenges both Tiresias and Creon. In pairs, choose one of these scenes and sit opposite each other. Read through the dialogue, trying to maintain quite a fast pace in your delivery. As you read the text, identify the most important words to stress and make a note of these. Try to find ways to emphasise these to an audience through subtle changes in your voice. Avoid using gesture during this exercise because it can make you ignore variations in your delivery. Perform this work to the rest of the group but suggest that the audience keep their eyes closed, ensuring that their response is focused purely on the vocal skills of the actor. Discuss the most effective examples and note why they were successful.

In order to ensure that the events took place in a logical order, Greek playwrights used the notion of reported action to reveal elements of the plot which took place in the past or off stage. Essentially, it is a form of narration which also helped to convey some of the more complex events which may have been difficult to stage. Look at the messenger's speech which describes Jocasta's hanging and Oedipus' blinding. Begin by identifying when the messenger is narrating the action and when he is commenting on it. Suggest ways in which his tone might vary. Now look at pace. Where might his delivery speed up or slow down? Explain the reasons for your choice. Focus on other vocal skills and document the decisions you have made on a photocopy of this section; insert this into your notes.

Oedipus' moment of recognition in the play occurs during the conversation between the Corinthian and the Shepherd. The danger with these characters is that they can appear superficial in nature at such a crucial part of the play. Looking at their dialogue in this scene, identify the nature of their first meeting. Try improvising that encounter and then find ways to show the memory of that day in the delivery of the lines in the text.

## Web link

Read the parody of stichomythia in 'Fragment of a Greek tragedy' by the English poet and classical scholar, A. E. Housman, available at http://ccat.sas.upenn.edu/jod/texts/housman.html

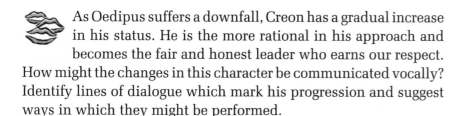 As Oedipus suffers a downfall, Creon has a gradual increase in his status. He is the more rational in his approach and becomes the fair and honest leader who earns our respect. How might the changes in this character be communicated vocally? Identify lines of dialogue which mark his progression and suggest ways in which they might be performed.

## Non-verbal action

Although the words of the text are essential to the unravelling of the plot, the movement and appearance of the characters were essential in communicating meaning to large Greek audiences. In a contemporary performance, the text allows for both moments of subtle, naturalistic gesturing and much more stylised movement to convey the mood of the piece.

Working in pairs, decide on one person to be a sculptor and the other a blob of clay. The sculptor's aim is to create an image of a successful leader by moving the 'blob of clay' in order to ensure its face and body position communicates this to an audience. After a couple of minutes, present the images to the audience and evaluate them. Swap with your partner and try to create the image of a challenged leader. Look also at the notion of leaders who are aggressive, frustrated and humbled. Try to identify moments in the text which link to these images.

During long passages of text, the movement of the chorus could suggest the action that is being described. The movements do not need to be literal; their role should not simply be to mirror the action on stage but try looking at the extract where Oedipus describes the killing of his father. How might the images created by the chorus reflect the tension in the scene?

The injury to Oedipus' ankles, which were pinned when he was exposed as a baby, is referred to several times during the play and is said to be the reason for his name, which literally means 'swollen foot'. The shepherd notes that even all these years later, his misshapen ankles are still obvious. Will you portray the king as limping or at all affected by the injury?

## Visual, aural and spatial elements

It is important to remember that productions of plays in ancient Greece were part of a religious festival that all citizens would attend. In Athens, the Theatre of Dionysus would probably have held up to 14,000 people. The style of performance reflected the demands of such a space, with bold characterisation, masks and

**Web link**

A useful website for learning more about ancient theatre is http://didaskalia.net/studyarea/study.html

grand costumes aiding communication of ideas across the large semi-circular auditorium. Reducing the play to a traditional proscenium-arch theatre or even a small studio space for a modern production can create problems, and it is therefore important that you remain clearly focused on the impact you are trying to achieve.

Select the traditions of Greek theatre that you think best suit your interpretation, rather than slavishly regurgitating all of the traditional elements for the sake of demonstrating your knowledge of the past. Your notes should be a personal exploration. In order to do justice to your design, you could use an A3 sheet that will allow you the flexibility to sketch, write and even stick on images that have influenced you. Remember that it is the ideas rather than the artistic quality that will gain you marks, although it is important that the presentation is clear. Be decisive: say exactly how your production would be staged rather than giving alternatives as this can become confusing.

Sophocles is said to have been the first dramatist to introduce scene-painting to represent the setting.

For more information about Greek performance spaces see page 10.

It is generally believed that in Greek performance spaces there was a raised stage at the back that separated the protagonists from the chorus, who remained on a large circular dancing area called the orchestra. The protagonists could move between the orchestra and the stage, which emphasised the social divide, but also the downfall from greatness. Would you wish to use such a platform in your design? How would Oedipus descend to the chorus at the end of the play? Spatially, the dynamic between the audience, the chorus and the protagonists is well worth exploring in this section. Should the chorus remain on stage, venture into the audience or even be above the seating area, providing a link between the mortals and the gods?

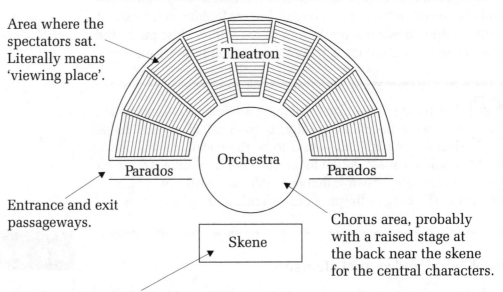

Area where the spectators sat. Literally means 'viewing place'.

Theatron

Orchestra

Parados

Parados

Entrance and exit passageways.

Skene

Chorus area, probably with a raised stage at the back near the skene for the central characters.

The skene was a construction at the back of the orchestra representing the building outside which the play was set.

Obviously, traditional performances were in the open air and used natural lighting. Would you look to recreate this realistic lighting or is a more stylised interpretation appropriate? Consider how shadows might be used to emphasise the theme of hidden truth.

**Lighting**

Traditionally all main characters were performed by three actors who relied on the details in the mask and costume to distinguish between roles. Are your performers going to be masked or unmasked? Remember that you will have to present the blinded Oedipus in the final scene. Keep in mind that using masks ensures that emotion has to be portrayed entirely through means other than facial expression. Explain the reasons for making your choice. Does your costume suggest any particular period, ancient or modern, or allude to the spiritual elements of the play?

**Costume**

Modern productions often use a mask for the bloodied eyes. If you do this, you will have to decide whether all your actors will wear masks throughout the play or whether you will just use a mask for this scene.

The portrayal of Tiresias can be problematic. The image of the blind prophet needs to be powerful and his dialogue with Oedipus needs to commence the king's downfall. How is this stage presence achieved? In Peter Hall's production at the National Theatre in 1996, Tiresias was a ghostly white figure pulled on by a rope attached to his waist. Try to find pictures of this production on the internet to generate ideas.

The use of sound does not initially appear central to the piece, yet it could significantly aid the creation of mood and atmosphere. How could the sense of Thebes' plague be created? How might the grandness of Oedipus' entrance through the palace doors be exaggerated by sound? What instruments could be used incidentally to emphasise the action of particular scenes? Bear in mind that traditionally the chorus sang in Greek theatre, accompanied by instruments.

**Sound**

## Interpretation

As you have worked your way through these sections, your understanding of Greek theatre should have improved and this process should be evident in your notes. The interpretation provides you with the opportunity to galvanise your ideas and present your thoughts in a coherent response to one specific part of the text.

The sample interpretation overleaf looks at the final scene which highlights Oedipus' downfall and provides an opportunity for you to communicate a strong vision. You should begin by stating the intended impact of the scene before giving specific information about how it would be realised in performance.

## Interpretation: Oedipus Rex by Sophocles

*Intended impact of scene: to present the extent of Oedipus' downfall by emphasising the Aristotelian concepts of fear and pity.*

*The play will be performed in the open air, being true to its original performance conditions and emphasising the final image of Oedipus' impending banishment.*

*During this scene, the music, which has underscored some of the action, will be absent. The sounds of the wind and a distant rumble of thunder will set the mood.*

**Creon**: That's enough. No more tears in public. You must go inside.

**Oedipus**: No, not yet, just a moment longer–Even against your better judgement.

**Creon**: No, everything must be done correctly, the proper thing at the proper time!

**Oedipus**: On one condition! That I have your promise.

**Creon**: My promise?

**Oedipus**: To send me into exile.

**Creon**: That is the gods' decision not mine. I shall follow their instructions.

**Oedipus**: Don't force me in there, when the gods hate me.

**Creon**: If they hate you, they will cast you out.

**Oedipus**: But do you agree? Will you do what I ask?

**Creon**: No. I shall do what I say I will do.

**Oedipus**: Well. I'm in your hands.

**Creon**: Then go in. But leave the children here.

**Oedipus**: The children? Don't take them away from me! Don't do that!

**Creon**: Don't give me orders! Those days are over. Your orders have brought you to this. Now you must learn to obey.

*Creon gestures to the attendants, who take Oedipus into the palace. Creon follows them, leading the two children.*

*Creon's confidence should be communicated both physically and vocally. Movement needs to be controlled, with bold movements of the arms emphasising the power of enough. His voice needs to be deep in pitch, well projected, with a confident tone.*

*Oedipus' desperate language should make the audience reflect on the initial images of the character. The actor's tone should be higher and less fluent, occasionally pausing to convey the sense of intense pain.*

*Oedipus' costume should contrast with the fitted charcoal suit of earlier scenes. The jacket should be removed, the white shirt dusty and bloodstained. In rehearsal, we experimented with different methods of conveying his blindness. We tried using a stick, the actor stumbling onto stage, and a stylised mask. My preferred interpretation was him being brought on by attendants – an image which is mirrored here as he is removed in a more forceful manner, emphasising the audience's sense of fear and pity.*

## A Doll's House

When her husband, Torvald, is gravely ill, Nora Helmer secretly borrows money to fund a holiday in Italy to allow him time to recuperate. She repays the debt through regular instalments, using money she has saved from her allowance. However, when Torvald recovers and is made manager of the bank, his first task is to sack Krogstad, who coincidentally is the person who loaned Nora the money. This loan was falsely obtained, since Nora forged her father's signature, and Krogstad threatens publicly to embarrass both her and her husband unless she manages to get him his job back at the bank. Torvald refuses to be influenced by his wife and consequently the truth is revealed. His anger at his wife's actions is only calmed when the threat of blackmail is revoked but by this time Nora has realised that she never loved her husband and she leaves.

*A Doll's House* by Norwegian playwright Henrik Ibsen (1828–1906) is a realist play that was written in 1879 in both Rome and Amalfi in Italy. Throughout his life, Ibsen struggled to be accepted by the Norwegian theatrical establishment. His reaction against the prevailing notions of theatre of the time meant that his works were initially dismissed. Consequently, he spent 27 years living abroad in Italy and Germany. When he wrote *A Doll's House*, he gained European recognition for the first time and it was this that paved his way for a return home.

### Social, cultural, historical and political context

The emotional turbulence of Ibsen's life is reflected in the complexity of his characters. His mother's over-reliance on religion and his father's depression are elements that are reflected throughout his writing. His acting style demanded a truthful performance that encouraged the audience to identify emotionally with the characters' internal states, rather than simply relying on physical gesture to convey feelings.

The psychologically realistic nature of *A Doll's House* and its exploration of individualistic ethics versus socially determined ethics make it an excellent play to discuss in both a historical and a modern context. Ibsen's focus on human nature and its response to complex situations make this a text that is as relevant today as it has always been. Add to this the context of the feminist movement and the rights of women, and you have a rich range of resources to draw upon.

Many of Ibsen's protagonists share common features. Essentially, they are members of a bourgeois family who appear to have lost direction in life. They have a choice to make: either they can continue in their current state of dutiful emptiness or they can elect a different way of living which may lead to self-discovery, but may also lead to loneliness or isolation. It is this conflict between two states that forms the heart of his work.

### Further reading

The translation used here is by Michael Meyer (Methuen Drama, an imprint of A&C Black Publishers 1985).

Norwegian 19th-century drama was similar to melodrama in style. A simplistic moral overtone dominated the play; good actions were rewarded and bad behaviour punished.

### Web link

A good starting point for the discussion of themes and issues within the play is www.gradesaver. com/classicnotes/titles/dollshouse/ Remember, however, that using extracts of work from the internet without identifying their practical significance will not earn you many marks and may count against you.

As always, it is important that you do not rely entirely on research. You need to consider the implications that all information has on the rehearsal and performance of the text. The nature of your response should play to your strengths. Your notes should be a practically focused response, which could include images, diagrams, quotations, practical examples and analytical prose.

> " These women of the modern age, mistreated as daughters, as sisters, as wives, not educated according to their talents, debarred from following their missions, deprived of their inheritance, embittered in mind – these are the ones who supply the mothers for the new generation. What will be the result? "
>
> Ibsen.

Look at Ibsen's play *Ghosts* (1881) and the character Mrs Alving. What similarities are there with the role of Nora Helmer? How does Ibsen use these women to challenge the beliefs of society?

 Ibsen was forced to write an alternative ending to *A Doll's House*. Nora's decision to leave her husband shocked the 19th-century audiences and the actress who took the role of Nora when the play toured Germany insisted that the ending be changed. In the amended script, just as Nora is about to leave, Torvald insists she take one last look at the children asleep and explains how they will wake the following morning motherless. The thought of leaving them is enough for her to abandon her plans and return to the role of 'doll' wife. Consider how this might change the meaning of the play and why this outcome might have been demanded.

## Response to a practitioner

**Aristotle** The structure of the play obeys many of the guidelines associated with the philosopher Aristotle's discussion of Greek tragedy. The unities of place and action are followed, and the only interruptions to time are the natural divisions at the end of each act. Ibsen uses the breaks between acts to move the audience forward to the next moment of tension and the focus on the 60 hours or so during the Christmas period adds particular impact when the play revolves so much around money, hidden secrets and family.

**Scribe** Ibsen's structure is further influenced by the concept of the **well-made play.** This was a common structure in the 19th century and was made famous by Eugène Scribe (1791–1861) who used the format to develop nearly 500 plays.

There are many rules that govern the nature of such a play, but essentially the action can be broken into three simple sections: exposition, development and denouement.

### Web link

A useful discussion of Scribe and the elements he used is given at www. wayneturney.20m.com/scribe.htm

1. The **exposition** reveals the facts of the situation. Act 1 in *A Doll's House* introduces all the main characters, outlines past events and provides a context for future action.

2. The **development** is sometimes referred to as the 'complication', since new information is introduced that makes the protagonist's situation more difficult. Rank's confession of his true feelings and Krogstad's dismissal followed by his posting of the letter all take place in Act 2, heightening Nora's emotional turmoil.

Dénouement is originally a French word meaning 'undoing a knot'. Compare it with the Aristotelian idea of recognition: see page 71.

3. The **denouement** is the unravelling of the plot, dealing with each of the strands of the play and leading the audience to a natural conclusion. Ibsen does bring together the different strands – Krogstad and Linde talk, Rank announces his death, metaphorically thanking Nora 'for the light' she has brought to

his life, and Torvald and Nora talk about the issues raised within the play. However, it is not a natural conclusion: it is a discussion that leads to an unpredictable future for Nora and her family. The playwright encourages the audience to hypothesise about what might happen in the future.

---

**?** On a piece of paper, write down the headings 'exposition' (Act 1), 'development' (Act 2) and 'denouement' (Act 3). In small groups, examine the three areas of the play and use quotations from the text to highlight how Ibsen uses the well-made play structure. Look at how Act 3 in particular appears to lull the audience into thinking that everything will be resolved.

---

In addition to these structural influences, most contemporary performances of the play would be closely linked to the work of Stanislavski, who aimed to ensure all performances conveyed a sense of emotional truth. He believed that the external actions of the characters needed to be balanced with internal feelings through a complex system of rehearsal.

---

In pairs, apply Stanislavski's techniques to the end of the play, beginning on Torvald's line 'May I write to you, Nora?'. Rehearse this extract looking specifically at objectives and emotion memory. Is it possible to convey his sense of loss? How hard is it to sympathise with his character? Perform the scene to the rest of the group and get feedback on the effectiveness of each portrayal. Draw conclusions on the relevance of Torvald's character to men in contemporary society. Are today's men governed by a different set of social rules? Look at Stanislavski's ideas and any ways in which they link with Ibsen's views on theatre, and explain how you might use them in a 21st-century production.

---

## Characterisation

The main focus of the play can be clearly identified as the relationships between Nora, Torvald and Krogstad. These three characters drive the action and their behaviour is constantly referenced by others.

---

In your notes, place the three characters' names in the centre of a page. Find quotations from other characters which comment on them; these could be lines addressed directly to them or said without them knowing. Once you have identified their key character traits, make suggestions as to how these might be revealed in performance.

> " I must disclaim the honour of having consciously worked for women's rights… To me it has been a question of human rights. "
>
> Ibsen, at a meeting of the Norwegian Association for Women's Rights.

Much of the tension that is created in performance relies on the audience reflecting on the language and actions of characters in previous scenes. In groups of three, find two scenes where Nora discusses the same issue first with Krogstad and then with Torvald. For example, in Act 1 look at how Nora confesses to Krogstad that she forged her father's signature and Torvald's explanation of Krogstad's previous misdemeanour: 'He forged someone else's name. Have you any idea what that means?' Choose short extracts from the different scenes and rehearse them in a way that might highlight the contrasting emotions of Nora. Perform the scenes to the rest of your group and ask them to comment on specific moments where the tension was at its greatest. In your notes, discuss how these three characters' actions help to highlight the themes of the play. In this extract, for example, lies and deceit are emphasised particularly.

When discussing Torvald's behaviour, the critic Bjorn Hemmer suggests: 'It is not the human being in him which speaks to Nora at their final confrontation, it is society and its institutions and authorities which speak through him.' What elements of Torvald's language in Act 3 could suggest he is indeed representing the common view of Norwegian society? Is this a fair perception of his character? Is he a tool for conveying this aspect of the playwright's message or is the role more complex than this? Consider how you might direct the actors during this section and what issues you would explore.

The critic Egil Tornqvist has suggested that Nora and Linde are 'parallel figures moving in opposite directions'. Look at the characters' relationships and the difference in how they start and end the play. Do you agree with Tornqvist? Ibsen deliberately draws comparisons between characters and their situations. Both Krogstad and Nora forged signatures and both contemplated suicide. Torvald and Rank (for different reasons) both try to maintain an external image of calm despite their inner turmoil. Select one or two such relationships and in your notes explore the comparisons and contrasts within them through specific reference to the text.

The main subplot is the relationship between Krogstad and Linde. The action of the play is cleverly structured to ensure they do not meet face to face until Act 3, but each character refers to the other in their opening scenes:

**Mrs Linde:** Nora, who was that man? … It was him then … How he's changed.

**Krogstad:** I saw your husband cross the street … with a lady … was not that lady a Mrs Linde?

### Further reading

'Ibsen and the realistic problem drama' by Bjorn Hemmer, in *The Cambridge Companion to Ibsen* (Cambridge University Press 1994).

### Further reading

Egil Tornqvist's book *Ibsen: A Doll's House* (Cambridge University Press 1995) is a detailed analysis of the playtext and its impact through performance. The language is easy to read and he makes interesting points that you could refer to in your notes.

In pairs, focus on one of these scenes. Consider how you could subtly convey to an audience a sense of the emotion experienced by Linde or Krogstad. Remember, Linde might be embarrassed by her past actions and Krogstad would not want to show himself to be weak in front of Nora. Rehearse the extract, keeping movement to a minimum. Now try working on the opening of Act 3. Look at Ibsen's stage directions and try to create Linde's anxiousness. When Krogstad enters, he is clearly confused.

Consider how this confusion might be performed. Experiment with him being aggressive, cold and cautious. In your notes, explore the role the subplot has in commenting on the main action within the play.

The children and the nurse seem inconsequential to the main plot yet their presence highlights the ramifications of the other characters' actions. Think about how these characters might make the audience reflect on the action within the play.

## Language

Although there are many different translations of the text, essentially they all try to remain true to Ibsen's original use of language. In order to write a good response, it is important that you identify the different styles used in the text and the impact they may have on the audience. However, you must remember that your notes are a record of how you have explored the text so try to support your ideas with practical examples from your work on the play or suggestions on how the language might be performed. You should be able to recognise the use of:

➤ Complex or simplistic language

➤ Heightened or poetic language

➤ Metaphor, imagery and symbolism

➤ Questions

➤ Pauses, different sentence lengths and changes in vocabulary

➤ Subtext (the meaning beneath the text)

➤ Characteristic words or phrases

➤ References to the natural world

➤ Specific patterns of speech for each character.

Remember this should be a personal exploration, so focus on the areas you find most interesting. See the example overleaf.

| Use of language | Quotation | Practical application | Impact on audience |
|---|---|---|---|
| Frequent use of questions to highlight Torvald's confusion in Act 3. | 'Nora, what kind of way is this to talk?' 'What kind of way is this to describe our marriage?' 'Nora, how can you be so unreasonable and ungrateful?' | Both characters sit formally at table, centre stage. Nora to hold eye contact but to use gestures sparingly, implying her control. Torvald is clearly uncomfortable sitting down and talking seriously. With each question, his vocal tone should become increasingly desperate, with less fluency in his delivery. | The contrast between the characters should be immediately evident. Torvald's questioning is an attempt to regain his status but his desperation only serves to reinforce how he is lost and confused. |

Nora uses language to manipulate the male characters in the play with varying degrees of success. Working in groups of four, choose three moments where Nora is alone on stage with Krogstad, Torvald and Rank in turn. Find a quotation that highlights how she tries to manipulate the characters in each scene. Sit each of the male characters on a chair and consider how the manner in which they sit communicates how they respond to the manipulation. Try acting each of the lines, thinking carefully about the tone of voice used and the stress put on certain words. How does Nora's proximity to the characters affect the power of her manipulation? Comment on what you have learnt about her language in your notes.

In small groups, focus on the difference between Torvald and Rank. Make a list of the phrases Torvald uses to refer to his wife. What do you think references to animals in the natural world might suggest to an audience about their relationship? Now look at the scenes with Rank and how Nora appears to be in control. Draw comparisons between sentence length, vocabulary, use of pause and questions. Does either character change their use of language when their status changes?

A Doll's House is often considered to be a transitional play, between the sensationalism of melodrama and realism. Krogstad, in particular, is a character who could fit comfortably in both genres. On one hand, he is the stereotypical villain, making threats and discussing the horrors of suicide. However, he could also be considered to be a victim of circumstance who has been hurt by Linde and needs his job to survive. Look at the duologue between Nora and Krogstad in Act 2 up until the line: 'Don't worry, I'll show him all the respect he deserves.' In pairs, work on two different versions of the scene with Krogstad as a villain and then as a victim. Perform them to the class and discuss which is the most appropriate.

## Vocal awareness

If you are to remain true to Ibsen's style, then the delivery of the text will be naturalistic in nature. The skill in the performer will be to identify the subtle alterations in tone and rhythm which highlight the changes in the psychological state of the character.

Look at the first exchange between Nora and Torvald at the opening of Act 1. Focus on the opening six lines of text up to and including Nora's line, 'Just now'. Assume that this is a unit, in Stanislavskian terms, and with a partner decide on an objective for each character in the form of 'I want ...'. Rehearse this short scene in pairs, playing the objective to the full, reflecting it in the vocal delivery. Once you have done this, turn to the end of Act 3 and look at the four lines beginning with the phrase, 'May I write to you, Nora' and finishing on 'Nothing. Nothing.' Decide on new objectives for the characters. Perform both scenes to the rest of the group. Ask them to suggest the objective you had been using and once it is identified ask them to identify moments when they found it to be particularly successful. Paste these extracts into your notes, identifying the objectives and the subtle changes you made to the vocal delivery. Such close attention to details will enable you to demonstrate a command of Stanislavski's ideas.

The dominant form of the play is **duologue**, a conversation between two individuals. Ibsen repeatedly uses two characters to highlight the moral conflict of each scene. Even when the characters superficially appear to be in agreement, conflict should be conveyed through subtext. For example, when Nora dominates the first conversation with Mrs Linde, the latter should show frustration at her frivolous nature. Consequently, when Nora is left on stage on her own, the change in form increases the impact of the words. Get into groups of three or four. Each member of the group should choose one of Nora's soliloquies. Rehearse them as an ensemble performance that highlights the confusion in Nora's mind. Try overlapping or repeating words. Consider how the size and speed of physical actions might convey character. Is there a logical development in her words that shows an emotional progression throughout the play or do her thoughts remain consistent throughout?

The relationship between Torvald and Nora often appears more like father and daughter than husband and wife. Ironically, the greatest sexual undertones are evident in the exchange between Rank and Nora in Act 2. Nora is trying to manipulate Rank to protect her from Krogstad's financial threats.

Her behaviour is flirtatious and Rank at times appears to be embarrassed by her approach. Discuss in small groups how the actors might show these emotions vocally. How might the tension increase around the line 'Why did you smile?'

## Non-verbal action

If the actors are to convey the reality of the Helmer household to an audience, then they need to understand the space and create an imagined environment in which to perform. Ibsen provides an intricate description of the key elements of the set but it is important that the actors spend time fleshing out the scene.

> " Any tendency for the actors to congregate downstage should be avoided, and their relative positions on stage should change whenever it appears natural; generally, every scene and every visual image should be, as far as possible, a reflection of reality. "
>
> Ibsen.

 Creating the room. The members of your group should take a chair each and use it to mark out the Helmers' room. Standing outside of the space, they should now take it in turns to describe the detail within it. They should elaborate on Ibsen's directions, giving a sense of colour, style and some of the precise detail which could suggest information about the family life. Once the room has been created, chairs and tables can be added into the space to signify the different objects that exist. Individuals from the group should now decide on physical actions that have taken place within the space. They should not be episodes from the play but moments from the past, helping the group to imagine how the relationships have evolved with time. It may be necessary for the person creating the freeze to identify the characters but resist the temptation to explain the image verbally. Draw stick versions of the images in your notes to show some of your ideas.

The name of the tarantella dance stems from the Italian town Taranto where they believed the only cure for the bite of a tarantula was a frenzied dance that would leave the participant exhausted but cured.

### Web link

A sample of tarantella music can be found at www.sicilianculture. com/folklore/tarantella.htm. More information about how to perform the dance is available at www. streetswing.com/histmain/z3tartla. htm

The use of dance and music through the tarantella scene at the end of Act 2 is an interesting device in a realistic play. On the most basic level, Nora uses it to prevent Torvald from going to the letter box and discovering Krogstad's letter. Symbolically, however, it is extremely significant. Consider why Ibsen chose to use the tarantella as a device. What does the history of the dance say about the marriage? How does it reflect Nora's mental state? Remember that Italy was where Torvald was taken to recover from his illness and is the source of Nora's financial difficulties; the dance and her costume are constant reminders of this.

 At the end of Act 1, Torvald's suffocating power over Nora is highlighted as she tries to plead Krogstad's case. The conversation is halted by the phrase 'Give me your hand'. From that moment onwards it is as if the debate is over and her spirit is quashed. In pairs, experiment with different ways of staging this moment by not just looking at the taking of the hand but also the physical actions both before and after the line.

Rank's tuberculosis is addressed in Act 2. Despite the morbid suggestion of a calling card with a black cross on it, he is clearly eager to hide his pain from Torvald. However, he is happy to reveal the true nature of his suffering to Nora. Research the symptoms of the disease and consider ways in which Rank's movement may alter when he is alone with Nora.

The practicalities of having children on stage means that their physical presence is sometimes cut. Nora could talk to them as if off stage or she could try to physically create their presence through mime. Experiment with both styles and decide which you prefer.

## Visual, aural and spatial elements

In order to bring *A Doll's House* to life, you need to consider how it might work in a three-dimensional space. Visual elements will include the environment of the Helmers' house as well as the costume and make-up worn. The spatial elements will include staging, traditionally the proscenium arch, and the size of the performance space. In addition, subtle use of music and sound effects may add to the changes in mood of the piece. Remember, unless there are two intervals, you will need to indicate the passing of time between two acts. Consider how the sound of the final door slamming could be amplified to ensure maximum effect.

This is the most creative of the written sections and is a chance for you to explore fully the practical implications of the play. At the beginning of Act 1, Ibsen gives specific information about the staging of the play. It is possible to begin your design by following his instructions. However, you do not need to mirror his ideas. You could choose to stage your play in the round. Consequently, the positioning of the different seating areas will need to be considered to ensure balance. Use an A3 sheet to present your ideas and illustrate your stage design in the middle. This will act as a focal point, with all of your other comments about visual, aural and spatial elements placed round the outside.

Ibsen gave considerable thought to the use of visual symbols to add resonance to the action and to explore facets of the characters. Look at the role of stage props in the play – behind every object on stage there lies a meaning. The stove is a symbol of warmth that certain characters gather around when trying to forget the harsh realities of the cold world outside the house. The macaroons highlight Nora's deceitful nature at the start of the play, since she eats one in front of the audience and yet tells her husband she didn't stop at the cake shop. The Christmas tree is in many ways a metaphor for Nora herself. She enters with it at the start, but hides it from her husband. It is centre stage at the end of Act 1, where it is prettified to highlight the happiness of their home, but

### Further study

Mabou Mines' *Doll House* is a striking interpretation of Ibsen's play deconstructing the traditions of Naturalism in a production which casts six-foot-tall women alongside men who are nearly two foot shorter. Search the internet for articles on the performance and make notes on what it was trying to say to a contemporary audience.

### Your design

Don't panic if you can't draw. Straight lines and two-dimensional drawings are perfectly acceptable.

### Visual symbols

is stripped and dishevelled in Act 2. How might these elements influence the use of stage space in particular moments of action? How might the image of a doll's house be created? What style of furniture, windows, fabric might help to emphasise this theme? Many doors are suggested by the text so think about entrances and exits. How might they be used to increase tension?

Consider the **costume** of the characters. What colour, style and fabric would best suit your performance? Are the costumes detailed and realistic or are they used to symbolise character? Consider how the costumes change as each of the characters changes. How does Torvald's appearance in Act 1 contrast with Act 3? When Nora states 'I've changed', how might her costume reflect the psychological change that has taken place?

How might **sound** contribute to the play? Consider the tarantella music, the door slam and the sense of the party continuing upstairs. In a non-naturalistic presentation, consider how music might underscore the monologues. If you are highlighting Nora's doll-like behaviour, this could be achieved through the sound of a music box or a violin playing pizzicato.

**Lighting** could be essentially realistic, with warm (straw-colour) general covers of lighting used in the majority of scenes. However, the use of the light in Act 2 with Rank and Nora implies a reduction in intensity. You may also wish to isolate Torvald at the end of the play and consider how lights shining through lattice windows might imply a cage or cell.

## Interpretation

You should have been demonstrating a practical understanding of the play throughout your notes but this is an opportunity to ensure that all aspects of the assessment criteria are explored.

In order to communicate your understanding of *A Doll's House* to your teacher, it is a good idea to conclude your notes with a section where you explicitly interpret a section of the text.

The nature of Ibsen's writing means that it is probably good to choose a section of text from Act 3, where the different plot strands are being resolved. The sample interpretation opposite gives suggestions on how your comments may look. This is by no means a comprehensive annotation of the text. Use some of these ideas as a starting point but develop them in greater detail. Remember, while it is good to refer to Stanislavski's ideas, do not forget to say how his approach altered your performance.

# Interpretation: A Doll's House by Henrik Ibsen

*Intended impact of scene: to emphasise the change in Nora's physical and psychological state.*

*When approaching this scene in rehearsal, we used Stanislavski's technique of units and objectives; this scene is divided into three discrete units by dotted lines. Unit 1, Nora: I want to understand. Torvald: I want to control my behaviour. Torvald: I want to explain what I'm thinking. Torvald: I want reassurance from my wife. Unit 3, Nora: I want to be respected.Torvald: I want to assert my authority.*

Nora's entrance should display a clear change in the tempo-rhythm of her gestures. The fidgets of the playful housewife have been replaced by a greater physical control.

The image of them both sat down at the same level should be new to the audience. For the first time, they appear to have equal status on stage.

**Helmer:** … What's this? Not in bed? Have you changed?
**Nora:** *(in her everyday dress)* Yes, Torvald. I've changed.
**Helmer:** But why now – so late –?
**Nora:** I shall not sleep tonight.
**Helmer:** But, my dear Nora.

**Nora:** *(looks at her watch)* It isn't that late. Sit down there, Torvald. You and I have a lot to talk about.
*She sits down on one side of the table.*
**Helmer:** Nora, what does this mean? You look quite drawn –
**Nora:** Sit down. It's going to take a long time. I've a lot to say to you.

**Helmer:** *(sits down on the other side of the table)* You alarm me, Nora. I don't understand you.
**Nora:** No, that's just it. You don't understand me. And I've never understood you – until this evening.

Nora's psychological change is reflected in her appearance. Her dress which previously touched the floor, giving the impression of her gliding across the room, is now ankle-length. Her hair is tied back, creating a more mature approach.

The phrase 'sit down' is a stark contrast to Torvald's 'Give me your hand' in Act 1. The actor playing Nora should hold eye contact, gesturing to the chair, speaking in a polite but firm tone.

### Further reading

Kafka's life is well documented. For more specific information read *Franz Kafka: A Biography* by Max Brod (Da Capo Press 1995).

## Metamorphosis

*Metamorphosis* is set in mid-Europe, probably just before the First World War. The story concerns the Samsa family, who have the following characteristics:

> **Father:** a large and robust man

> **Mother:** a loving but pained woman

> **Greta:** the daughter, a sensitive spirit hoping to become a violinist

> **Gregor:** the son, a travelling fabric salesman.

The story quickly turns into a nightmare when Gregor wakes up one morning to find that he has turned into a large beetle. The play is then divided into two views of what happens next: we see and hear how the members of the family try to deal with this problem and Gregor talks directly to the audience to tell of his dilemma.

Although the metamorphosis of the title refers most obviously to the transformation of Gregor into an insect, by the end of the play each member of the family has undergone their own transformation. No longer able to live off Gregor's wages, the family discuss getting jobs themselves. Father is once again the man of the family, the object of his wife and daughter's respect and love. Greta grows as she assumes responsibility for her brother's care and all three remaining members of the family remark at the end on her blossoming into womanhood. Though Gregor gains clarity in his mind about his family's attitude towards him, he deteriorates physically, especially after he is injured by his father.

### Social, cultural, historical and political context

Steven Berkoff (born 1937) is a great advocate of stirring the audience's imagination to get them fully engaged and involved in a play, rather than allowing them to sit back in a passive manner with all of their thinking done for them by the performance.

*Metamorphosis* is an unusual playtext because it is the dramatisation of a short novel by a different author. The story was written in German (as *Die Verwandlung*) by Franz Kafka (1883–1924) and published in 1915. There are various areas of his life that have a direct relevance to the play. He was born into a German-speaking Jewish family in Prague, which was then part of the Austro-Hungarian empire. He was dominated by his father, who never really accepted Kafka's talents and abilities. Kafka worked for an insurance company for most of his life, until tuberculosis forced him to retire, and therefore experienced routine and monotony. He struggled with the dual identity of being an insurance worker and a writer.

### Web link

www.iainfisher.com/berkoff.html is a comprehensive website with a useful photographic gallery, information on Berkoff and his plays and some really clear research papers on his life and work. www.stevenberkoff.com is Berkoff's own website, and carries photographs and information about his plays. A useful site for more information about the life and works of Kafka is www.pitt.edu/~kafka/links.html

### Think about...

Consider the similarities between Berkoff's upbringing and those of Kafka and the character Gregor.

The ideas of alienation and being an outsider, the futility and monotony of work, the struggle to be heard and understood are all areas from Kafka's life that impact directly on the story and the play adapted from it.

Steven Berkoff was born in London in 1937 but his parents were Russian-Jewish immigrants. His early life was fairly nomadic since his parents moved to different locations around London and also spent a short spell in New York, all before he was 15. He felt lonely and isolated as a boy and his many moves prevented him from establishing friendships. His relationship with his father was strained and his father found it difficult to show any emotional connection with his son. After leaving school, Berkoff went through a series of jobs such as selling biros, office clerk, messenger boy and an assistant in a clothing shop. It was while working as a clothing salesman in Germany that he first came across a copy of Kafka's *Metamorphosis*. Berkoff's own childhood and the conflicts he faced are similar in many respects to Kafka's own dilemmas, and it is easy to see how Berkoff found an empathy with the content and themes of the original text.

Berkoff is an unusual writer in that he is also a director and an actor. His journey into writing plays was inspired by the fact that he found it hard to get parts in plays after graduating. He was also disillusioned with the theatre establishment and the way in which plays were written and cast. He found himself discontented with the bourgeois nature of theatre in Britain, and the style of acting and form of playwriting.

---

In small groups, look at the quotation below. Do you feel that it is appropriate to see the play in these terms? How might you attempt to communicate this or an alternative vision to a modern audience?

> Of course, literary critics and commentators tend to see the story as an allegory of the outsider, the handicapped or sick, the mentally disturbed or anyone who cannot conform to the norm acceptable to a society that is distinctly uncomfortable with damaged goods, or individuals. And Kafka was both.

Steven Berkoff, *Meditations on Metamorphosis*

---

## The response to a practitioner

Berkoff has created a unique theatrical method of working with words and images. The language that he uses in his plays is very poetic and graphic in terms of its imagery. It has roots in his upbringing in London, and the rhythm and rhyme that regional slang can create, as well as a more literary referencing of a Shakespearean quality at times, especially when dealing with universal themes such as love and death. The physical demands of Berkoff's plays, which are very evident in *Metamorphosis*, reveal the influence of European theatre, and particularly Antonin Artaud, for whom creating meaning through image and movement was more important than the spoken word.

Berkoff has not always met with critical acclaim in Britain. His work is highly praised in continental Europe but has received a

**Berkoff**

**Further reading**

Try Berkoff's *Overview* (Faber and Faber 1994) and *Meditations on Metamorphosis* (Faber and Faber 1995).

**Further study**

Read some of Berkoff's other plays and see if you can find similarities with *Metamorphosis* or identify any of the issues discussed in this section. His *The Trial* (1971) has a similar origin to *Metamorphosis*, as it was also originally a novel by Kafka.

much less enthusiastic critical response in his home country. This may be because in many respects he fought against the British theatre establishment. His ideas never really fitted in with the kitchen-sink drama, agit-prop theatre, or the commercial shows of the 1960s and 1970s. He is still seen as the enfant terrible of British theatre and his work is often labelled as indulgent, controversial and over-stylised. His recent pieces *Requiem for Ground Zero* (2002) about the 9/11 tragedy, and his rewriting of the final days of Jesus in *Messiah* (2000) are testimony to his unique approach to plays and the mixed critical acclaim with which his plays frequently are met.

Find out about the other movements in British theatre in the 1960s and 1970s, especially kitchen-sink drama and agit-prop theatre, and consider how different this was to Berkoff's work in style and content. Find some recent reviews of Berkoff's productions to see how they have been received.

Although there are many aspects of Artaud's influence in Berkoff's style, the structure of the story shows many of the elements of Brecht's epic theatre (see pages 26–28). It is important in your notes to demonstrate an understanding of the Brechtian device of performance storytelling that allows us to realise that the actors are representing characters. The audience is required to make imaginative links with the action rather than just accept the action as real. In small groups, look at the sections of this book which refer to Brecht and Artaud (pages 24–40). Make a list of the different elements of each practitioner's style and find examples from *Metamorphosis* to illustrate their approach. Do you think Berkoff is influenced more by one practitioner than another?

From the playtext, it can be difficult to imagine the nature of Berkoff's performances. There was a BBC production starring Tim Roth as Gregor which was broadcast in 1987 although this is not available to buy; it is also not an entirely successful piece of drama as you do not get a complete sense of the play's impact in performance. You may be lucky enough to see a production in which Berkoff has been involved or you could consider buying a DVD of one of his plays. Research his style and make notes on what you learn.

## Characterisation

The action in the play is seen through the eyes of the Samsa family, although after the metamorphosis there is a clear divide in the storytelling. Berkoff provides us with an insight into the family's fears of what Gregor has become while Gregor himself frequently comments on his mental state. It is this inherent duality which makes the play both challenging and interesting.

Look at the opening stage directions. Berkoff outlines the opening mimes, 'condensing the personality into a few seconds'. Look at the description of the mother's action. The use of language is quite deliberate: 'describes a sad face – leaves a pained heart and angst.' Perform this image to your group bearing in mind what you've learnt about Berkoff's style. What is the difference between 'describing' and 'showing' a 'pained heart'? How might this be explicit in your mime? How is the image of the 'pained heart' shown? How does the mother 'leave' it? Using the same level of detail, look at the physicality of the other characters and draw stick characters in your notes to reflect the physicality in this opening.

The family's change in attitude during the play is as striking as Gregor's physical metamorphosis. Look at the roles of Mr Samsa, Mrs Samsa and Greta. Find quotations from the beginning of the play to illustrate their attitude to Gregor and their life as a whole. Try to find examples from the end of the text which reflect a change in their state of mind. Try condensing the dialogue of the three characters into a monologue lasting no more than 200 words which reflects their journey during the play. You may choose to use direct address to the audience or imagine other characters on stage. Include a copy of this in your notes with important lines of dialogue annotated.

The transformation of Gregor into a beetle is the pivotal action of the play and the catalyst that allows the audience to see the changes in the other characters. How this transformation is achieved theatrically is vital to the success of the play. The play is not a literal story and does not demand that we physically see Gregor changed into a beetle. This would be far too simple a technique for the audience. They must imagine his grossness and feel the family's disgust. Therefore Berkoff chose to represent the beetle physically through the actor's use of voice, body and space. This allows the actor playing the beetle to slip easily into human form when he needs to perform a flashback or to communicate with the audience. It also makes it easier to tell the story and communicates that the story and its message are more significant than the characters themselves.

Kafka is very vague about the form of the beetle in the original German, using a word meaning 'vermin', rather than a specific term meaning dung beetle or cockroach, as translations often do. His language is designed more to stress the monstrous, gross, but helpless and slightly ridiculous nature of the insect that Gregor has become.

Lie face down on the floor. Now pull your knees up and cross your arms in front of your face so that you are resting on your forearms, knees and shins. Through this simple and yet physically demanding position, Berkoff was able to mimic the legs, head and thorax of the beetle. The actor's fingers, arms, head, upper body and legs could all work in isolation and begin to emulate the movement and manner of an insect. Move your head mechanically and in a jerky fashion. Push your arms forward and drag your body forward, supported by your knees. Try to create a continuous movement with this action. Berkoff also found that by swapping his crossed arms and having them on the correct side of his body, but forcing his elbows up by pushing his shoulders down, he could find another dynamic that enabled him to 'ooze' as well as crawl. Experiment with this physicality – you may find it incredibly hard and tiring. Look at Berkoff's introduction to the play to see his recommendations for physicalising the beetle and try to follow them.

## Language

Even though *Metamorphosis* is layered and driven by physical work, words and dialogue are still important. The characters are very much represented as caricatures, yet they also have moments of revelation where the audience witnesses their personal journeys within the play. The language the family uses can be divided into four distinct areas:

1. **Direct address to the audience.** Explaining exactly what they are thinking and feeling. Gregor frequently tells the audience his thoughts, since he has no one else to speak to.

2. **Speaking in third person.** Again, this is addressed to the audience, but the characters take on the role of narrator, which allows us to understand that they are telling a story and that it is the story that is important.

3. **Naturalistic dialogue.** The characters talk to each other in a manner that allows us to believe they represent a real family and real people.

4. **Stylised and rhythmic language.** This device is often used to support a theme or mood.

This is a device in the style of Brecht's alienation technique, which requires the audience to think about the situation and events of the play (see page 27). When the characters take on the role of narrator, their words are often a direct translation of Kafka's original story.

The various uses of language that Gregor is given within the text show the complexity of the types of language that pervade *Metamorphosis*. He is able to talk to the audience as part of the narrative form of the piece, allowing the audience to think about his character and his predicament. Gregor is also able to talk to himself through soliloquy. In a sense, this allows him to be the universal representative of a human being, a sort of everyman figure. Finally, Gregor talks to the family, although here, while the audience can generally hear him quite clearly, the family can apparently hear only grotesque sounds and noises characteristic of a beetle. By the end, the family refer to their son and brother as 'it' rather than 'him' or 'Gregor'. In groups of three or four, create a performance of some of Gregor's most important lines of dialogue and sounds to demonstrate his vocal deterioration.

The use of rhythm and repetition is part of the language format of the play and is usually accompanied by a physical realisation described by stage directions. This use of language not only communicates meaning through the words, but also through their delivery. Rhythm and repetition support and reveal the themes of monotony and routine, and create a ritual that is a very important part of the Samsas' life. Consider the scene in which the Samsa family realises that Gregor needs stale and rotten food now that he is a beetle, and begin to gather together all the old scraps they can find. The language pattern changes here and we begin to get a glimpse of a rhythmic list accompanied by a physical depiction of the food being collected. In fours, rehearse this scene beginning with 'What do you suppose they … he eats?' up to the image of the family eating their breakfast normally. Try to identify the changes in rhythm and the impact they would have on the audience.

**Think about…**

Give examples of the following types of language within this unit, stating who uses it and why: direct address to the audience; internal monologue; naturalistic dialogue; ritualistic dialogue; and rhythm/repetition in dialogue.

## Vocal awareness

There is a distinctive style to Berkoff's vocal work which is significantly distanced from Naturalism. The onomatopoeic quality of the language is just as important as the meaning of the words themselves. As you work on the text, guard against any realistic delivery. You should create a style of performance which distances the audience from the characters, presenting the action rather than allowing the audience to become fully absorbed in it.

In order to be successful with the text it is important to work bravely. Stand in a circle as a group and explain that you are going to experiment with the sounds of different words. You are going to take it in turns to interpret the same word in different ways by shouting it, singing it, elongating it or whispering it. After each group member does this, the others will repeat it like a chant. Repeat the exercise with each of the following words and phrases: 'Gregor', 'Chief Clerk', 'dreaming', 'I can hear you' and 'dead'.

The family are clearly rattled by the presence of outsiders. Berkoff's choice to use a single location traps Gregor, the family and, indeed, the audience. This claustrophobic aspect is accentuated with the arrival of both the Chief Clerk and the Lodgers. Their tone becomes increasingly anxious, their language less fluent and the hierarchy within the family is disrupted. Look at the moment from the Chief Clerk's entrance to Gregor's line 'Leave me in peace'. Rehearse the scene in groups of four or five, identifying the changes in the actors' delivery.

Not all the language used in the playtext is concerned with words. The stage directions often refer to the sounds of the play, such as knocking, tapping, ticking, banging or even the implied sound when the family are listening to Gregor's movements in his bedroom. Consider how meaning and mood can be communicated through such a soundscape. Look at the whole of the breakfast scene but this time starting at the beginning and continuing up to and including Gregor's speech 'Oh I could weep with joy and satisfaction…'. In groups of between four and six, try using the acoustic of your fingers against a door, or a table turned on its end to represent a door, to create the following sounds:

➤ A large insect running on the floor

➤ A large insect eating

➤ A large insect running up the wall and across the ceiling

➤ A large insect dropping from the ceiling and scuttling off.

Then, using naturalistic dialogue, consider how the Samsa family might respond to these noises. Show that:

➤ Mrs Samsa is worried

➤ Greta doesn't want to upset Gregor

➤ Mr Samsa is too scared to do anything himself.

How important are sounds in the play? What does the family hear? How do they feel? How can you show what they feel? How much of the text is spoken word and how much is stage direction? How important is the language of imagery and sound within the play?

## Non-verbal communication

Movement and images underpin all of the verbal work – just by flicking through the text you will come across many stage directions that indicate this. Through his instructions, Berkoff allows you to conjure up images and actions that should accompany, support and lead the words.

If, as it is sometimes argued, *Metamorphosis* is a metaphor for an individual's inability to cope with the stresses and routines of contemporary life, then it is important to gain an understanding of what these might be. In groups of four or five, create a movement collage of the pressured life of a given individual. Think about the daily routine but move away from a simple realistic presentation. Consider the more grotesque aspects of commuting on a train, working in a factory, meeting deadlines. Think in particular about the tension in the images you choose. Draw stick diagrams or take photos of the images you use and include these in your notes. Is there any way of suggesting some aspects of these pressures in your production?

 Berkoff regularly uses images to express, rather than explain, a character's emotions. Look at the following images and try to recreate them in your group. Identify which are the most successful and why. Choose one of the images and document it in your notes.

| Page | Image Description |
|------|-------------------|
| 81 | Actors as marionettes – Father smokes and drinks, Mother sews, Greta reads. |
| 82 | Other travellers at breakfast when Gregor returns with the morning orders. |
| 82 | Image of family going to meet and their parting. |
| 88 | What to do – hands flapping behind backs. |
| 89 | Total family confusion – reaction to Gregor's voice. |
| 89 | Image on A, B and C. Reasons why family were so upset. |
| 93 | Frantic eyes and outstretched hands following Clerk. |

Divide the play up into units – you should try to create between 15 and 20 units. Give each unit a title that sums up the action of that unit. Working in groups of between four and six, try to represent the action of each unit as a freeze or still picture. What is happening in the unit? What are the characters thinking and feeling? What are you trying to communicate through the freeze? Use movement to link the freezes together and think about how movement can also create meaning. Try using music to accompany the realisation of the units. Establishing what you think are the most important moments of the play will help you to gain a deeper understanding of the plot. Think about how Brechtian devices such as alienation, third person speech and representation allow the importance of the story to be communicated.

## Visual, aural and spatial elements

**Set**

Berkoff gives incredible detail about his vision for the set of the play. The text begins with a detailed page on the requirements of a skeletal framework of steel scaffolding. This fulfils many of the functional and symbolic requirements of the play, in that it represents an abstract sculpture of a giant insect, it solves the problem of the split space needed, and it even suggests the use of stools for family functions. Stage instructions in the text are layered. Berkoff often sets out the physical action of the episode, then the dialogue, and then the image that is required. These generally simultaneous instructions need to be layered together to complete the action of the scene.

**Function and symbol**

Function refers to those elements that have to be in the design because the stage instructions (or the play) demand them. Symbol is the way in which the functional elements are designed, or the extra things that the designer brings to the play in order to create meaning or to emphasise themes. In *Metamorphosis* there has to be, for example, a living space for the family; an area that suggests Gregor's bedroom; a division between the two living spaces; some suggestion of location and time; some simple props to allow simple family functions such as the meal to happen. However, the set itself needs to represent and suggest elements of the deeper meaning, themes and moods of the play. These are:

➤ Surrealism and the dream-like/nightmarish quality of the story

➤ Insects and all the repellent and repulsive feelings that come with them

➤ Routine, monotony and futility

➤ The passing of time.

**Lighting**

Lighting is very important in communicating the action to the audience. In its most raw element, it allows the action of the play and the characters to be seen by the audience. For example, the use of lighting could distinguish between the living area and Gregor's room; sharply focused light could create isolation for the person in that beam; cross-fading of light or black-out can indicate the passing of time or the end of an episode; the speed of the appearance of light can startle, shock or have other effects on the audience. Stark and snapped white light contrasting with black-outs are a major feature of the stage directions. The monochromatic set may enforce the idea of a dream or even match the colouring of a beetle.

**Think about...**

Consider how the use of colours in lighting can create symbolic meanings. Red, for example, can represent anger, rage, madness and so on.

Go through the playtext and write down a lighting plot purely based on the stage directions. Use the following chart to help with format:

| Lighting effect | Action | Reason |
| --- | --- | --- |
| Light backcloth | Family enter | Creates silhouettes: physical representation of characters important |
| Front light comes up | Revealing family | Moving from surreal to real |
| Lights snap on | Revealing Gregor as normal | Scenes of pre-insect light |

**Costume**

The costumes in *Metamorphosis* need to:

➤ Allow the actors to move and work very physically

➤ Indicate class status

➤ Indicate a location

➤ Indicate a period

➤ Allow the actor playing Gregor to slip between being a human and a beetle with ease

➤ Indicate the notions of Surrealism

➤ Emphasise the monochrome nature of the play.

Sound and music are an important part of the layering of *Metamorphosis* and can have the following functions:

➤ Support or lead movement or ballet sequence

➤ Underscore a monologue or dialogue to enhance mood

➤ Link scenes to show the passing of time

➤ Indicate flashback or flash forward

➤ Create a mood.

The play demands a certain style of staging as we have discovered from our previous exploration of form, structure and plot. This style is best achieved through allowing the actors to create with their own bodies what is required by the text and through relying on the imagination of the audience rather than on a complex set. In Berkoff's opening address on stage setting, at the front of the text, he clearly states: 'The stage is void of all props – everything is mimed – apart from three black stools.' The actors are required to use their voices, bodies and the space available to create the world that the characters exist in.

 Imagine that you are the set designer for a production of *Metamorphosis*. How do you think the set should look? Consider:

➤ The function of the space: what must be there

➤ The symbolism you could use: what the space could look like

➤ Those stage directions that demand a specific look.

Draw the set as you feel the playtext demands. Then try to draw an alternative set, incorporating your conclusions about function and symbol.

## Interpretation

The episodic nature of Berkoff's writing means that there is no real climax to the action. Gregor gradually fades from existence rather than meeting a high-profile death. However, the change in the family's character at the end of the play is more marked. Consider how you might convey this.

The final action before Gregor's death is the scene with the Lodgers. The family are desperate for money and more material objects and inviting members of the outside world seems to suggest a greater confidence. Consequently, this is an excellent scene in which to bring together your different ideas for the text.

### Sound and music

**Further study**

Try finding a CD that would work effectively with the style and action of *Metamorphosis*. For example, try listening to the soundtracks to the films *Evil Dead*, *Edward Scissorhands* and *Beetlejuice*.

### Staging

Berkoff will generally not allow chairs into his rehearsal space because it allows the actor to relax mentally and physically, instead of becoming fully aware of and engaged with the space they are working in.

When working on the staging elements, try to consider the following words and phrases: stylised, grotesque, imagery, choreographed movement, ballet, total theatre, physical theatre, Theatre of Cruelty, Surrealism, clockwork, ritual.

In the BBC production, the hairstyles at the beginning had been extreme; by the end they were much more normal and the delivery was relatively realistic.

## Interpretation: Metamorphosis by Steven Berkoff

Intended impact of scene: to emphasise the family's growing confidence and disregard for Gregor.

There should be a lavish nature to the Lodgers' costumes which is mirrored in their flamboyant gestures. They should be impressive and disgusting.

The Lodgers should speak with exaggerated received pronunciation (RP). Their formal tone and stressing of consonants should contrast with the more relaxed delivery of the Samsas.

---

**1st L:** It's warm

**2nd L:** Pleasant

**3rd L:** A little cramped, but it'll do.

*(They all take the family stools)*

**Mrs S:** We'll try and make it comfortable.

**Mr S:** It's a very friendly household – say the word and we'll do our best.

**Greta:** *(giggles)* What funny faces!

**Mrs S:** Ssshhh!

**1st L:** We'd like to be called at 8 o'clock.

**2nd L:** Prompt!

**3rd L:** Breakfast hot and ready at 8:15!

**2nd L:** Prompt!

**1st L:** Coffee, rolls and cheese.

**2nd L:** Marmalade, if you please.

**3rd L:** And toast.

**Mrs S:** I think we'll manage that all right.

**1st L:** We're sticklers for order.

**2nd L:** Especially in the kitchen.

**3rd L:** Can't bear slovenliness.

**Mrs S:** You tell us what you need.

**1st L:** When we've examined our quarters.

**2nd L:** We'll tell you of our objections.

**Mr S:** *(uncomfortably)* Hmmph! *(clearing his throat)* There's er ... one thing you should know before making a decision.

**1st L:** Yes?

**Mr S:** We ... er ... keep a pet in the back room.

**All Ls:** Oh yes?

**Mr S:** I wondered if that would bother you?

**All Ls:** Oh no, we're fond of pets.

---

*Annotations:*

Mr Samsa's stuttering delivery should alter the pace of the scene; all eyes should turn to him in a slightly claustrophobic manner. The sense of intimidation should be strong but eventually he receives their approval.

Gregor, the pet, can remain. The Lodgers should conclude with an aggressive bark which makes Mr Samsa jump and then laugh nervously at their humour.

As the Lodgers call out their requirements, the family should be positioned behind, bent over in half supplication. The father should mime taking notes, ripping off sheets and delegating the jobs to the others.

The Lodgers should move, wherever possible, as one. Sitting on their chairs should be a statement of their immense self confidence. The Samsa family should watch slightly bemused and yet in quiet admiration of their arrogance.

Greta's giggle is a final reminder of her child-like innocence. The actor should position herself downstage to imprint this image in the audience's memory before she changes.

The pace of the delivery is important at this point. The Lodgers should speak quickly although the family should look as if they can cope with their demands – an ironic contrast to their slovenly behaviour at the beginning of the play.

## Evaluation of live theatre

The exam board wants you to experience as much live theatre as possible. By going to the theatre you will begin to see in practice the choices directors make when dealing with texts, the approach actors bring to their roles and the decisions designers make when creating set, costume and lighting.

Watching live theatre will also help you to make sense of the way you have explored texts in this unit and open your eyes to the way that directors, actors and designers deconstruct a text on the page, bringing meaning to the words, action and characters.

You should already have worked practically on two texts and written exploration notes on how they could be performed. Now, in this part of the unit you are going to write reflectively about plays that have actually passed through this process and been performed. You should not see the evaluation of live theatre as an extra part of the unit, but rather as a continuation of your earlier thinking. Your evaluation needs to show understanding and knowledge of all the areas covered in your exploration notes:

➤ Use of language

➤ Non-verbal communication

➤ Vocal awareness

➤ Characterisation

➤ Social, cultural, historical and political context

➤ Visual, aural and spatial elements

➤ Interpretation.

You should be able to use theatre language and terminology confidently, and understand the roles played by a theatre production team and how they contribute to a production.

> Make sure you have read and understood the Understanding Theatre chapter in this guide, pages 8–48.

### What should my evaluation look like?

This piece of written work must not exceed 1,000 words and a successful evaluation could be shorter. You can use appropriate sketches, diagrams and other illustrations to support your work and help communicate meaning.

The evaluation of live theatre along with the other elements of this unit (practical work and exploration notes) will be assessed by your teacher; the whole unit is worth 40% of the total AS mark.

This piece of written evaluation can be completed at any point during the course but must be submitted with the rest of the unit by the coursework deadline.

### What should the evaluation try to do?

This written evaluation should get you to think about theatre performance in terms of decisions and choices.

You need to be able to:

➢ Analyse how characters, narrative and ideas are conveyed through theatre

➢ Recognise the contribution made to a piece of theatre by directors, designers and performers

➢ Understand how the social, cultural and historical background of a playtext creates relevance for its audience.

If this seems a little bit confusing then you can think about the way in which a production has been created in more simple terms, as a 'page to stage' process:

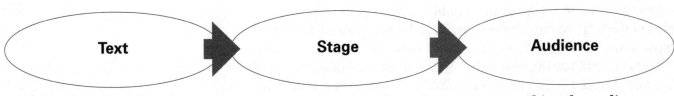

| **Interpreting the playtext** | **Performing the play** | **Reaching the audience** |
|---|---|---|
| *How do we make meaning in theatre?* | *What are the conventions of staging and the tools of the actor?* | *How is the play made relevant for its audience?* |
| *What choices does the director, designer or actor have when bringing the playtext alive from the page to the stage?* | | |

## Preparation

**Reading reviews**  Reading reviews in broadsheet newspapers or magazines will help you to understand the nature of theatre criticism and will improve your literary and theatrical vocabulary. However, it will not directly help you to analyse the creation of meaning in theatre, as this unit demands. Reviews can be too concerned with forming positive or negative judgements. This unit, by contrast, is not simply about making value judgments, but about understanding what makes effective meaning in the theatre.

**A live production**  Be aware that you must see a live production; you cannot settle for writing about a play you have seen on television or on a video recording. The whole essence of this unit is about the live interaction between a production and its audience.

**What to see**  Although you are only required to submit for assessment an evaluation of one live production that you have seen, this should not prevent you from seeing a number of productions. In fact, it would be highly beneficial to your understanding of theatre to see a range of performances during your year of study.

Create a list of different genres and see an example of each:

➢ A play that deals with serious issues

➢ A musical play

➢ A Shakespeare play

➢ A play with a targeted audience – such as a children's play

➢ A touring piece that has to work in a variety of different spaces

➢ A more experimental piece using different forms of theatre in the storytelling.

Many pieces of theatre resist simplistic categorisation – some of the plays you see will be a combination of more than one of the genres above. What is important is that you see a wide range of work in a range of different spaces, which prompt varying responses from their audiences.

**What is available**

Going to the theatre depends very much on where you live, what is available and what you can afford. You do not have to restrict yourself to professionals; choosing to evaluate a school or amateur production can prove to be just as valuable. You might see a production of either of the two plays which you have studied practically in this unit, in order to support your understanding of them.

> A good choice of play in performance will really help you to respond to the key areas in this unit and enable you to shape an effective answer.

Whatever you see, and whatever you ultimately choose to write about, seize the opportunity to analyse and evaluate in an enthusiastic and positive, yet also critical, way. Write about how effective the choices and decisions made by the director, actors and designers have been.

**Where to start**

Understanding how to break down a piece of live theatre into areas that you can write about should begin even before you enter the theatre and is part of a more gradual process of thinking about theatre. In fact, you may not realise it, but you have already begun this process. The AS course is designed to start you thinking about how theatre is made and why it is made in particular ways. You already have a great deal of experience from which to draw: in this unit you have looked at different approaches to performing playtexts practically and your exploration notes will have given you experience of justifying the decisions you have made. In Unit 2 you will take a playtext and a monologue or duologue, and make appropriate decisions as directors, designers and actors as to how to bring them to life on stage.

**Creation of meaning**

There is a theatre anecdote about a production of Chekhov's *Uncle Vanya* – the opening scene of which is set in a garden:

> The curtains open and in the middle of the beautiful set of natural-looking trees and shrubs is a modern, metal stepladder with a theatre light hanging down above it. The audience begins to analyse why the lantern can be seen and why a modern stepladder exists in a garden of trees, which can be seen to represent Russia at the end of the 19th century. One critic decides that it is a symbol representing the industrialisation of an essentially agricultural Russia, while another is convinced it is an act of genius on the part of the designer, and depicts the rise of the working classes over the land-owning classes. However, before they can speculate any further, a technician walks onto the stage and apologises profusely for leaving the ladder there: he was replacing a lamp in one of the lanterns and didn't realise

the time. He informs the audience that the curtains are going to close again and that the play will begin properly without the lantern and ladder on stage.

While the truth of this tale may be questionable, nevertheless the point it illustrates is valid: everything you see and hear in a performance is deliberately there in order to create meaning for the audience (unless it has been left on stage by a negligent technician!). It is for the audience to try to interpret the signs and symbols and work out what the messages communicated by the play are.

## Test yourself

Although you must write about a live performance for your final piece, it is good introductory practice to test your analysis skills on a recorded production. Create notes using the headings given on the next two pages for the musical, *Jesus Christ Superstar.*

**Further viewing**

Get hold of a copy of the new stage production of *Jesus Christ Superstar* on DVD (Universal Pictures UK 2000). It is a film version of an actual theatrical production (make sure that you do not confuse it with the 1973 version, filmed on location in the Middle East).

**Before viewing the production**

Before you start watching the production, write down some thoughts about what you know about it using the following headings:

➤ **Location:** where is it set?

➤ **Time/period:** when does it take place?

➤ **Action/events:** do you know any of the key events?

➤ **Characters:** who are the main characters and what do they look like?

➤ **Themes and issues:** what is the intent of the story and what can we learn from it?

**While viewing the production**

As you watch the production, write down some observations using the following headings:

➤ **Set:** how is location created and what does the set remind you of?

➤ **Staging:** how does the action move about the set and how are events staged?

➤ **Characters:** what do the characters look like and do they match your preconceptions?

➤ **Costume:** do the costumes worn by different groups of characters carry any strong connotations?

➤ **Lighting:** how does the lighting work to create effects, moods and atmosphere? How does this inform the audience of place and time? Does the lighting create symbolic meaning?

**The set**

The set plays a major part in defining a performance space. The set for *Jesus Christ Superstar* locates the action in ancient Galilee by suggesting the form, shapes and colours of Roman architecture. However, it also appears modern: the use of scaffolding and graffiti makes an audience think about modern Palestine and Israel, and the conflicts which exist in the region today. It alludes to the period in which the play's events occur and also brings new relevance and meaning to these events by referring to struggles which exist today.

**Staging**

The staging dramatically alters the effect of the set. The set is defined by the action within it, the lighting used, the characters populating it and the words that are spoken and sung. Although the same spaces are used throughout the musical, the audience is still willing to accept that they represent different locations.

**Characters**

*Jesus Christ Superstar* has a multicultural cast (departing from the story as told in the Bible). This has a number of different effects:

➤ It reminds us that it is a piece of theatre and not reality; it is the message communicated by the story which becomes important rather than the individuals within it

➤ It implies that the story has universal significance; it is not simply relevant to one country or nation

➤ It gives the story modern significance, suggesting that it could be about people today in any political or international conflict.

**Costumes**

The production uses an eclectic mixture of costumes. Many costumes hint at the traditional garments which would have been worn in ancient Galilee; however, there is also a prevalence of modern dress, for instance there is a suggestion of modern combat gear in the costumes worn by the disciples. The costumes of the Romans are influenced by the uniforms of ancient Rome as well as evoking Nazi Germany through their colour, cut and insignia. The priests and Jews wear garments which suggest clothes worn by Hasidic Jews in the 1930s, when propaganda was used to incite anti-Semitic feelings.

The use of costumes which combine influences from various historic periods, have the following effects:

➤ They root the story of the production in its original period

➤ They make reference to other periods in history in which the Jews suffered persecution

➤ They establish connections with the modern world, for instance with modern day conflicts and terrorism.

> The use of modern weapons in conjunction with spears and swords also has a similar effect.

Well-chosen costumes can be very effective in creating new meaning and relevance for an audience.

**Lighting**

In order to evoke the religious and spiritual significance of Jesus the lighting which is directed on him is often enhanced with a bright white effect. Mood and atmosphere are created using volume and colour. The location of each scene is denoted with angled lighting, which reveals whether the scene is outside or inside. Lighting is also used to give the impression of there being many buildings, windows and doors in a busy, yet dilapidated city.

**Intent**

What do you think the director wanted the audience to come away thinking about the production? Were they concerned with conveying historical detail or with investigating who was the 'real' Jesus, or were they more interested in showing that the struggle against oppression and the fight for freedom still goes on in other guises? Write a statement describing what the production was trying to say to the audience about the story of Jesus and Judas.

**Interpretation**

If all productions of the same play were identical, theatre would be very dull and there would be definitive versions that could be videoed and watched on television. Performances would not take into consideration changes in theatre trends, performance styles, new actors, cultural changes, historical events, social injustices and current events. Theatre is a living art form that reflects the here and now. The possibility of bringing new meaning to any play, or making the audience view it with new eyes and ears, through the process of interpretation, is what keeps theatre alive.

Having created some notes using the headings suggested above for a recorded production, you will begin to see that the director, designers and performers make decisions in order to make the production relevant and thought provoking for a modern audience.

## Suggested recorded productions

**Romeo and Juliet**

Choose another film version of a play to test your analysis skills. A good one would be a film of a Shakespeare play, especially one you know quite well already. Try the above exercise for yourself and see if you can 'read' the director's and designers' interpretation.

**Further viewing**

*Romeo and Juliet* (20th Century Fox 1996).

You could look at Baz Luhrmann's *Romeo and Juliet*, starring Leonardo DiCaprio and Claire Danes. When watching the film consider the headings below; don't just observe what is done but try to decide *why* decisions have been made:

➢ **Location**: where is the film located and why?

➢ **Time/period**: when is the film set and why?

➢ **Action/events**: how would you describe the action of the play? How is music used and why?

➢ **Characters**: how are the main characters presented and costumed and why?

➢ **Themes and issues**: what do you think is the main theme of the play and how is it communicated through the performance?

While this template of questions is useful for any film version of a play, it is especially suited to Shakespeare's plays because they are open to many different interpretations in terms of time and location. Look, for instance, at Ian McKellen in the title role of *Richard III* (1995) or Julie Taymor's *Titus* (1999) as alternatives to *Romeo and Juliet*.

**The Gruffalo**

The DVD of Tall Stories' *The Gruffalo* is another suitable production with which to analyse the notion of effective theatre as it is a recording of a theatre production. Obviously the camera dictates what you see and how you see it, but it still provides a great starting point to evaluating live theatre. The piece sets out to retell the picture book of the same name in a magical, humorous and theatrical way, with the aim of engaging and entertaining a young audience. Your evaluation of the production should consider: does it succeed in achieving this aim?

**Further viewing**

*The Gruffalo* (Universal Pictures UK 2005).

Complete notes under the following headings. Again, remember that you should not just be observing what is done, but you should be trying to make the leap to deciding *why* these directorial and design decisions were made:

➤ **Location:** where is the story set? What does the set look like and why? How does it compare to the illustrations in the picture book?

➤ **Action/events:** how would you describe the action of the play? How are songs used in the production?

➤ **Time/period:** what sense of period is created by the set, the costumes and the action?

➤ **Characters:** what decisions have been made about the costumes and the characters? How have the different animals been represented?

➤ **Themes and issues:** what do you think is the main intent of the play and how is it communicated through the performance?

## Evaluation notes

It is unlikely that you will be writing your final live evaluation immediately after watching the production. It is therefore important to make extensive and detailed notes on each of the productions you see in order to keep them fresh in your mind, ready for when you begin to write your evaluation.

It is always good to have a fermentation period after seeing a production, in which you mull over thoughts about it so as to reach a balanced and objective assessment; writing notes will help in this process. If you have the opportunity, discuss the production with your teacher or group members, to clarify your own thinking. Use your notes to prompt topics for discussion.

The guidelines given below for taking structured notes can be applied to any production that you see – use them to shape your own notes.

## Pre-show expectations

Begin your thinking about the production before you even get to the theatre.

Is it a **theatre** you have visited before? Do you know anything about its layout, the relationship between the stage and the audience, its size or where you will be sitting?

Is it a **play** you know? Have you seen it before? Have you read it? Do you have an idea of how it might look in performance?

Who is performing the play? Is it a **company** that have been brought together for the purpose of performing this play? Are they a repertory company that have performed other plays together? How long have they been performing this play?

Does the **poster** give any clues about the content of the play, the issues dealt with or the style in which it is performed? Examine the poster again after you've seen the production to refresh your memory; how did the production compare with the pre-show expectations created by the poster?

**Further reading**

*The Gruffalo* by Julia Donaldson and Axel Scheffler (Macmillan Children's Books 1999).

Asking good, focused questions is the most important thing when it comes to evaluating live theatre. Arriving at your chosen production with a clear set of questions will help you to create a thorough evaluation.

On pages 113–119 you will see some sample evaluation notes, to give you an idea of what your own should look like.

**Questions**

## In the theatre

### Space and layout

Make sure you have read and understood the descriptions and diagrams of the different types of stage layout featured on pages 43–45 of this guide.

Try to understand and assess the stage layout. There are various traditional stage layouts, each of which encourages a different relationship with the audience and suits a different type of theatre.

The effectiveness of a production is reliant on the relationship between the acting space and the position of the audience. Many modern productions are taken on tour, and this means that they are placed at the mercy of the various spaces they are visiting. While a production may be perfectly suited to the small, intimate space it was originally designed for, it may not be quite so effective when placed within a large proscenium-arch theatre. An example of this scenario is the production of *The Blue Room* which was originally produced at the Donmar Warehouse in London in 1998, starring Nicole Kidman. The play is a series of vignettes in which two actors perform a variety of duologues, playing different characters, all of whom are linked to one another. The play relies on the intimacy of the relationships and the believability of the characters in order to show the complexities of love and modern relationships. While the production worked beautifully in the intimate thrust layout of the small Donmar Warehouse, where the audience was in close proximity to the performers and hence could sense the electricity between them, once the play was reworked and toured to large proscenium-arch theatres round the country, much of its intimacy was lost.

Consider how the stage layout affects your relationship with the play. Draw the layout so that you can remember it.

### The programme

Some programmes can be very expensive and may only include colour photographs of the show and biographies of the actors, which will not be particularly helpful. Others contain a director's or designer's statement, an interview with one of the main actors or some background contextual information about the play and when it was written. All of these will help you make notes after the production.

The programme will also hold the details of the production; these are essential for your piece of writing. You will need to write them at the beginning of your written evaluation. They include:

➤ **Title** of the play

➤ **Date** you saw it

➤ **Where** you saw it.

You will also find a cast list in the programme. This, again, will be very useful for your evaluation: you will need the names of the actors when it comes to analysing how they created their parts, otherwise your response will be vague and confusing.

## During the play

### Set

As the performance begins, spend some initial time thinking about the set. Remember that the entire set may not be revealed immediately and it may change considerably during the performance as scenes and locations change. Ask yourself some basic questions:

➤ How does the **set** create or define the performance space?

➤ Does it suggest a particular **location** (or various locations)? How does it do this?

➤ Does the set suggest a particular **time or period**? How?

➤ How does the set assist the **action** of the play (think, in particular, about exits, entrances and levels)?

➤ Does the set suggest or create a believable world for the **characters** to live in?

➤ Does the set use **literal/naturalistic techniques** to create the world of the play, or is it more symbolic?

➤ Does the set suggest or contribute towards an overarching **mood**, through use of shapes, colours, materials, scale or distortion?

➤ Does the set contain any clues about the **themes and issues** in the play?

If you know or have studied the play beforehand, think about how the playtext describes the setting of the action, and whether it offers any suggestions about how this should be realised in the set.

Sometimes, even if the playtext does provide set details, the production may decide to depart from these and create a radically different set idea. A good example of this is the National Theatre's production of *An Inspector Calls* in 1992. The playtext indicates that the action is set in an Edwardian living room, however this production chose to create a much more surreal setting and have a number of houses set on stilts which opened like dollhouses to reveal rooms inside. This expressionistic set suggested a new interpretation of the story, which emphasised the isolation and aloofness of the family, the nightmarish qualities of the inspector and the family's doll-like manipulation. When the family's world falls apart at the end of the play, the set reflected this by literally falling down around them.

The difference between what the playtext offers as a suggestion for the set and the set which the production actually creates is the **interpretation**.

Think about the set under two headings:

**Function.** What does the set need in order to be able to fulfil the requirements of the action of the play? The playtext may demand certain things such as exits and entrances, levels and certain specific locations. How does the set in the production you have seen serve these basic functional requirements?

**Symbol.** What elements of the set are additional to what is written in the playtext? A designer will make decisions and choices in conjunction with the director about the emphasis their production

Some texts, such as Arthur Miller's *The Crucible* (1953), offer detailed instructions as to how to create the set, right down to where the walls, doors and windows should be positioned, and what their colours and textures should be. Some, such as Shakespeare's plays, offer very little.

will have regarding the themes and action of the play. These decisions will affect the whole concept of the set. The set can create moods, suggest themes and support staging styles through the objects and shapes chosen, its use of materials, colours and textures, and its use of scale and proportion. It might be naturalistic, to evoke the real world, or it might be abstract, to suggest an impression of a world.

How would you describe the set of the production you have seen, and is it trying to suggest meaning? Soon after seeing the production, draw some plans and illustrations of the set so that you can clearly remember it later. Draw a bird's-eye-view plan of the set and indicate where the scenic elements are. Then draw a 3D impression of the set, looking at the stage from the point of view of the audience.

**Staging**

The staging concerns the way in which the story is told and the way in which characters move within the set.

The staging of the production is dependent on:

➢ The **genre** of the production: is it a musical, a comedy, a play trying to show modern reality?

➢ The **content** of the playtext: is it about love, war, the supernatural?

➢ The intended **audience response**: is the production trying to make the audience think, feel, laugh, cry?

From your previous study in this unit, you probably already have a basic grasp of some of the choices concerning staging and the way in which they can be applied to the playtext. Consider whether the production has been influenced by one of the following practitioners:

**Stanislavski**. Does it seem that the production you are watching is trying to mimic reality? Do the characters speak and move naturalistically? Do you feel like you are watching a slice of real life (whether in the past or the present)? Do you feel emotionally engaged with the action and characters of the play?

See pages 15–24 for more information about Stanislavski.

**Brecht**. Does the production you are watching seem to be dramatising a grand, epic story? Do the actors play a number of characters? Can you see them changing from one costume to another in order to change characters? Do the actors use song to comment on the action or to move it along? Do the characters speak directly to the audience as well as each other?

See pages 24–32 for more information about Brecht.

**Artaud**. Does the production you are watching challenge the way in which the audience and the action relate? Does the movement and language used in the production seem unique or special in that way that it tells the story? Does the way in which the events are presented shock you?

See pages 32–40 for more information about Artaud.

There are, of course, many other major influences in terms of staging. Try using the internet to find out more about:

**Steven Berkoff and physical theatre**
www.stevenberkoff.com
www.iainfisher.com/berkoff.html

**Jerzy Grotowski and poor theatre**
www.owendaly.com/jeff/grotdir.htm
www.geocities.com/akatsavou/grotowski_en.html

**Pinter, Beckett and the theatre of the absurd**
www2.arts.gla.ac.uk/Slavonic/Absurd.htm
http://dana.ucc.nau.edu/~sek5/classpage.html

**The history of staging**
www.win.net/~kudzu/history.html
www.videoccasions-nw.com/history/theatrer.html

**The influence of world theatre**
www.csuohio.edu/history/japan/japan12.html
http://allsands.com/History/Objects/kabukitheatre_suf_gn.htm

What is essential to your understanding and appreciation of staging is that in modern theatrical productions directors draw on a huge vocabulary of ideas; they will often mix and match staging forms and conventions to suit an individual production. Equally, the beauty of modern theatre is that directors increasingly draw from influences beyond the confines of theatre history; they use influences from pop music, videos, cinema and rock concerts to find ways of staging theatrical ideas. Look for the diverse influences at work on a production and refer to them when you're discussing staging.

As you look at lighting, sound and music, costumes and props, remember that they are all expressions of the **ruling idea**, the concept behind the interpretation of the playtext. This is concerned with where the play is set, when it is set, how it looks and how it will be staged. Most importantly, it is concerned with what the production is trying to say to the audience, and thus it is made manifest in the set and staging of the play.

The primary function of lighting is to allow the characters of the play to be seen by the audience. In some productions this is all that is required. Brecht often used normal house lighting for his plays because he didn't want the lighting to detract from the simple telling of the narrative; lighting can create a magical world and he preferred his audience to be reminded of their own, real world. Brecht's denial of theatrical lighting is an acknowledgement of its power.

The lighting that supports performances can be used in an exaggerated way, for example in support of a big show like Ben Elton's *We Will Rock You* (2002). It can also be used in a more subtle and almost unnoticeable way, for example in support of the same author's *Popcorn* (1996), which takes place primarily in a living room.

---

**Web link**

The French-Canadian director Robert Lepage is just one modern director who uses cinematic imagery and technology in his productions, such as *Needles and Opium* and *Elsinore*, to explore new meanings and relevances for his audiences. You can read him in conversation with the former director of the National Theatre at www.nationaltheatre.org.uk/?lid=2627

**Lighting**

The lighting of a play can have a number of different purposes:

In creating **locations**, the lighting of a play can:

➤ Define a location quickly by focusing on one area

➤ Indicate change of location over time by fading to black and then up again

➤ Indicate quicker change of location by cross-fading between different areas and levels

➤ Use a gobo to project a specific sense of location such as forest branches, city skylines or a church window

➤ Indicate an epic, large-scale location by being used on a cyclorama.

In creating the movement of **time**, lighting can:

➤ Define changes in time through fades

➤ Indicate a time of day by using colour and intensity of light

➤ Show a change in season through altering colour and intensity

➤ Be used on a cyclorama to give an indication of time of day.

To determine the **audience's response** to a production, lighting can:

➤ Confront

➤ Blind

➤ Shock.

To support the **reality of the set**, lighting can:

➤ Be directly linked to a source on stage, such as a lamp or a candle

➤ Imply sources of light through windows and doors, supporting the time, location and mood of the production.

Lighting can create its own **mood, atmosphere and tension** by use of:

➤ Different types of colour and levels of intensity

➤ Different angles and directions

➤ Filtering effects and smoke.

It can create **symbolic meaning** in support of the action of the play by use of angle, colour, intensity and effect, for example:

➤ A simple use of a red gel to indicate an act of murder or of rage

➤ A floor flood facing a character to create a huge shadow on the back wall or cyclorama to indicate a growth in that character's ego or a giant metaphorical presence on stage.

When you are watching your productions, examine the use of lighting and decide whether any of it fits into the categories explored above. Remember: the lighting in a production is always a series of deliberate choices in support of the play. Work out what decisions and choices have been made.

---

Write down the different uses of lighting in the show you have seen and give specific examples of when they were used, how they were used and why you think they were used. It can help if you illustrate the examples with drawings.

---

## Sound

Sound and music work in a very similar way to lighting, in that they can:

➤ Create a **location**, such as a busy street or the countryside through use of selected sound effects

➤ Support the events of a scene by creating a soundtrack to underscore the action and create **mood**

➤ Heighten the **emotional intensity** of a scene by using an evocative or poignant sound, melody or song

➤ **Comment** on the action by contrasting with the action of the scene

➤ Move the action forward by reflecting the passing of **time**

➤ Create **symbolic meaning**, as in *Equus*, in which the ritualistic sound and chanting express its themes of religion and sex.

## Costume

Different types of plays will give different opportunities for costumes. However, whether the play is set in modern Britain or Elizabethan England, whether it is naturalistic or abstract in staging, the costumes will have been designed or chosen to reflect a number of things. Like lighting and sound, they are a part of the ruling idea. They are likely to be intended to:

➤ Reflect and support **character**

➤ Suggest a **period** and **location**

➤ Suggest or support the **themes** being explored

➤ Indicate the style of **staging** of the play.

> For example, a king could be represented only by a crown. The character of the king never changes, but the actors playing him do. In this instance, the costume is the audience's sign of recognition for that character and the costume itself becomes the representation of the character.

For the latter point, if actors are doubling (each playing more than one roll) and using costume to differentiate the characters they play, then the costume *becomes* the character. An audience is able to identify a character through costume.

The degree to which the costume does any of the above will depend on the type of production you see and how much scope there is for interpretation. When observing costume, look for obvious signs of character representation, location and period representation, but also examine colour, shape, texture and material to see what is being suggested about the person who wears it.

**Props**

The props used within a play can be thought of in a number of clear ways. They too can support the location and period of the play in a very literal sense: a gramophone in a living room will give a sense of a specific period in time. They can also have a symbolic value: the gramophone, for example, may also represent memories of the past for one of the characters through its music, and thus become a symbol of the past.

Equally, props can have significance if placed ironically within a production. Our gramophone could be placed in a modern setting, where it would stand out, forcing the audience to think about what point the director might be trying to make.

Props can also have a representational value in terms of being many things within a production. The gramophone could be used as a hearing aid; it may become a witch's hat, a beautiful shell on a beach, a weapon. The way in which a prop is used will give you many clues as to the style of the production. And, as with costume, props can be key signs as to how to recognise characters. Props such as handbags, hats and walking sticks can be used to help actors create characters and help the audience identify them.

---

Think carefully about what props are used in the production you are watching and how they are used. Do they have a value greater than what they literally are? Not all props will carry this value but some may. Describe when, how and why the props are used and draw illustrations.

---

**Actors' performances**

The characters within a play often carry the story, and their actions and words are what draw us into and engage us with the events of the production. It can be very difficult to distance yourself from the characters and try to decide *what* the actor is doing, *how* they are doing it and, most importantly, *why* they are doing it. It is very important that you avoid making value judgements about the performance, such as 'He was very good' or 'I didn't like her'. You need to address what the actor was doing and whether it was effective.

A good way to start thinking about an actor's performance is to break it down into clear questions:

➤ What did the actor do with their **voice** to create the character?

➤ How did the actor **move** to create their character?

➤ What did the actor **look like** in creating their character?

➤ How did the actor **relate** to the other actors and the space in creating their character?

➤ Did the actor make you **feel** anything for their character?

➤ Did the actor make you **think** about anything through the way they created their character?

These questions force you to regard the actor separately from the character. They also force you to consider the performance in distinct sections, under which we can begin to build supplementary questions to aid our analysis of the performance. Consider the more detailed questions in the following table:

| | |
|---|---|
| **Voice** | Could you hear what the character was saying? Did the actor use an accent or a dialect? Was the characterisation sustained throughout the play? How would you describe the voice of the character: was it soft/loud, gentle/harsh, natural/mannered? Did it change during certain scenes? Did you always feel that the voice was appropriate to the moment or action? |
| **Movement** | Was gesture and body language used effectively? What type of movement did the style of production or the character demand? Was the movement appropriate to the character and to the moment or scene? Did the character's movement change during the course of the play for any reason? Did the actor use any props in his creation of the character and how did they affect movement? |
| **Costume** | What was the costume of the character? Did the costume change and, if so, for what reasons? Did the costume represent anything or give you clues to the style, themes or meaning of the play? What were the textures and colours of the costume? |
| **Relationships** | How did the actor relate to the other actors or characters on the stage? Did you feel the actor had any real engagement with the other actors? How did the actor use the space to communicate his character? How did the actor relate or communicate with the audience? |
| **Feeling** | How did the actor's performance make you feel? Did you feel sympathy or even empathy for the character at any point? Did you like him or hate him and why? Think of a specific scene or moment when you felt something, and explain what and why. Did the style of acting affect the way you felt? Did you feel alienated from the character or did you feel close to them? |
| **Thinking** | Did the way in which the character was presented by the actor make you think about the themes of the play, or about yourself and your position if you were in the play and what you would do? Were you psychologically engaged or just emotionally engaged or both? Think of occasions when you were challenged to think and describe what they were and why. |

Can you think of any words or phrases that sum up the style of acting you witnessed? Try to relate these terms to the practitioners and concepts that you have already explored on the course.

Remember, however, that simply using these terms is not enough. You cannot just describe *what* is being done; you must give examples from the production of *how*, by describing a scene, moment or event from the performance, and ultimately *why*, by explaining an actor's role in the overall interpretation and in terms of the directorial aim, or ruling idea.

You need to build up a vocabulary of descriptors for acting styles. Make sure you are confident with the meaning of the following terms: believable, introspective, sensitive, reflective, stylised, physical, controlled, animated, intense, calculated, demonstrative, stereotypical, melodramatic, mannered, indulgent, ineffectual.

**Interpretation**

The interpretation refers to the journey which is made from page to stage. In order for you to understand this journey fully, you need to have an awareness of what the play looked like as a text. It would be a good idea, therefore, to try to find a copy of the playtext, read it, and consider what the stage directions and instructions tell you about how it should be created on the stage. Do you think the performance does justice to the script? How was the performance different from your expectations?

Is there a ruling idea that comes through in the production? What do you think the director was trying to say about the play? What was your overall response to it? Were there any significant moments or scenes? Did you recognise any influences from areas of theatre that you have already studied? Did you recognise any influences from any other cultural sources? How would you describe what the production was trying to do?

> Again, it would be good here to use a vocabulary of terms that you have come across in exploring other areas of the course: for example, you might describe the production as thought-provoking in the style of epic theatre, emotional in a naturalistic way or shocking in the vein of total theatre.

### Further reading

*Theatre Studies: An Approach for Advanced Level* by Simon Cooper and Sally Mackey (Stanley Thornes 1995) offers some excellent approaches to analysing performances. It also gives some clear examples of performances that have been analysed.

Try to write down the narrative of the play as soon after seeing the production as possible. While this may seem tedious and not particularly worthwhile, remembering the basic outline of the story at a later date can be difficult if you cannot get hold of a copy of the script. Remembering the action, events and scenes of the production will be vital when you come to writing your evaluation, and saying *how* elements of the production were achieved.

### Web link

The plot of *Blood Brothers* is fast-moving and quite complicated, in that it covers a period of a number of years. There is a terrific website that covers the details of the plot: www.d.kth.se/~d97-ask/blood/Synopsis/synopsis.html

## Sample evaluation notes

You should now be equipped with a system of analysis that allows you to watch a production and begin to break it down, through the use of manageable questions under manageable headings. You will then be able to use your notes in preparation for writing your evaluation of live theatre.

Look at the sample evaluation notes opposite on a performance of *Blood Brothers* in order to get a clear idea of how to put this into practice. Bear in mind that your notes do not have to resemble these exactly – you will probably want to include more sketches and pictures.

# Blood Brothers the musical, written by Willy Russell and performed at the Phoenix Theatre, London.

### Pre-show expectations
THEATRE: Knew very little about Phoenix Theatre, just that it was old Victorian theatre so could expect an end-on proscenium-arch layout with audience in stalls and circle.
PLAY: Had read play so knew that it was piece of musical theatre about twins separated at birth and brought up in differing households in modern-city setting.
COMPANY: Brought together specifically for this production. Linda Nolan, from pop group the Nolans, playing the central role of Mrs Johnstone – wasn't sure about pop playing lead role, thought it might prevent me concentrating on story.

### Poster
- Two male hands locked together in a brotherly handshake. Background: cityscape with an epic blood-red sky.
- What this told me: play will be about togetherness and love of two males; sense of significance of them being brothers.
- Cityscape located play for me – recognised building as one in Liverpool.
- Blood-red sky gave real sense of play's epic nature; also suggested it would be dealing with issues and themes even greater than two hands locked together in foreground.

### The space and layout
- As anticipated: large Victorian theatre with wide stage and large seating capacity.
- Didn't feel that distant from the stage, as in second row of the stalls, but those in the audience further away may not have felt the same intimacy.
- Seemed to be some compromise with the proscenium arch – stage jutted out past the arch into an apron in attempt to reach audience.
- These theatres originally intended to allow large audiences to enjoy spectacle of Victorian melodrama – fitted needs of Blood Brothers as epic story with spectacle and declamatory acting styles.

### The programme
Clear indication of cast of actors and parts they played.
List of songs, their order, who sang them.
Explanation of setting simply stated 'The play is set in Liverpool'.
No detail of specific location or when it will happen or change.
Two really interesting articles that help my understanding of the play:
1. By Willy Russell about how and why he wrote Blood Brothers. Gave insight into play's structure and use of songs. Built up expectation that it would try to use songs in different way from normal musicals and attempt to be different in form and structure.
2. About Liverpool and Willy Russell. Helped me realise tradition of writing, humour and music in Liverpool, and understand significance of placing the play specifically in Liverpool during 1950s to 1980s, and not just in any city or time period. Made me wonder whether Blood Brothers could work in any city setting.

### The set
- Clearly defined PERFORMANCE SPACE. Stage surrounded on three sides by raised platform. Side platforms house band and musicians but were disguised as rows of houses. Back platform was walkway in form of iron bridge.
- Houses on stage right seemed run down and working class; houses on stage left seemed to give impression of being larger and grander.

- Large, flat floor space between platforms was raked but initially empty.
- Large backdrop showed cityscape similar to that on poster, indicated city location.
- Cyclorama backdrop also presented huge sky as shown in poster.
- Mrs Johnstone's home generally represented by area outside house and alleys around it.
- Mrs Lyons' home represented by bringing inside of house into flat floor space, using flying false wall, carpet and various items of furniture.
- Two sides of houses suggest two different types of street: one very working class and one more middle class — supported themes in story and different backgrounds of twins after separation.
- Combination of fixed set (defining space) and moveable set (working within fixed area) created own magic — made me think less about the literally quality of story and more about message behind it. Always aware that was piece of theatre — reminded me of Brecht.
- Use of levels and fixed set area allowing Narrator to roam and move effortlessly supported atmosphere of supernatural — promoted notion of superstition at heart of Mrs Johnstone's actions.
- Set suggested TIME PERIOD in not-too-distant past — architecture and style of houses suggested 1950s. BUT: action of play moves in time, tracing characters as they grow up — set dealt with this in number of ways. Although basic platforms/houses remained same throughout, number of changes were indicated through other means — backdrop changed in second half, showing move to more rural setting outside city.
- Internal setting of the houses: brought out into empty floor space between platforms on movable trucks and by using movable props.
- As time passed different items of furniture used.
- As LOCATION changed for Mrs Johnstone, a different internal setting was brought out — new kitchen. Showed improved social position.
- Large floor space used very inventively to show number of locations: different streets, beach, park. Moveable items brought on and off to give an indication of setting — bus, funfair, various rooms, prison cell, town hall.
- Set provided whole range of exits and entrances and levels: really aided STAGING of play. Narrator (omnipresent, and watching and commenting on the action) could use levels and alleys to keep appearing and disappearing, and to watch from a distance.
- Play's STRUCTURE made up of series of episodic scenes showing characters as through large number of years; pace and momentum really important. Set aided this: large floor space, many exits and entrances from it, and the levels around it allowed scene changes; could overlap scenes, one ending and disappearing off one way while another set up from another way — ensured momentum and engagement with audience.
- Set suggested world in which characters live, but didn't present it as a literal world. Style of play and passage of time during it demanded locations could be suggested through quickly changed sets, represented by lighting, props and words.
- Style of set in conjunction with staging made me very aware of production as piece of theatre — made me think about story being told rather than just lives of characters. Messages and themes become very universal — although story about people, began to take on epic status.
- Clearly met functional demands of play — provided clear definition of locations, and provided space and levels for action to flow freely and quickly.

The staging
Some clear conventions and devices at work in production.
- Piece of theatre that has songs — all have particular role within production.
- Play spans 30 years, but same groups of actors play all parts/ages. Clearly named parts (Mrs Johnstone, Mickey, Eddie etc.) play same part all the way through (so twin actors have to play twins at 7, 14, 28 onwards). Also multi-role — play number of parts, e.g. milkman, gynaecologist, bus conductor etc.

- Play begins with end: audience immediately realises that twins are going to die but has no idea how that happens or why.
- Narrator provided to pass information directly to audience. Also makes comment on action of play and gets audience to think about what has happened and why.
- Locations suggested by props and moveable sets brought on and off by actors — audience fully aware they're involved in watching a story in a theatre. Familiar device from Brecht: concerned with confronting audience with themes and issues of paramount importance to society; even though play concerned with individuals, story concerned with larger, more universal messages.
- Blood Brothers very moving experience. Characters presented so that feel for them and sympathise with them as people as well as feel angry and upset by themes of play.
- Set allows staging to move quickly and sustain pace of play despite epic move through time and location.

## The lighting

- Lighting played important part, as large open stage space became many different LOCATIONS very quickly — light helped define different locations by focusing audience's attention to certain areas of stage.
- Action moved quickly between two houses placed on stage right and stage left — supported by cross-fading lights.
- Audience's attention quickly changed to Narrator standing on raised platform at back by cross-fading light to him.
- Location also indicated by type of light: city scenes used more yellow, phosphorous lighting, often dimmed, gelled blue to indicate night time; country scenes much brighter, tried to create more natural light using straw-coloured gels.
- Simple gobo helped create size and atmosphere of prison cell.
- Lighting used to indicate passing of TIME by fading up and down accompanied by music and/or words.
- Lighting indicated changes in time of day with colour gels and changes in seasons by use of colour and angle.
- Lighting large cyclorama sometimes supported time of day/night, sometimes supported city/country location.
- Lighting used very much to create MOOD and tension. Cyclorama coloured in vast washes of blue and red to support supernatural feel of Narrator and to indicate superstition and sometimes hate being expressed on stage.
- When action in small rooms, cells or alley, lighting evoked mood and atmosphere through use of obtuse and interesting angles.
- When key action on stage that was part of themes and issues of play, lighting heightened moment by changing from natural light of room or location to more symbolic colour and sinister angle.
- Lighting also used in conjunction with songs and music: when action more stylised through use of song and movement, lighting changed from more natural light to more obvious light effect to support change of style.

## The sound

- Sound very important contributor to both action and atmosphere. Very cinematic soundtrack: music for much of performance, supporting scenes, heightening mood and emotion; songs carried much of the narrative and commentary.
- Great deal of underscore — supported dialogue and heightened mood e.g. when children playing in park or when Sammy and Mickey were robbing local shop. Music integral part of mood creation.
- Narrator's role always supported by music. Role both inside and outside action of play; spooky music accompanied his appearances generally gave warning that he was commentating on something bad happening in a prophetic way.
- SONGS like 'Marilyn Monroe' and music sequences like 'Forever 18' pushed action of the play forward and covered many years in lives of characters by passing information to audience.

- Songs like 'Shoes Upon The Table' made significant and effective comment on action and brought audience's attention to meaning of action.
- Songs like 'Easy Terms' and 'I'm Not Saying a Word' heightened emotion of scene and used melody and lyric to make audience feel something for characters.
- Music often introduced in action before or after song was sung – creating a motif that audience recognised. Narrator's music generally made audience aware of his entrance or that something significant was happening. Music from 'That Guy' heralded encounter between Mickey and Eddie.
- So music took on very strong role and importance in itself and linked feelings, people and action to audience.

The costumes
- Costumes clearly indicated class and status – defined very clearly difference between Johnstone and Lyons families, from early childhood, through school years right up to ending when twins were young men working.
- Also clearly indicated passing of time from 1950s to 1980s as reflected real fashion trends.
- Narrator's neutral, black, timeless suit gave him evil, haunting and supernatural presence.
- Costumes used to define the age developments in characters.
- Ensemble of actors used costumes to define different characters they were playing.

The props
- Props important in giving audience clear idea of location and setting of scenes.
- Simple furniture represented Mr Lyons's middle-class home; washing line represented poverty Mrs Johnstone faced.
- Benches quickly appeared and represented a bus (rather than whole bus appearing).
- Chairs represented seating in cinema.
- Table and chair represented cell.
- Gun: seemed to have metaphorical and symbolic value. Toy gun made significant early in play as reason Mickey and Eddie become friends when playing Cowboys and Indians; Mickey, Eddie and Linda sneak off with Sammy's airgun to shoot at statue in park as their friendship develops; Eddie gives Mickey toy gun as parting present when leaving for country; Mickey, Eddie and Linda shoot gun at the funfair as part of their growing up sequence; Mickey forced into using real gun by Sammy in order to earn some much-needed money; Mickey shoots Eddie and is shot by police at end. Gun represents play, friendship, trouble and ultimately fate of both twins – pivotal prop.

Choose central performances to think about. In *Blood Brothers*, Mickey would be a good performance to consider in conjunction with either his twin Eddie or his mum, Mrs Johnstone.

The performances: Mickey, played by Stephen Palfreman

Voice:
- Playing a character at the ages of 7, 14, 18 and older is quite a challenge. Used his voice to great effect in representing different stages of his character.
- Dialect definitely rooted in Liverpool – gave real sense of location.
- Voice at 7 was full of real enthusiasm and excitement. Had taken idea of innocence and fun and really exaggerated and animated his voice by using pace, volume and heightened tone to create a voice that was not trying to be realistically like a 7-year-old but give the impression of a 7-year-old.

- At 14: voice deepened, tried to be much more cool and sophisticated, but were moments when he was so excited it almost reverted back to 7-year-old's voice – showed his character still had enthusiasm and energy of a child.
- At 18: voice became measured and controlled. Struggling with own feelings and trying to understand words around him – voice reflected that uncertainty.
- As older man: had gone through mental and emotional trauma – voice reflected time in prison and loss of dignity and self-worth. Almost reverted back to pace, volume and heightened tone of 7-year-old, but this time through pain, not excitement.

Movement:
- Physical gesture and movement were really important part of the way character was communicated in different stages of his development.
- As 7-year-old: managed to communicate tension and pent-up energy that 7-year-old has. Brought physical life to character through scratching and stretching of sleeveless jumper and use of invisible horse to move from one space to another.
- Some stereotypical observations communicated? Character was larger-than-life – but in context of the set, staging and size of space, character was effectively communicated and represented.
- As 14-year-old: body language and posture much more laid back – desire to be seen as cool, especially in context of relationship with Linda. Showed tension beneath cool exterior at times – explosions of physical action and gesticulation expressed frustration of character. This made for great comic effect.
- Actor showed real physical control as character developed though teens: body language and movement much more measured – reflected clearly the character maturing.
- As Mickey got involved in robbery, spent time in prison and became unwell before leading to final showdown with Eddie, actor showed real physical regression to the pent-up energy and frustration of his early portrayal. This time nervous energy contained within character not waiting to burst out and play – this time it wanted to explode with anger and rage. This journey superbly handled and motivation behind the physicality was clearly explained through music and dialogue.

Costume:
- Social status of Mickey at all ages clear from costumes; it contrasted well with costumes worn by twin brother, Eddie.
- Clearly indicated location – e.g. school scene at 14, growing-up sequence, later in prison, and finally when working in factory.
- Costume at its most effective when showing ageing process – clearly defined periods of time that character passed through.
- Actor used costume very well in depicting his age and his mental state, e.g. punishment his ragged, sleeveless jumper took when he was 7 showed his energy and frustration after his mother had told him off; way he played with his shorts after being released from prison showed fragility and insecurity of his mental state.

Relationships:
- Great feeling of ensemble within group of actors. Playing variety of roles helped build up ensemble feel and quickly made the actors familiar to audience.
- Passing of time and development of characters also made them very familiar – shared their experiences of extreme happiness and sorrow.
- Nature of play and its inherent tragedy also seemed to bring company closer. Although certain characters were in relationships of animosity, there was real sense of reconciliation and respect at curtain call – lifted the play.
- All actors seemed very comfortable with each other and with space they were playing in – must be result of working together on play for extended period of time, but production didn't seem tired.

Personal response: emotions

- Stephen Palfreman's Mickey constantly made me feel emotional. At all stages in his age development, the performance was getting response from me.
- As child: humour, but great poignancy as relationship with Eddie was built up only to be shattered by events outside Mickey's control.
- Early part of play was spent building relationship with audience through combination of great joy and happiness and then great sadness.
- It was Mickey who initially talked directly to audience when explaining about brother and family. In many respects, though mother tells the story, it is through his eyes that story is revealed and through him that we live events: our sympathy and emotional link is to him.
- Much of emotional attachment to Mickey was because he was victim of fate: could have been with Eddie if Eddie hadn't been given away, or could have been like Eddie and enjoyed comfort of financial security if he had been given away.
- Even when he suffers a nervous breakdown we still sympathise and share his pain because still victim of fate in tragic-hero style.
- Sense of poignancy for audience made more extreme because know that ultimately Mickey will die – saw it at beginning.

Personal response: thoughts

- Also engaged by Mickey on psychological level.
- Share the story through him and begin to understand what he is thinking.
- Share his thoughts about Linda – wanting to love her and not being able to express that love.
- Share emotional breakdown and suspicions regarding Linda and Eddie.
- Understand what he means when cries out at end to his mother 'Why couldn't you have given me away?'
- Mickey forces audience, even more than Narrator, to confront why things have happened and think about how we would have behaved in similar situation or how we could change his fate. The Narrator merely passes comment upon them.

Acting styles

- Difficult to sum up acting style – seemed to be a mix of styles.
- Characters clearly defined and represented through costumes.
- Named characters larger than life and at times stereotypical; represented through clear use of voice and movement.
- Did not appear to be trying to be naturalistic – clear representation of age and type and at times spoke directly to audience.
- Did display whole range of emotional experiences – shared with audience who could sympathise and even empathise.
- Although characters were servants to wider story, we still cared very much about them.

The interpretation

- Production had very epic feel.
- Set spectacular; music and song brought a real grand spectacle to arguably simple story.
- Theatrical conventions made audience think about themes and issues of story.
- Ability to see band and mechanics of piece of theatre never detracted from story – in fact made story more powerful because always aware that it was story – made us think about 'what if it were true?'.
- Simple story about simple people but had much grander allusions. Felt like it was story about audience and society. Made audience really care about characters and action they were involved in, then sped us forward in time to next significant moment in their lives and immersed us in emotion of that moment.

- Story strikes clear chords and resonances with its audience: story about injustice, friendship and love – all themes mean something to all of us, are universal.
- Space and style of staging told me I was going to enjoy an epic piece of story-telling that would make me think. But because sat so close to stage and felt I was in intimate space, and because characters and story had touched something in me, felt I witnessed something both epic and personal.

## Evaluation of live theatre

Once you have completed your notes, you can use them to help you to write your evaluation of live theatre. Going to see live theatre can be a thrilling experience. Your live-theatre evaluation should try to reflect upon and celebrate this experience. Make sure you evaluate a production that really challenged you, made you think, made you feel something or even shocked you. Remember, however, that your written reflection should be a positive analysis of a production's effectiveness and not just a series of criticisms.

You will be able to create your own question in discussion with your teacher for this piece of written work; essentially, your piece needs to evaluate how effective the production was in what it was trying to do. You should use your notes as the skeleton for the body of your evaluation.

Here is an example of a Unit 1 evaluation of a live theatre piece using the thought processes outlined in this section and in response to *The Woman in Black* by Stephen Mallatratt as performed at the Fortune Theatre, London. The structure given is just one possible way of approaching this piece of written work.

**Web link**

See the following two links for further information and resources regarding *The Woman in Black*: www.thewomaninblack.com and www.pwprods.co.uk/images/education/wib_pack.pdf

The Woman in Black is a play written by Stephen Mallatratt in 1987 but based on the novel by Susan Hill and is a ghost story that borrows much from the classic work of Charles Dickens and M. R. James in its setting, structure, period and intent. The story and this adaptation sets out to tell a tale in a very matter-of-fact way with great clarity. It builds to a horrifying climax and is intent on leaving its audience chilled. It is a fictional tale but told in such a way that the audience are led to believe that it is true and that we have witnessed a cathartic event.

> Try to keep your introduction clear and concise and show knowledge about the context of the play.

I couldn't have imagined a more appropriate theatre for the telling of this story. The Fortune Theatre is a small, old Victorian playhouse hidden down a side road in London's Covent Garden. The theatre inside was presented as an aged, run-down, rarely used space with old props strewn across the stage and a dirty gauze hung across the back. It was a small proscenium-arch theatre in which we sat very close to the stage in an end-on format; this immediately created an atmosphere of claustrophobia and intimacy. I felt like I had gone back in time when I entered the space and this added to the atmosphere of the story, which is set in Edwardian times, giving the whole evening an eerie sense of the past. The action of the play

> Write in the first person as this indicates that the piece is a personal response. Try to show an awareness of the theatre space and its relationship to the audience and the story of the play.

If you refer to actors, be clear which parts they are playing and make a clear distinction between the actor and the character they are creating. Don't spend too long on plot but try to show an awareness of theatrical form and structure, and whether there is a wider purpose behind the play's structure.

cleverly takes place in the theatre which heightens the tension and draws an audience into the imaginary world of the actors. A middle-aged London solicitor, Arthur Kipps, played by Paul Chapman, is seeking the advice of a younger actor, played by Daniel Coonan, on how to tell the tale of terrible events he experienced 30 years earlier, to an audience of family and friends. The young actor quickly encourages Kipps not to tell the story but to take part in a dramatic retelling of it in which the actor will take on the role of Kipps, while Kipps himself will play all the other characters encountered in the story. The story is then slowly revealed to the audience through the rehearsal of various scenes. There is a simple, yet sophisticated theatricality about the structure of the play: the story is prepared and acted out for an audience that is yet to arrive, however an audience is already there.

The actors' performances were incredibly effective but simple. At all times the audience were aware that they were watching a story, allowing the actors to use simple costuming, props and staging effects to indicate characters and locations. What became important, as in all good stories, was the imaginative link between the actors and the audience.

As Paul Chapman's Kipps began to be more comfortable with what he had been asked to do, and the range of characters that he had to play in his own story, he became increasingly deft at doing so. He created the character of Kipp's superior by donning a simple, black morning jacket and by formalising the intonation in his voice. He was then able to transform into Keckwick, who drives the horse and trap, by wearing an old hat and cloak and crumpling his body to indicate an old and weather-beaten man, complete with rural accent to regionalise his character. I accepted this completely because I was always aware that I was witnessing an actor and another man telling the story. Arthur Kipps's journey within the piece is from a man uncomfortable and inexperienced at acting out parts in a story which hold great horror for him to a man who can quickly and subtly change from one character to another. Paul Chapman communicated this journey well; he began his characterisation with great hesitancy and in constant need of encouragement from Daniel Coonan's Actor and finished the piece as an accomplished performer relieved to have told the whole story at last.

Daniel Coonan's journey began as a supercilious and sceptical young actor who feels it is his professional responsibility to make the story more theatrical and interesting to its intended audience. As the story evolved he visited Eel Marsh House as a young solicitor and came face to face with the horror of the Woman in Black and began to be drawn to the reality and intensity of the story. This was cleverly supported by the arrival and appearance of an actual Woman in Black who started to make appearances. The Actor believed this has been arranged by Kipps as a surprise, but this was not the case. One such moment in the story was when the Actor accompanied the local solicitor to the grave of Alice Drablow and she appeared behind him, only to be seen by him as an audience. Daniel Coonan, through his shocked facial expression, was able to communicate fear, surprise and delight.

Identify acting styles and give specific examples to show how the actors achieved those moments and characters. Refer to voice, facial expressions and body movement to describe how characters are created. Discuss how costumes and props can help create and support characters. Write about why specific moments are effective.

The play was simply staged with a combination of set, staging lighting and sound. Because we were being told a story, the props that already existed on stage were used as a variety of other props. One excellent example of this was the use of a large wicker basket as a table in the early office scenes and then as a horse and trap in a later scene by the actors sitting on it sideways and moving as if they were on a horse and trap, with one character driving and the other being a passenger. This effect was subtly supported by the use of a soundtrack of a horse and cart. This quickly indicated where we were and what we were watching without the complexity of a sophisticated set. Alternatively, the production could have used more literal and extravagant scenery, but in the context of the piece being rehearsed. However, because it is a story that is being told by an actor and another man, this would not have been any more effective.

The soundtrack was an integral part of the piece and many of the tensest and scariest moments were created through sound effects. Within the context of the story, the actor had hired a sound man to help with sound in the rehearsals and the performance. The soundtrack created busy London streets and atmospheric seaside sounds, and most memorably a soundtrack of a horse and cart and a woman and child drowning in the marsh. This was incredibly eerie, as there was nothing visable, which left everything to the imagination. The lighting was also a vital part of the telling and atmosphere of the story. A theatrical gauze was used across the stage which meant that when it was lit from the front you couldn't see behind it, while when it was lit from behind you could see through but with a blurred, eerie effect. This contributed to one of the most effectively scary moments in the piece when the Actor as Kipps went behind the gauze to discover a child's bedroom in beautiful condition only to be drawn in front of the gauze to investigate a noise. When he quickly returned behind the gauze to go back to the room it had been turned upside down. The cross-lighting between the gauze allowed this very quick effect to be achieved.

I felt engaged yet scared by this production; this impact was as a result of a combination of factors. I was drawn into and engaged by the production as a story: the actual theatre surroundings in which we were sat and the theatrical structure of the story made it easy to believe. The success of the actors in creating two very believable characters made me feel that I was witnessing a terrible story being retold in a past world. The way the story made me use my imagination through use of words and props prompted me to engage on an intellectual and emotional level with the story. The sudden, infrequent use of sound effects, such as the scream that occurred just before the Actor went to open the door to the child's bedroom, kept me on edge, wondering what would happen next. The narrative twist that the Woman in Black appears, but only to the Actor and the audience, added an extra degree of eeriness – especially when I got home and went to bed that night.

Choose and describe key elements of the set and staging of the show. Try to discuss what was done, how it was done and why, with reference to specific examples. You can't talk about everything in the plays so you must make choices about key scenes and moments to illustrate your points. Try to suggest alternative ways that things might have been done to show that you are aware of the choices and decisions that have been made by the director.

Try to make some final personal statements about the success or otherwise of the production. Summarise its overall effectiveness and say why certain aspects were successful.

This evaluation would benefit from the use of illustrations supporting the space and set descriptions, and to illustrate key moments – the exam board encourages you to support your words with appropriate diagrams and illustrations.

# Theatre Text in Performance

## What do I have to do?

### The unit

Unit 2: Theatre Text in Performance is the most practical element of your AS course. To quote the examiners, in this unit you are expected to 'demonstrate skills in a performance environment'.

The unit is divided into **two** sections with 40 marks allocated to each:

1. **Section A**. You will need to decide whether you wish to be assessed on your contribution to **performance** or **design**. Performers will present a monologue or duologue. Designers will produce a considered approach to one of the following areas, based on a text that is being explored by a performer: costume, lighting, mask, make-up, set and props, or sound.

2. **Section B**. Once again, you have a choice between **performance** and **design**. Your choice does not have to be the same as the one you made in Section A. Performers will develop a performance of a published text, working in groups of between three and nine. Designers will work with the group focusing on at least one of the following areas: costume, lighting, mask, make-up, set and props, or sound.

This element of your course should not be seen in isolation. It is very much a part of the progression of both your AS and A2 course, and you need to think carefully about how it fits into the exam as a whole.

**Links with Unit 1**

You should have covered Unit 1: Exploration of Drama and Theatre before starting Theatre Text in Performance. It should have made you think about how plays are written and constructed, and how they can be interpreted. This process of thinking is called **deconstruction**: the process whereby you break a play down to see what it is made of, how it is made, what it is trying to say and why. Your study for this unit should have made you aware of:

➤ How the play can be made relevant to both performer and audience by an understanding of its **social, cultural, historical and political context**

➤ How the story is communicated through different types of **language**

➤ How the **characters** are portrayed and their significance in the development of the plot

➤ How the decisions about **voice and movement** affect the play's meaning

➤ How the play could **look** and **sound** according to the different ways in which it could be staged

➤ How the final interpretation can communicate the desired **impact**.

You must apply those skills and thinking processes you have gained in Unit 1 to this second unit. Because of the early work done, you should now be in a position to take a monologue or a duologue and a playtext that you do not know, and deconstruct it with a mind to casting, rehearsing and performing it.

## Section A: an overview

### Acting

You must choose a monologue or duologue from a different playtext from those studied in Unit 1 or the play which you perform in Section B of this unit. Whether you choose a monologue or duologue you should read the whole play from which it comes, and do some research into it and its author to be able to place it within a social, historical, cultural and political context.

You must choose a section or sections from the play for your monologue or duologue that are coherent and make sense in the context of the whole play. You should rehearse and learn the monologue or duologue and present it in performance conditions.

You will perform the monologue or duologue to the visiting examiner in front of an appropriate audience. Ensure that the audience is supportive and are able to create good performance conditions.

You will also have to complete a written concept for Section A that must be no longer than 500 words, which you must send to the examiner a **week** before their visit. The concept will be a rationale to support the interpretation, preparation and final performance of your monologue or duologue. It should include:

➤ Evidence of an understanding of the complete playtext with an **analysis** of your chosen character's development throughout

➤ An **explanation** of your preparation process and intended interpretation

➤ A clearly **annotated** final monologue or duologue, which justifies the decisions you have made in your interpretation.

Throughout the preparation and rehearsal period for your monologue, duologue or design skill it would be useful to keep a log of all the things you have done in preparation for the final performance. This should cover:

➤ Initial choice of play

➤ Reading of the complete text

➤ Your concept for it

**Choosing your monologue or duologue**

You will not be expected to present the monologue or duologue in full costume, as you would do in a performance of the whole play, but you should make a token gesture towards costuming, to support the creation of character.

See pages 133–134 for an example of an annotated monologue and pages 143–147 for an example of an annotated duologue.

**Log**

➤ Rehearsal process

➤ What you have learned or gained from each rehearsal.

For each rehearsal session, create a log entry using the following headings:

➤ **Target**. What we were hoping to achieve in the session

➤ **Action**. What we did and how we did it (you may wish to use illustrations to show any blocking or physical work)

➤ **Thinking**. What decisions were made as a consequence of the work done in the session

➤ **Concept**. Thoughts on the overall vision of your piece.

## Design

If you choose to design you must still make sure that you work on a different playtext from the ones studied in Unit 1 or the play which you have chosen for performance in Section B of this unit.

A similar preparation process applies to design, as to acting. You must read the whole play and research both it and its author to gain social, historical, cultural and political awareness. You should choose only one design skill from the list provided by the exam board. Even though you only have to complete your design for one section of the play which will be presented to the visiting examiner, you must still prepare a design plan for the complete text, as if you were going to design the whole play.

You must also prepare in advance for the examiner a 500-word rationale to support your interpretation, preparation and final demonstration. This should include:

➤ An overall design concept for the complete playtext

➤ A rationale for the final design decisions.

The exam board provides a clear and useful design-skill grid which outlines the choices of design skills available and the minimum requirements to be successful in these skills.

➤ **Basic research**. Research and make sure you are familiar with the basics of your chosen skill. Log your findings in your notes.

➤ **The design process**. Week by week, record your contributions to the journey of the play through initial exploration, rehearsal and performance, as well as your relationship with the director, other designers and the actors.

➤ **Past designs**. Find out about previous designs of the show you are working on, and analyse and record them in your portfolio.

➤ **Your design**. Create your design, informed by your research and the notes you have made throughout the exploration, rehearsal and performance process.

You may use other students to deliver the text in the demonstration to the visiting examiner.

**Web link**

See the exam board website, www.edexcel.org.uk

## Performance concept

Think of the written performance concept as a series of headings which you can use to write about your chosen text and extract:

### 1. The story and structure

Give a brief outline of the play and how the story is told through the structure of scenes. This will give you an overview of the play, and force you to consider its plot and the journey made by your character throughout the play.

### 2. The place of your extract

Explain where your chosen extract is in the structure of the play. Show an understanding of what has happened in terms of the action before your chosen scene and, most importantly, how your chosen character has been developed up to this point. What has happened to your character up until your scene will have a huge influence on the way they behave, what they say and how they think and feel in your extract.

### 3. The original staging and style

Show that you have researched how the original production was staged and the style of this performance. An awareness and understanding of an early or original performance of the text will help you to explain your own interpretation; you might be bringing fresh meaning to the text or trying to recreate its original meaning.

### 4. Your staging and style within the extract

Show an awareness of acting styles and the tools of the actor, and how you can use voice, body and space to create meaning. Refer to how the set and the staging in your interpretation would bring meaning to the piece. Show an awareness of other design elements such as costume, lighting and sound, and how these elements would contribute to the overall effect of the extract and the play.

### 5. Your hope for the piece

Describe how you would like your audience to respond to your interpretation of the play and specifically your extract. Show an awareness of the themes and issues raised by the play and be sensitive to how you would like your audience to think and feel while engaging with the extract.

## Design concept

There is a whole range of design skills that you could choose for this section, such as masks, make-up, costume, set, lighting and sound. Your written design concept will only be a part of the overall assessment of this section of the unit.

You will also be assessed on:

➤ The realisation of your design

➤ Documentation appropriate to your chosen skill

➤ A presentation to the examiner of the design process.

Think of the written design concept as a series of headings which you can use to write about your chosen text and extract:

### 1. The story and structure

Give a brief outline of the play and how the story is told through the structure of scenes. This will give you an overview of the play and enable you to consider the role your design will have in the play as a whole.

### 2. Your design skill

Explain the potential importance of your design skill within the context of a production and the relationship of a designer to the director. Show how you would hope to influence both the functional and the symbolic elements of the text in creating a look and a meaning for the production.

### 3. Past designs of the show

Find out about previous designs of your chosen text and comment on how they have affected the look and meaning of the production. This will give you an opportunity to talk about how design elements contribute to the overall meaning of any production and specifically your text.

### 4. Design ideas that have influenced you

Describe how you have brought ideas together to use on this text. Talk about the influence of practitioners, and other productions you have seen, researched or been in. Choose two or three brief examples of specific effects you want to achieve in your interpretation of the text itself.

### 5. What you want to achieve

Set out some clear targets for what you want your design skill to achieve in this production, in terms of:

➤ The look of the show

➤ The meaning of the show

➤ How it will engage with the audience.

## Sample performance concept

Here is a written performance concept for an actor playing Audrey in Dennis Potter's *Blue Remembered Hills* in the duologue with Angela.

> 1. The story and structure
> The story revolves around a group of seven-year-olds who are playing in the forest. The play opens with Willie, eating an apple and pretending to pilot a war plane, when he encounters Peter, falling from a tree as a parachutist. After a fight over Willie's apple – in which Peter attempts to show how powerful a bully he can be – the two eventually spot a squirrel and chase it up a tree. They are joined by John and Raymond, and the group of lads attempt to force the squirrel down the tree and eventually manage to trap and kill it. Meanwhile, in a barn nearby, Donald

Duck is playing with Angela and Audrey. As they engage in their fantasy game of 'Mummies and Daddies' we see how vulnerable a child Donald is as he suffers some vicious teasing from the two girls. The killing of the squirrel and the girls' baiting of Donald have just been rehearsals for a much more horrific persecution at the end of the play when Donald is locked in a barn which is set on fire.

## 2. The place of your extract

The extract we are performing as our duologue comes just after Audrey and Angela have teased Donald, and they have left him crying and wanting his father who is a POW. These early scenes show how fickle they are and how heartless they can appear to be in their treatment of each other and their desire to be grown up. They are pushing their squeaky and broken-down pram on a path though the forest and debating who their best friend is. The scene begins to build the momentum for the final teasing of Donald, which leads to his death.

## 3. The original staging and style

Blue Remembered Hills by Dennis Potter was originally written for TV and first broadcast in 1979. It was set in the Forest of Dean at the time of the Second World War, during the long, hot summer of 1943. Although the play has the appearance of Naturalism, the original TV production was a highly stylised piece in which adults played the seven-year-old children. This device made the story, which charts the loss of innocence, very funny but also even more poignant, and allowed the audience to distance themselves from the events and think about them even more carefully.

## 4. Your staging and style within the extract

Any performance of the script runs into the immediate difficulty of converting a TV script into theatre. The play is a series of episodes that move from location to location in the forest very quickly. We have tried to use simple staging, lighting and music to try to convey period and place. We have used a set of tea chests, a pair of pallet gates, and some branches and leaves to give the play a rural, period feel. At the same time, this simple staging has also allowed us, as actors, to use our voices, bodies and the space to indicate age and the rural quality of the play.

## 5. Your hope for the piece

We have tried to create clear characters and we have deliberately caricatured the children in order to make it clear that these are adults playing children. We hope that the extract captures:

- A sense of childhood, the past and the country, through characterisation and accent
- A sense of the forest and vastness of the adventure that the children have, through simple staging and lighting
- A sense of poignancy and sadness at the loss of innocence, and a real sympathy and empathy with the girls and what happens to them.

**Monologue or duologue?**

When you approach this aspect of the unit, you have a difficult decision to make – whether to choose a monologue or duologue. Obviously, if there is an odd number in your group, one person will have to do a monologue by default. However, your decision should always be an active one, based on an understanding of your performance skills. Some individuals thrive when working with a partner, enjoying the sense of sharing, discussing and compromising, while others become easily frustrated and enjoy the autonomy that a monologue provides.

There is another influencing factor which you should consider. If you are contemplating studying drama at a higher level then you may be asked to perform at least one monologue at audition. The experience of performing in front of an examiner would serve as good preparation for this.

## Monologues

### Choosing wisely

Once you've decided that you are going to work on your own, it is important that you identify a passage of text that interests you. The time limit specified by the exam board for the monologue is two minutes, which translates approximately to one side of text, or approximately 300 words. This is a rough guide but when choosing a monologue it is best to err on the side of caution. A straightforward reading of the text will be quicker than your final performance. You need to allow for changes in pace and pause; gestures and movements may slow your delivery and you do not want to be rushing. Delivering your piece too quickly will negatively affect your marks.

It is also important to ensure that the monologue is right for you. Use the following points as guidance for your selection:

**Style of play.** You will already have experience of performing the texts of different playwrights. You may enjoy the notion of naturalistic performances or feel more comfortable with more physical theatre. Use these personal preferences as a guide when selecting the text.

**Age of the character.** Although there is no specific guidance on this matter it is best to play a role which is within your realm of experience. Performing characters a lot older than yourself may expose weaknesses in your acting ability.

**Mood of the piece.** Some members of your group may have impressive comic timing; others may be able to capture the fragile nature of an individual's mental state. By all means, choose a challenging passage of text but consider which area will suit your personal strengths.

**Nature of the delivery.** Look carefully at the text. The section could be delivered to other actors on stage or directly to the audience, or both. Each of these is a different skill and you need to anticipate the demands that they will place on you as an actor.

**Further study**

There are many monologue books available which are specifically designed for preparing students for audition speeches. A particularly useful text is *Audition Speeches for Young Actors 16+* by Jean Marlow (A&C Black 2002).

## Contextualisation

It is important not to see your speech in isolation, but rather as a short section of a complete performance. The decisions you make need to be appropriate for a whole production of the playtext. The portrayal of your character in your chosen scene needs to be consistent with their behaviour in the rest of the play. If you choose to mime all props, this needs to be fitting to all of the play's action. Lavish costumes or set may be visually impressive but they could be wholly inappropriate for the action that precedes and follows your chosen extract. Reading and understanding the entire text is vital.

> Some monologue books use extracts from plays that are no longer available in print. Make sure you can acquire a copy of the play before finalising your decision.

**Initial reading**

In your initial reading of the playtext make sure you have a pen and paper handy. Look for any clues about your character. Look at the dialogue of all characters, considering the words that are spoken and the action that is implied. Read stage directions carefully; short phrases could provide essential information about a role. Create a list of all of your character's attributes, noting pages of the text which may be particularly important.

Once you have analysed the text closely, you will have created your own impression of the role and its place in the play. These initial decisions are important and you should be careful not to lose sight of these as you progress. Sometimes, students can become so focused on the delivery of an individual line that they forget what they should be communicating to an audience

**Research**

The text is only one part of the information you will need in order to create a successful performance. It is vital that you supplement the text with any additional understanding that can be gained from individual research. Address as many of the following points as possible:

➤ Read **other plays** by the same playwright: don't forget to look at the introductions to these texts to see if they contain any additional information about the writer's style.

➤ Find **biographical information** about the playwright: are there any clues about how their style has been influenced by their experiences?

➤ Use the **internet** to find any relevant information: this could include reviews of productions of the play, programme notes, newspaper interviews and images.

> It might be appropriate to alter the period in which your performance is set, although it is important that this can be applied to the whole text.

➤ Look at the **historical period** in which the play is set: how might this affect the manner in which you perform it?

➤ Research the **issues** that are raised in the extract: try to find personal accounts from individuals who have experienced similar things to your character.

All of this information will help to ensure that you have a secure foundation on which to build. Any decisions you subsequently make about the performance will be based on the information you have gathered, rather than being an unfounded impulse which could lead to a rather generalised portrayal.

The final question to ask yourself is what this extract says to a contemporary audience. What is its relevance to the way we behave today? Consider this point quite carefully as the most successful actors will be fully aware of the impact they are looking to have on their audience.

## Getting started

The exercises outlined below are suggestions on how to approach the work. They may not all be appropriate for every monologue although there is always some benefit in trying every activity and then rejecting it when it doesn't appear to be useful. Although this is essentially an individual task, you may choose to join with one or two other members of your class, sharing your ideas and offering constructive suggestions on how to improve.

**Walking round the room**

While this exercise sounds quite simplistic on paper it is an extremely successful way of accessing the subtle changes in your text. The rules are relatively straightforward.

Holding the text, you have to walk round the room reading the lines of the monologue. You should read the lines relatively neutrally without stressing key passages of text or experimenting with delivery. The focus should be on the playwright's words rather than your interpretation of them. However, as you are walking you should be looking at each sentence in turn rather than worrying about the fluency of your delivery. Every time you feel there is a change in the character's psychological state you should stop, pause, turn to face another direction and then continue with your delivery. This turn should not be rushed as if you were walking round a corner; it needs to be deliberate, emphasising the change. Once you have finished the monologue, mark these points of change on your text. As you rehearse your lines, make sure you are aware of these points as possible changes in the tone or rhythm of your work.

**Identifying important phrases**

An entire monologue can appear daunting and so it can be easier to think of it as a series of episodes encapsulated by a key phrase. Look at your text and identify short lines which chart the progression of the action. You may choose anywhere between five to ten lines. Now look at these lines from your character's perspective. What do they reveal about the changes in tone? Focus on the delivery of the lines, rehearsing them as a mini-monologue, with pauses between each line to make sense of any abrupt changes in emotion. Consider the gestures that might be used to emphasise moments.

**Applying freezes**

This could be done in conjunction with the previous activity or as a separate task. Consider the physical appearance of your character. How do they stand, sit, walk and gesture? Create an opening image. Do this taking careful consideration of your character's posture and body position. Do not necessarily rely on the first image you create. Shape the work and consider it carefully. On which line of dialogue are they likely to move from this position? What change in their mood would cause this movement? How is this represented in their new physicality? Chart these movements as a physical monologue showing how the role develops during the piece.

Each individual has a natural vocal rhythm, a way of delivering words which affects their everyday speech. As an actor it can be difficult to break this habit. Students often apply their own rhythms to the text without deciding whether or not it is appropriate for the character. The easiest way to demonstrate this point is to record other people delivering the monologue. They needn't be drama students. They could be friends or family members. Listen to their delivery and try to copy the rhythm patterns of their speech. Make a note of any changes in their delivery which you think might be appropriate and try applying them to your own performance.

**Experimenting with rhythms**

The key to achieving the most successful performances is exploring the text through play. No matter whether you are looking at a comic or emotionally intense extract, as an actor you need to be willing to explore and experiment without fear of failure. Without this approach, there is always the danger of the work becoming stale. Try performing the piece in the following styles:

**Experimenting with style**

➤ Melodrama

➤ Australian soap opera

➤ News bulletin

➤ A children's television presenter

➤ Stand-up comedy routine

➤ Wildlife programme

➤ A speech by the prime minister to the House of Commons

➤ A bedtime story.

Each of these should encourage you to vary your vocal delivery and you may find a word or short phrase that particularly suits one of the styles.

There is no doubt that the exploration of the text should mostly be a practical activity, in which you make judgements through your experience about performing the extract. However, there is also a necessary place for moments of reflection during the rehearsal process. This should involve returning to your original notes and checking that you are not losing sight of your initial impressions. You should also take the opportunity to consider the shape of your piece; a simple but effective way of doing this is to present your work as a series of graphs. The 'x' axis should be time – the 120 seconds of your performance. The 'y' axis can be varied depending on your needs; label it 1 to 10. Try drawing a graph to show how the pace of your piece alters with time ('10' being the fastest delivery), labelling key changes in the graph with quotations from the monologue. Look at movement with '1' being extremely static. You could focus on the mood of the scene by considering the tension you want the audience to experience throughout. The purpose of this exercise is to highlight the need for variety in your piece.

**The shape of your piece**

Weaker students will not demonstrate a range in their work; by explicitly identifying the shape of the piece, you should be able to avoid falling into this trap.

## Emotion memory

Whether you are giving a naturalistic or more stylised performance, there is still a need to identify with the emotions of the character. Stanislavski emphasised the need for 'truth' and this should be present in all performances. Take time to empathise with your character's experiences. Think about the situations you have been in that are similar and try to recall how you felt and how those emotions were revealed in your movement and voice. If you cannot recall appropriate emotions use your knowledge of your behaviour to imagine the way it would make you feel. When would the emotion come to the surface and when would you be able to hide it?

## Applying objectives

The more naturalistic extracts allow for a traditional Stanislavskian approach where objectives in the form of 'I want…' can be applied to the different units within the monologue. While this might appear to be a time-consuming process, students often find that they save time in the long run by creating a more considered piece of work.

> Look at pages 15–24 for a detailed discussion of Stanislavski's system.

## Creating space

The performance space is vital in establishing the appropriate mood for your performance. If you are working with someone who is designing a set for your extract then their ideas must complement, rather than restrict, your performance. Think about the following:

➢ What elements need to be on stage: do you need furniture or could the space be represented by stage blocks?

➢ How big is the space in which your character is working? Is it the same size as your performance space?

➢ Do you need to imagine that certain aspects of set or props exist? How might you do this?

It is important that you are clear in your own mind what your performance space will look like. Use a written description, a stage plan or a visual image which represents your character's world.

## Annotating the text

There is an argument to say that over-rehearsing an extract stifles the creative process and prevents the actor from fulfilling their potential. In extreme cases, this can be true. However, this notion shouldn't be used as an excuse for laziness or a lack of preparation. The most able students should be in thorough command of their performance and should, for example, at every point be able to state when they move, what they move and why. An easy way of identifying this is by annotating your text with all the decisions you have made and you will quickly be able to see where the less-rehearsed passages of text are.

Opposite is a monologue for you to consider as a starting point for your own decision-making process.

# Molly Sweeney (female)

Despite being blind since childhood, Molly was content with her perception of the world. Her routine is threatened when she marries her husband Frank, who persuades her to have an operation that may restore her sight.

Born in Omagh, Northern Ireland, in 1929, Friel has been a successful playwright for over 40 years. His more recent work, which includes *Molly Sweeney*, has become less epic and political in nature and more focused on everyday human dilemmas.

**Molly:** When Mr Rice did arrive, even before he touched me, I knew by his quick, shallow breathing that he was far more nervous than I was. And then as he took off the bandages his hands trembled and fumbled.

'There we are,' he said. 'All off. How does that feel?'

'Fine,' I said. Even though I felt nothing. Were all the bandages off?

'Now, Molly. In your own time. Tell me what you see.'

Nothing. Nothing at all. Then out of the void a blur; a haze; a body of mist; a confusion of light, colour, movement. It had no meaning.

'Well?' he said. 'Anything? Anything at all?'

I thought: Don't panic; a voice comes from a face; that blur is his face; look at him.

'Well? Anything?'

Something moving; large; white; the nurse? And lines, black lines vertical lines. The bed? The door?

'Anything, Molly?' A bright light that hurt. The window maybe?

'I'm holding my hand before your eyes, Molly. Can you see it?'

A reddish blob in front of my face; rotating; liquefying; pulsating. Keep calm. Concentrate.

'Can you see my hand, Molly?'

'I think so ... I'm not sure ...'

'Now I'm moving my hand slowly.'

'Yes ... Yes ...'

'Do you see my hand moving?'

'Yes ...'

'What way is it moving?'

## Context

*Molly Sweeney* in *Plays volume 2* by Brian Friel (Faber and Faber 1999).

## Playwright

The National Theatre of Scotland produced a version of the play in 2007. Look for reviews of the performance and any information about the intended impact of the play.

The play is written as a series of monologues with the three characters seated when not speaking in Friel's interpretation of his play; Molly is the only character to give the appearance of looking at the others. Frank and Mr Rice only make eye-contact with the audience. When would you choose to reference them and when the audience?

Friel is explicit in the stage directions as to how to portray Molly's blindness: 'Most people with impaired vision look and behave like sighted people. The only evidence of their disability is a certain vacancy in the eyes or the way the head is held.'

Molly had been content with her blindness and had to be persuaded to consider the operation. Is that scepticism in evidence in this extract?

Removing the bandages is a powerful image. Would Molly recreate this moment as if she was Mr Rice or show the impact it has on her?

'In *Molly Sweeney*, Friel, gently and subtly, creates an allegory for Ireland's current cultural dilemma. Molly Sweeney – what more Irish name? – stands onstage literally between the twin impulses of modernization and romantic nostalgia, represented by the former international medical star Mr. Rice and the idealistic but hapless Frank. And she is destroyed by her desire to please both.' Karen Devinney, *Monologue as Dramatic Action*.

The gradual increase in Molly's excitement should be evident in changes in pace and tone. Where might these changes occur?

Molly both converses with Rice and narrates. How might you distinguish between these forms as an actor?

'Yes … I do see it … up and down … up and down … Yes! I see it! I do! Yes! Moving up and down! Yes-yes-yes!'

'Splendid!' he said. 'Absolutely splendid! You are a clever lady!'

And there was such a delight in his voice. And my head was suddenly giddy. And I thought for a moment – for a moment I thought I was going to faint.

## The Pillowman (male)

The National Theatre production in 2003 starred David Tennant in the role of Katurian. He has recently found television fame in *Doctor Who*. It may be helpful to imagine the same playful spirit being applied to this role

### Suggested text

*The Pillowman* is set in a totalitarian state, and depicts the aggressive interrogation by the police of a writer due to the unnerving similarity between his macabre stories and the apparent murder of three children. While the play's playwright, Martin McDonagh, was born in London in 1970, his Irish heritage permeates his plays. He creates worlds in which tragedy and farce exist in equal measure, distorted realities which reflect the obsessions of contemporary society in an often satirical and insightful manner.

Look at the monologue spoken by Katurian, when he stands up to read his story to the interrogator, Tupolski, beginning 'Once upon a time in a tiny cobble-streeted town on the banks of a fast-flowing river…' and ending '…leaving the boy, the rats, the river and the darkening town of Hamelin far behind him'.

Consider the following points:

➤ How would the pace of delivery vary in order to keep the audience engaged throughout the complex tale?

➤ Despite the threat of violence hanging over him and his brother who is held in the neighbouring room, Katurian is extremely proud of his stories. How could you show his simultaneous fear and enjoyment in this scene?

➤ There may be some moments in the narrative which you could illustrate with movement. Which gestures would you use, and when, to add emphasis to the story?

➤ There are effectively two audiences listening to Katurian's story – Tupolski the interrogator and the real audience of the play. Consider which lines are delivered to which audience.

➤ The stage directions preceding the monologue explain that Katurian stands up to read his story. Think how he might use the performance space without appearing threatening.

### Further reading

Look at *The Lieutenant* of *Inishmore* (Methuen Drama 2001) – a similarly gruesome and hilarious play by Martin McDonagh.

## Duologues

### The difference between monologues and duologues

With a monologue you are addressing the audience or other characters on stage who, while they are engaged by you, do not respond with words of their own. With a duologue, on the other hand, your main point of focus is another character, on stage with you, and with whom you establish a dialogue.

Therefore, an important aspect of choosing a duologue is that you will be choosing to work with another student from your class. For some it is much easier to work with a partner because you can share thoughts and motivate each other. Think carefully about how best you work before making a final decision.

The duologue offers a completely different theatrical challenge from the monologue. You will have to build a relationship and rapport with your partner and this interaction must compel the audience to engage with you as characters. The relationship and emotion you build together on stage, through speech, facial expressions, physicality, action, silences and space, will determine how well your audience engage with your chosen extract. You must therefore not only consider which play to do but also with whom you would like to work. Think about which other students share your approach to drama and the same work ethic. With whom would you be comfortable sharing ideas and concepts?

### Choosing a duologue

Consider what you have learnt from the course so far, especially from Unit 1. Think about the practitioners and plays you have studied and seen in performance.

Be honest with yourself as you go through the following:

➢ **Character.** What are your strengths when it comes to characterisation? Which types of character have you enjoyed watching, studying or performing in your practical work? Do you want to play a character who is close to your own age or one who is older?

➢ **Styles of performance.** What dramatic styles have you encountered so far? Which have you enjoyed the most or been most at ease with?

➢ **Content.** What would you like to tackle, in terms of action and events?

➢ **Themes and issues.** Would you like to deal with historical or modern-day themes and issues?

➢ **Mood.** Do you want the duologue to be serious, emotional, shocking or funny?

➢ **Emotion.** What kind of response do you want to elicit from your audience? Do you want to make them sad, angry or make them laugh?

➢ **Region/accent.** You might like to choose a play from a different

> Remember that, if you are performing a duologue, you will need to consider both your and your partner's strengths and weaknesses; the choice must be agreed upon by both of you.

country such as the United States or Ireland, or region such as Liverpool or East Anglia, to display your strengths and talents to their best advantage.

By considering all of these factors you will be able to build up a wish list of criteria when it comes to choosing a play. You will then be able to find a script which is suitable for you and your partner, and effective in allowing you both to display your strengths.

## Consider the duologue

Remember that you are choosing an extract from a play that is only five minutes long. The duologue must, within this time, give you and your partner the opportunity to impress the examiner in **three** key areas:

➤ Vocal skills

➤ Movement skills

➤ Characterisation.

You will be marked on these three areas, in conjunction with your written performance concept and how it relates to your actual performance.

When selecting an extract, choose a scene, unit or moment from the play that has **impact**. Find a scene, unit or moment that is:

➤ Important to the journey of the characters

➤ A climax in the action of the play

➤ Of emotional importance.

Try to avoid scenes that are heavy on exposition, even though such scenes may appear tempting as they make the play's plot clear to the audience. Try and find an extract that contains some sort of emotional transition or psychological journey for the characters so that you can demonstrate a full range of acting skills.

You should also avoid editing key moments from the play together just for the sake of impressing the examiner. This section of the exam is about understanding the selected moments' place in the whole play and, through what you do with your chosen scene, suggesting to the examiner how you would hypothetically develop the character throughout the rest of the play. It is not about trying to create an adaptation of the play. Your written performance concept will support the hypothetical journey through the whole play; this duologue performance is just about the selected scene – which is why your choice of scene is so crucial.

## How to find a play

Before you choose an extract you must choose a play. You should already have made a short list of criteria for the type of play you are looking for, such as content, action, style, period, issues and mood. One way of clarifying your thinking on which play to choose is to brainstorm the kinds of plays you are interested in, in the form of a word map.

It might look something like this:

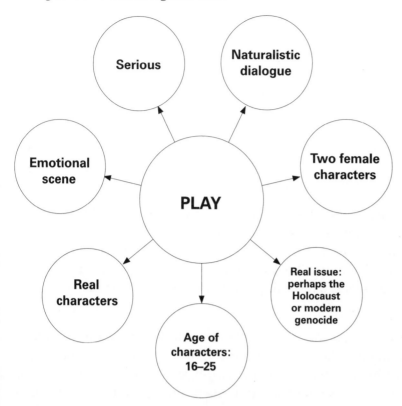

Once you have identified the key elements of the play you are looking for, you can act on this information.

Your **teacher** is always an excellent resource for play selection and should be your first point of call in gaining help and advice. They will be able to give you some ideas about plays in a particular style or genre that might be suitable for you and your partner.

You might be able to use the **practitioners and plays you have studied in Unit 1** as a starting point. While you cannot choose any of the plays you have studied in this unit, you could use another play by the same playwright or find other plays in a similar style. You might also choose to use the text of one of the productions that you have seen as a **live performance in your Unit 1 study**.

A visit to a good local **bookshop** with a drama section will also be able open doors to you, in terms of range and choice.

An **internet search** on, for instance, Google or Amazon, using an author's name, a key word or phrase like 'plays about genocide or the Holocaust' as search terms, may also begin to give you a range and choice of what is available.

While you should try to avoid choosing your duologue from a collected edition of duologues or monologues, such a book might be useful to give you an idea of plays that you might be interested in. You could then get hold of a copy of the play itself and choose a different scene from it which really grabs you.

## Understanding the context of the duologue

It's important to know well the entire play from which your duologue comes, so that you are able to deliver your scene with

**How to act on your word map**

integrity and conviction. Knowing and understanding what happens to your character before and after your duologue will help you to give a much clearer and richer performance.

Try to follow these four steps:

1. Read the play to gain an overview, then try to **summarise the plot** in a few sentences. Don't write too much: force yourself to be succinct and to the point. Now, using these sentences, tell another student from your group or your teacher what the play is about. Gauge their response: are they confused? Interested? What questions do they ask you? This should help to clarify your thinking.

2. Create a **scene-by-scene chart** or **unit chart** which breaks down the play into manageable sections (your chosen duologue will make up one of these scenes or units). Give each one of the sections a short title, describing what happens in it or where it takes place. This will provide you with a clear idea of where your duologue scene comes in the context of the whole play.

3. Now focus on your character and create a **journey graph** or **chart** which describes what they are thinking, feeling and what they want in each scene. Use the graph to plot the strength of their emotion or use the chart to write a sentence for their changing state of mind throughout the play. This will give you a clear indication of where your duologue comes in your character's journey during the play.

4. Now test the information and insights you have gathered so far by **hot-seating** with your partner. Sit opposite each other and take it in turns to get in role as your chosen character, while your partner interviews you about the whole story of the play. Make sure you stay in role as you're responding to the questions. This will really help you to create a strong, believable character who lives both inside and outside your duologue.

Don't overcomplicate your journey graph.

## Approaching the duologue

Once you have understood the place of your chosen duologue in the play as a whole it is time to tackle the realisation of the extract from page to stage. One way of approaching this is to think of the duologue in three distinct parts:

➢ Words

➢ Action

➢ Emotion.

Ultimately, of course, all these areas are closely linked and interwoven in the writing and they cannot be separated in performance; however, thinking of the piece in these terms will give you a variety of strategies with which to approach, understand and perform your duologue. The strategies and ideas can be combined or even used simultaneously depending on the type of play that you have chosen.

## Dealing with the words

You should start your approach to the duologue with a read-through with your partner. Remember that words in a play are different from words in a story in that they are intended to be read out loud.

As you're reading the words aloud, experiment with the dynamics. After your initial reading find a room with good acoustics, such as a bathroom or a music room, and whisper the duologue to each other. Make a note of the words and phrases that work well in this environment.

**Dynamics**

Now, go to a corridor or a large hall with your partner and stand at either end. Shout the duologue to each other. Again, note the words and phrases that worked particularly well with these treatment and consider why they did. Refer to the actual setting of the duologue (for instance, a bedroom, a living room, a street corner) and, if possible, practise the duologue in such a location. Discuss what effect this has upon the dynamics of the words.

The spoken text is intrinsically linked to the action of the play and the characters' feelings, so in order to make these areas clear it is important to know the value of the words.

**Meaning**

As you read through the duologue with your partner make sure you both understand the meaning of every single word. Don't shy away from difficult words or phrases. Work through the following steps together:

1. Rewrite the duologue in your own words. The best way to do this is to read it a few times on your own, in your head, then read it out loud together. Now, set the text aside and try to recreate the dialogue based on what you remember.

2. Go back to the text and highlight the words and phrases that you consider to have the greatest importance in the exchange. List these on a separate sheet of paper.

> You should do this exercise before you have begun the process of memorising the words.

3. Now improvise the duologue by using your list of important words and phrases as a guide; try to use all of these listed words in your improvisation.

4. Finally, return to the original duologue and begin the process of memorising the words. No real acting can take place until you have understood and learnt the text.

## Memorising the words

While memorising words is often a difficult process, it can be aided by exploring the action and emotion contained within them: knowing where you are standing, what you are doing or how you are feeling really helps to fix lines in your head and bring meaning to them. Below are outlined some suggested strategies for doing this.

Working on a duologue means that you have a partner to help you learn your lines, which can act as a tremendous motivation. If your partner happens to be absent, then ask friends to read the other part with you. You could also try recording the duologue onto a tape or CD leaving your section blank, so that you can play back

**Working with a partner**

the recording and fill in the missing part. Repetition is a great way to learn your duologue.

**Action**    You need to think about where the action in the duologue is set and make decisions about what you are doing in the space and how your character relates to your partner's character. These decisions are vital to your success in performing the duologue.

---

 **1.** Having read through your duologue again, create a sequence of freezes with your partner, representing five to ten points throughout the duologue. Make sure they are evenly spread throughout the action, taking into consideration the beginning, middle and end. Try to make them all different, by altering the dynamics of space and action in each one.

Think about:

> ➤ How you would physicalise your characters

> ➤ Where you would space them at different points in the duologue

> ➤ Are they touching or apart? Facing away from each other or towards each other?

> ➤ Are they sitting, lying or standing?

> ➤ Are there any moments of dynamic physical action, such as a slap, that you could freeze?

> ➤ When is the physical climax of the piece?

**2.** Add a third-person caption to each freeze, describing the action which has just occurred, or commenting on what the character is thinking or feeling. Choose a caption each, or decide on an appropriate one together.

**3.** Now add a word or line from the duologue that occurs just before or after each freeze. Keep the caption and add the line after.

**4.** You can now have some fun by trying to do all the freezes in sequence. Link them together using movements accompanied by music to create mood and emotion. Experiment with different types of music and see if this changes the atmosphere of the piece; you may even like to punctuate your sequence of freezes with different music so as to identify the various moods in the piece. This exercise also gives you a good opportunity to explore the physicality of your characters' expressions and movements – try both exaggerating and minimising your gestures.

**5.** Now choose a significant moment in the duologue and create a freeze for it together. Find an appropriate piece of music to accompany the freeze, which highlights its mood and emotion. Walk into the freeze, physically interacting with your partner's character, before you both freeze. This is a particularly effective technique for emphasising moments of pathos or sadness.

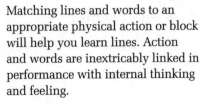

**Tip**

Matching lines and words to an appropriate physical action or block will help you learn lines. Action and words are inextricably linked in performance with internal thinking and feeling.

**6.** Finally read through the duologue again together, using the freezes almost as punctuation to block the sequence. At each freeze, ask yourselves why you have adopted the particular position. By doing this, you will be able to build up an understanding of your characters' motivation.

**Emotion**

Your performance of the duologue will not have any truth or integrity without an understanding of the character's emotional journey. You should have established a solid understanding of this through the work done earlier on the context of the play as a whole. However you must have a detailed knowledge of the character's journey in the extract to support your performance.

Once you have established a secure sense of the play as a whole, you need to consider your chosen duologue in more detail and break it down into smaller units. If you think of the larger units, or scenes, of the play as chapters in a book, then you could view the smaller sections of the duologue almost as paragraphs, each one representing a different action, thought or feeling.

If you struggle to divide your duologue in such a way, then try the following exercise. Assemble six chairs with your partner, so that you each have a row of three, facing each other across a space. Your first chair represents 'action', the second 'thinking' and the third 'feeling'. Read the extract from the duologue through, facing each other. Each time you think an action is required by your character sit in your 'action' chair; if you think your character has a new thought sit in the 'thinking' chair; and if you think your character has a change in emotion sit in the 'feeling' chair. Of course, sometimes there will be a combination of things (both action and feeling, for example) but in each case sit in the chair which best represents your character's dominant element.

**On the surface, under the surface**

Once you have memorised the extract and are beginning to work on acting it with your partner, try the 'On the surface, under the surface' exercise. This is a simple Brechtian exercise, in which you comment on your character in the third person. Choose three or four moments in the duologue. Both you and your partner should step out of role at these points, and comment on what your characters are doing, thinking and feeling and why. Then step back into role and continue with the duologue, until stopping at the next chosen moment.

This exercise prompts you to think about what is going on in the text of the play and also what is happening in its **subtext** – what is occurring under the surface of the words. An understanding of text and subtext is vital to creating a successful staging of a play.

## Emotional extremities

**Tip**

Understanding what the character is thinking and feeling in the subtext can help you remember the lines you are speaking in the text.

Another way to understand and exploit the potential of your duologue is to apply 'emotional extremities'. This is an exercise of exaggeration and can be used in rehearsal to explore the emotional potential of the piece. Once you have memorised the text and are working on the interaction between your characters, exaggerate any emotional moments by finding the extreme of each particular feeling. Overact the lines.

Identifying the extremity of an emotion enables you to locate the emotional truth in each line. In your performance you will probably choose to deliver your lines in a much more measured and restrained way, appropriate to your character and the scene, however the sub-textual emotion driving the line will still be apparent, as a result of your rehearsal work.

## Final preparation

As you approach the performance of your duologue it is important to keep it fresh. One way of doing this is to perform it in a number of different styles, which often raises important issues and brings new insights to the action and characters late in the process. Try out some of the following exercises.

 **Silent movie.** Perform your piece without any words at all, just exaggerated physical actions accompanied by some simple piano music in the style of a silent movie or dumb show. How clear is the content of your piece without words?

**EastEnders.** Using the words of the piece perform it in the style of a TV soap such as *EastEnders*. Try it in a loud and angry presentation style with urban accents as if it was in front of cameras that were close up to you. How does this style affect the intensity of the piece and your facial expressions?

**Props and costume.** You will not be expected to perform the duologue in the set or costume that the play would be performed in but you should make a token attempt to set and costume your piece. You need to think carefully about what you could wear and what props you could use to enhance and support the performance. Make sure you bring these ideas to the piece early so that you have a chance to experiment and work with them.

**Web link**

All of Shakespeare's plays can be found in their entirety at: http://shakespeare.mit.edu/. An excellent website suggesting examples of both monologues and duologues from Shakespeare plays is: www.shakespeare-monologues.org/

## Annotating the text

The plays of William Shakespeare offer wonderful opportunities for a whole variety of duologues for both genders, containing a wide range of issues and themes. The language in the plays is integral not only to character creation but also to the action and location of the play. Therefore, an approach that centres on dealing with the words of the play is the best way of accessing the text. An excellent example to look at, using the strategies outlined above, is the duologue for two female characters, Olivia and Viola from Act 1 scene 5 of *Twelfth Night*.

**Olivia:**

Give me my veil: come, throw it o'er my face.
We'll once more hear Orsino's embassy.

*Enter Viola*

**Viola:**

The honourable lady of the house, which is she?

**Olivia:**

Speak to me; I shall answer for her. Your will?

**Viola:**

Most radiant, exquisite and unmatchable beauty, I pray you,
tell me if this be the lady of the house, for I never saw her:
I would be loath to cast away my speech; for, besides that it is
excellently well penned, I have taken great pains to con it.
Good beauties, let me sustain no scorn; I am very comptible,
even to the least sinister usage.

**Olivia:**

Whence came you, sir?

**Viola:**

I can say little more than I have studied, and that question's
out of my part. Good gentle one, give me modest assurance
if you be the lady of the house, that I may proceed in my
speech.

**Olivia:**

Are you a comedian?

**Viola:**

No, my profound heart: and yet, by the very fangs of malice I
swear I am not that I play. Are you the lady of the house?

**Olivia:**

If I do not usurp myself, I am.

**Viola:**

Most certain, if you are she, you do usurp yourself; for, what
is yours to bestow is not yours to reserve. But this is from my
commission: I will on with my speech in your praise, and then
show you the heart of my message.

**Olivia:**

Come to what is important in't: I forgive you the praise.

**Viola:**

Alas, I took great pains to study it, and 'tis poetical.

---

The veil is an important prop: Olivia wears it to show she is in mourning and to disguise herself to confuse the messenger.

First important blocking position: Viola standing and Olivia sitting. The text indicates that there are other people in the room, therefore Viola should be looking around.

Olivia is playing games with Viola.

Viola has prepared this speech and her language, delivery and body posture should start off as formal and calculated before her informal, normal voice and more relaxed body gestures break through.

Olivia is more interested in the messenger than in Orsino's words. This could be a new blocking position: Olivia could come closer to Viola and inspect her.

Viola is made a little nervous by Olivia's questioning and voice; her movement should reflect this.

Olivia is asking whether Viola is an actor playing lines. Olivia has the upper hand and could circle Viola in an interrogative manner.

Dramatic irony, as the audience knows that Viola is in disguise. Viola is getting frustrated by not knowing if this is Olivia; her manner should show this.

Olivia admits to being the lady.

Viola hints that Olivia is doing herself wrong by not giving her hand away in marriage. She makes this comment as a woman and then returns to her role as messenger. Her voice and body should show this distinction.

Olivia backs away and sits again, restoring her role as lady and Viola as messenger.

Preparing herself for the speech, she could cough to clear her throat and adopt a new formal position.

Olivia reasserts her authority by a sharp, almost angry response. She has had enough of the messenger and Orsino. She makes to leave and stands up.

**Olivia:**

It is the more like to be feigned: I pray you, keep it in. I heard you were saucy at my gates, and allowed your approach rather to wonder at you than to hear you. If you be not mad, be gone; if you have reason, be brief: 'tis not that time of moon with me to make one in so skipping a dialogue.

**Maria:**

We did not have Maria here for the duologue so we cut this line but the sense of the passage was kept.

Will you hoist sail, sir? here lies your way.

**Viola:**

No, good swabber; I am to hull here a little longer. Some mollification for your giant, sweet lady.

**Olivia:**

Tell me your mind.

Viola physically represents herself by stepping forward.

**Viola:**

I am a messenger.

Olivia is angry and tired of the teasing. She feels that Viola is wasting her time.

**Olivia:**

Sure, you have some hideous matter to deliver, when the courtesy of it is so fearful. Speak your office.

**Viola:**

Viola wants to get Olivia alone and the servants to leave; she appeals to Olivia's curiosity and vanity.

It alone concerns your ear. I bring no overture of war, no taxation of homage: I hold the olive in my hand; my words are as full of peace as matter.

Again, Olivia is interested in Viola more than the words she brings; blocking must show this, in the way she looks or moves toward Viola who remains stationary.

**Olivia:**

Yet you began rudely. What are you? what would you?

**Viola:**

The rudeness that hath appeared in me have I learned from my entertainment. What I am, and what I would, are as secret as maidenhead; to your ears, divinity, to any other's, profanation.

Viola acted the way she did because of the manner in which she was received, but she hints at holding a secret using female imagery which interests Olivia and amuses the audience because they know she is a woman. Viola needs to present this line wryly and wittily.

**Olivia:**

Give us the place alone: we will hear this divinity.

*Exeunt Maria*

Now, sir, what is your text?

**Viola:**

Most sweet lady, –

**Olivia:**

A comfortable doctrine, and much may be said of it. Where lies your text?

A quick and pacey interchange which should show the two women fencing with words.

**Viola:**

In Orsino's bosom.

**Olivia:**

In his bosom! In what chapter of his bosom?

**Viola:**

To answer by the method, in the first of his heart.

**Olivia:**

O, I have read it: it is heresy. Have you no more to say?

**Viola:**

Good madam, let me see your face.

> This punctuates the interchange and should perhaps be accompanied with a pause.

**Olivia:**

Have you any commission from your lord to negotiate with my face? You are now out of your text: but we will draw the curtain and show you the picture. Look you, sir, such a one I was this present: is't not well done?

> Olivia is fascinated and flattered by the fact this messenger is interested in her face. The uncovering should be slow and teasing.

*Unveiling*

**Viola:**

Excellently done, if God did all.

> The second half of the sentence could be done almost as an aside.

**Olivia:**

'Tis in grain, sir; 'twill endure wind and weather.

> Olivia could respond with great control or with impetuous anger – try doing it both ways.

**Viola:**

'Tis beauty truly blent, whose red and white
Nature's own sweet and cunning hand laid on:
Lady, you are the cruell'st she alive,
If you will lead these graces to the grave
And leave the world no copy.

> Viola cleverly uses Olivia's own vanity as a reason for marrying; she could move towards Olivia or even touch her face.

**Olivia:**

O, sir, I will not be so hard-hearted; I will give out divers schedules of my beauty: it shall be inventoried, and every particle and utensil labelled to my will: as, item, two lips, indifferent red; item, two grey eyes, with lids to them; item, one neck, one chin, and so forth. Were you sent hither to praise me?

> After a moment of hesitation, indicating her interest in Viola, Olivia reasserts herself and moves away, becoming cold again.

**Viola:**

I see you what you are, you are too proud;
But, if you were the devil, you are fair.
My lord and master loves you: O, such love
Could be but recompensd, though you were crown'd
The nonpareil of beauty!

> Viola admits that Olivia is beautiful; this could be a speech to herself, rather than Olivia.

**Olivia:**

How does he love me?

> Olivia responds to the word 'love'; a turn towards Viola on that word would signify this.

**Viola:**

With adorations, with fertile tears,
With groans that thunder love, with sighs of fire.

> Viola returns to her prepared speech.

Olivia has heard all this before and has no patience for it. Her tone and gesture should show this. She acknowledges that Orsino is a good man but not for her. She is again bringing the conversation to an end.

**Olivia:**

Your lord does know my mind; I cannot love him:
Yet I suppose him virtuous, know him noble,
Of great estate, of fresh and stainless youth;
In voices well divulg'd, free, learn'd and valiant;
And in dimension and the shape of nature
A gracious person: but yet I cannot love him;
He might have took his answer long ago.

Viola tries a different tack, and her language and gesture become more immediate and personal.

**Viola:**

If I did love you in my master's flame,
With such a suffering, such a deadly life,
In your denial I would find no sense;
I would not understand it.

Olivia is becoming interested but more in Viola than in Orsino. She should soften her tone and look toward Viola.

**Olivia:**

Why, what would you?

This is perhaps a type of wooing that Olivia has not encountered before. She is attracted by the beautiful language and imagery that Viola creates. Throughout the speech this transition in her feelings must be shown. Perhaps on 'Olivia' she begins to show her interest by facially and physically responding. Viola could be unaware of the effect she is having on Olivia at this stage.

**Viola:**

Make me a willow cabin at your gate,
And call upon my soul within the house;
Write loyal cantons of contemned love,
And sing them loud even in the dead of night;
Holla your name to the reverberate hills,
And make the babbling gossip of the air
Cry out 'Olivia!' O, you should not rest
Between the elements of air and earth,
But you should pity me!

Olivia is now really engaged by Viola and comes towards her.

**Olivia:**

You might do much. What is your parentage?

Viola returns to a formal tone and moves away, scared that Olivia might realise she is in disguise.

**Viola:**

Above my fortunes, yet my state is well:
I am a gentleman.

Olivia is harsh towards Orsino but softened by the thought of Viola coming again, which should be shown in tone and gesture.

**Olivia:**

Get you to your lord;
I cannot love him: let him send no more;
Unless, perchance, you come to me again,
To tell me how he takes it. Fare you well:
I thank you for your pains: spend this for me.

A fee'd post is a paid messenger. Viola responds angrily on behalf of her master, perhaps aware that Olivia is now interested in her. She is angry that a woman's heart is so fickle, which is made all the more difficult in that she is herself a woman. Her exit is characterised by anger and formality.

**Viola:**

I am no fee'd post, lady; keep your purse:
My master, not myself, lacks recompense.
Love make his heart of flint, that you shall love;
And let your fervour, like my master's, be
Placed in contempt! Farewell, fair cruelty.

*Exit*

**Olivia:**

'What is your parentage?'
'Above my fortunes, yet my state is well:
I am a gentleman.' I'll be sworn thou art;
Thy tongue, thy face, thy limbs, actions and spirit,
Do give thee five-fold blazon: not too fast:
soft, soft!
Unless the master were the man. How now!
Even so quickly may one catch the plague?
Methinks I feel this youth's perfections
With an invisible and subtle stealth
To creep in at mine eyes. Well, let it be.
What ho, Malvolio!

> We chose to retain this final soliloquy even though Olivia is now alone on stage. The speech marks the end of the scene and articulates the subtext of the duologue. Olivia wants to know more about Viola and feels she is falling in love with 'him'. She should return to the chair and ponder this from a sitting position, exhausted and smitten.

## Suggested texts

There are many plays which lend themselves to a particularly visual and physical style, and which offer opportunities for a whole variety of duologues for any gender. The work of Steven Berkoff, for instance, contains an interesting mix of language and imagery and would be suitable to attempt with a more physical emphasis (as suggested in some of the earlier strategies). Berkoff's work often contains as much image and stage direction as text and it would therefore benefit from such an approach. However, you can successfully apply a visual/physical approach to any text, if this is where your skill and enthusiasm lies.

Look at the opening sequence in Samuel Beckett's *Waiting for Godot* between Estragon and Vladimir. Use the exercise in the 'Action' section of this chapter (page 140) to approach this extract. Think about the sequence as a physical slapstick routine between two characters. Create a series of freezes that punctuate the extract and then link them together with movement.

If you are interested in exploring the deeper, subtextual meanings within a text and taking a psychological, emotional approach to them, you may like to consider choosing a play that has a naturalistic setting and style. There is a wide array of classic and modern plays that enable you to focus on the psychological journey of the central characters; with such a text, focus your rehearsal work on strategies for dealing with emotion.

The work of American playwrights Tennessee Williams, Edward Albee and Arthur Miller provides excellent texts to look at, as do the British playwrights of the 1960s 'kitchen sink' era, such as John Osborne. You may also like to consider modern playwrights who combine naturalistic language and characters with more stylised settings, such as Mark Ravenhill, Nick Grosso and Jonathan Harvey. However, you can successfully apply an emotional approach to any text, if this is where your skills and enthusiasm lies.

Look at the opening of Act 2 of Arthur Miller's *The Crucible*, with John Proctor and Elizabeth Proctor. Refer to the exercise in the 'Emotion' section in this chapter (page 141), for guidance on how to approach it.

### Waiting for Godot (male and male)

**Further study**

To get a visual idea of the possibilities of this type of duologue look at some video clips of the comedians, Rik Mayall and Adrian Edmondson in the comedy series, *Bottom*. Mayall and Edmondson co-starred in a production of *Waiting for Godot* at the Queen's Theatre in London in 1991.

### The Crucible (male and female)

**Tip**

Annotate your script extract as a series of illustrations or floor plans, thinking about it as a sequence of movement. You should clearly state: what the action is or what the characters are doing to each other, how you achieved this through use of movement, levels or props and why you think this was an important moment for the characters, relationship or play.

**Final advice**    Try to choose a play and an extract that:

➤ Fulfils the rubric and timing of the exam

➤ Challenges you intellectually, physically and/or emotionally

➤ Suits you and your partner's strengths and talents

➤ You will enjoy working on and spending time and energy on with your partner.

## Section B: an overview

In Section B, you must have between three and nine performers in your cast. There is no limit to the number of designers per production. It is likely that your teacher will direct the play, although it is acceptable to have a student director. The play should run for 30–60 minutes, depending on how big your cast is. While it is important that you all get a chance to demonstrate your skills, the performance must not exceed the set time limit.

You will be involved in the process of designing, rehearsing and performing a play. For many of you this will be the most rewarding aspect of your AS course. It may also be the most difficult.

### Log

You should keep a log of all the sessions that you are involved in and the work that you cover. This includes lessons, discussions, group rehearsals and performances you have seen that may be relevant to the play – or style of play – you are studying.

This log should cover:

➤ **What** you did during the sessions. This could be an account of lessons, practical sessions or discussions.

➤ **How** you did the work. Show the style of work you were involved in, and be communicated through notes, illustrations and diagrams showing the different parts of the session.

➤ **Why** you covered this material. Explain the relevance of the work you have covered and explain the point of the exercises or types of work covered in relation to the text.

Write and draw these notes immediately after each session so that they are fresh in your mind. These observations are for your own benefit but they are also important when charting the progress of your work.

### Assessment

This aspect of your course is assessed and marked by a visiting examiner, who will visit your centre for the performance of the play. Your teacher will also need to video the performance and send that video recording to the examiner after the production.

This video ensures there is a record of your production so that if there are any problems or queries regarding your performance it can be used as a reference.

# Criteria

The examiner will assess you in **four** different areas (or assessment objectives) within each section. These areas will be different depending on whether you have focused on performance or design. Each area is worth a maximum of 10 marks. See the table below.

 The exam board sets out some specific rules and regulations to consider in terms of this unit, and while your teacher will be aware of them, it's worth your bearing them in mind:

**Dos and don'ts**

➤ The plays you choose for this unit **must** be different from the plays you have studied for Unit 1: Exploration of Drama and Theatre.

➤ The plays you choose **must** provide you with a sufficient challenge as a performer or designer. We will give you guidance on the choice and selection of plays later in this chapter.

| Assessment objective | Performance criteria | | Design criteria | |
|---|---|---|---|---|
| 1 | **Vocal skills** | You will be assessed on your control of 'pause, pace, pitch, tone, inflection and projection'. | **Use of materials and equipment** | You will need to demonstrate a full command of different 'equipment, techniques and applications'. |
| 2 | **Movement skills** | You will need to demonstrate appropriate physicality for the character using 'gesture, poise and stillness'. | **Realisation of design** | You will need to demonstrate a full awareness of the demands of the production, developing your design area with creativity and skill. |
| 3 | **Characterisation** | Your performance of the character(s) should be complete and sustained, demonstrating a full command of the play's style and contemporary relevance. | **Written design concept** | Your concept should show a comprehensive understanding of all aspects of the production including the style and genre of the piece. |
| 4 | **Written performance concept** | Your writing should illustrate an understanding of the play's 'social, historical, cultural and political context', and be a detailed documentation of both the rehearsal process and the intended impact on the audience. | **Design documentation** | Your writing will illustrate an understanding of the play's 'social, historical, cultural and political context', and be a detailed design plan for the production and thorough justification of the performed design. |

## Written performance concept

Out of the 40 marks available for Section B, 10 are allocated for the 500 words in which you summarise your concept of the text. This does not have to be continuous prose but needs to demonstrate a comprehensive understanding of the play's meaning to a contemporary audience and make detailed reference to the rehearsal process and the intended impact of the work. While some of this will be led by your teacher's ideas when directing the work, it must be a personal response which highlights your understanding of the text.

Consider using examples of the exercises explored through this chapter, illustrating ideas with brief excerpts of the text, images, photographs and moments of personal reflection. Reference your understanding of the playwright's style and the influences of practitioners during your rehearsal process. You will not be able to include every aspect of the process, but it needs to be a vibrant response which celebrates the text and emphasises your engagement with the work.

## Choosing a play

Although you may choose to devise your own performance piece at A2, here you must work with a playscript already in existence. The exam board does not prescribe which texts you should use: the choice is completely yours. However, it does stress that your choice of text is crucial; it is vital that you pick a script that suits your group and which will inspire you all creatively. So where should you look for advice on choosing a play?

Samuel French publishes an excellent guide to selecting plays for performance (*The Guide*, £8.50). For more details go to: www. samuelfrench-london.co.uk.

Of course, this very important decision may well have already been made by your teacher. If that is the case, they will have already gone through the following thought processes, which, if the play is still to be chosen, you will need to consider.

**Practical considerations**

Firstly, there are some **practical** questions to think about:

### 1. How many students are in your group?

It is always a good idea to try to find a play that has a cast the same size as your group. It is also advisable to try to find a play that has a sense of balance, in that the parts are of equal measure. This may not always be possible and there may be members of your group who actively seek smaller parts. However, you must remember that the examiner can only mark you when you are performing and that, therefore, everyone in your group must have time on stage in a role that challenges them and brings out the best in them.

The play and the part you choose offer you the opportunity to be challenged and show your understanding as an actor or designer. You must also be able to write about this experience in your written concept. Choose a play that will allow you to enjoy, intellectualise and reflect on the process.

### 2. What sexes are the members of your group?

There is nothing in the exam rubric that states you cannot have girls playing boys or vice versa, and examiners have reported that some interesting work was done in this area. However, the rubric encourages you to retain the artistic integrity of your chosen play and this may not always be best achieved by cross-gender casting. Think carefully before you take this decision and ask whether it suits or supports the intentions of the play. You may choose to have a female Hamlet in order to make a theatrical point or statement, but try to avoid making this decision out of a logistical necessity rather than an artistic concept.

### 3.  How do we make a play fit the time restraints of the exam?

Whatever play you choose, it must meet the time restraints of the exam (as a rule, 30–60 minutes depending on the size of your group, with larger groups nearer an hour). You must have an opportunity to show a sense of development as an actor. This is achieved by presenting the whole play or the essence of the whole play.

If you have chosen a play that is longer than an hour you could still show the essence of the play by:

➢ Selecting a continuous extract or a whole act or scene and representing missing moments or events from the play through abstract movement, narration or tableaux

➢ Selecting aspects of one particular plot or strand of the play by choosing particular scenes that support this

➢ Making careful cuts and edits that still leave a sense of the  story and character development. The cut moments from the play could again be told or represented through abstract movement, narration and tableaux.

Examiners say that candidates have done best when there was a sense that the entire play had been taught and explored, and then creatively edited. This could easily be achieved with a text such as *Metamorphosis* (discussed on pages 86–96 of this guide) in which abstract movement, narration and tableaux are already heavily used, or with, for instance, *Macbeth*, in which action-driven parts of the story could be effectively represented.

The time constraint is there as a help rather than a hindrance. A longer play will demand longer rehearsal time, more sustained focus and concentration during the performance, as well as greater production demands.

Secondly, there are some **artistic** questions to answer:

**Artistic considerations**

### 1.  What type of play do you want to choose?

Choose a play that will lay down some artistic challenges and allow you to work at a level appropriate for the AS course. You must also be able to write about the process of rehearsing and performing the play in your written concept.

Reflect on the work you've already done for Unit 1 and what you know of the key theatre practitioners. Use your interests as developed here to help you decide on a text. Consider the following questions:

➤ Have you been interested by a particular style of approach to the content of a play?
*For example: epic theatre and storytelling techniques, as discovered in your work on Brecht.*

➤ Have you been challenged or engaged by a particular theme or issue?
*For example: the role of individuals in society as explored in* A Doll's House.

➤ Have you been excited by a particular approach to rehearsal and the realisation of characters?
*For example: emotional truth and the work of Stanislavski.*

➤ Have you been inspired by a specific style of performance?
*For example: the Theatre of Cruelty and the work of Artaud.*

➤ Have you been engaged by a particular period of theatre history?
*For example: ancient Greek drama.*

➤ Have you considered your target audience and what may be most relevant for them?
*For example: an issue-based piece relating to young people.*

Try to find plays that lend themselves to the passions and interests that have been stirred by the work you have done so far.

## 2. How do you choose roles within the group?

Choosing roles and casting parts can be problematic, and a cause of tension within your group. This is something a group can do without at a time when group work and shared motivation is all-important to the success of the project. Be sensitive and prepared to compromise; balance your personal preferences with an awareness of what will be best for the production as a whole.

The first decision you need to make is whether you wish to be a performer or designer. Your teacher should direct this element of your course. If you do want to direct then bear in mind that this will be available as a possibility in the devising unit of the A2 course, in which student directing is encouraged.

## Design

If you choose to take on the role of designer for your group, you will need to decide whether to focus on one of the nominated skills or a combination of more than one element. The choices are: costume, lighting, mask, makeup, set and props or sound.

The role of designer in any of these areas is concerned with the journey of exploration, interpretation and realisation of the play. You would be expected to make a full and important contribution to all areas of rehearsal as well as the final performance.

The decision to take on a design role should be a positive one, based on a real enthusiasm and desire to explore the selected area. It should not be a default decision arrived at because you don't want to perform, don't like the play or don't like the characters in the play.

**Web link**

The different design skills have different criteria for assessment. A very comprehensive and clear grid of requirements is available from the exam board at www.edexcel.org.uk.

It is, in many ways, a more difficult role than performing, because you need to approach the tasks in a structured and self-disciplined fashion. You will be required to attend all rehearsals and contribute actively in these sessions, as well as working alone to build up knowledge and understanding of your chosen skill before implementing it.

Having said all this, acting as the designer can be incredibly rewarding in terms of artistic satisfaction, and can be an excellent way of securing good marks in this unit. Not only will you be judged by your contribution to the final performance, but you will also have an opportunity to give a short presentation to the examiner after the performance, outlining your thinking and the processes by which you made decisions.

## Performance

For those who have made the decision to perform, the process of casting the play can be critical to its success as well as to the harmony and work ethic of the group. Of course, this may be solved by your teacher making the casting decisions, but even if they do so, they will still go through some clear thought processes before arriving at this decision.

Don't be frightened of holding auditions among your group to see if anyone finds an immediate or natural affinity with any of the parts through reading them aloud or learning a short extract. Perform these pieces in front of each other so that there is a democracy and a sense of sharing from the beginning. Talk openly but positively about the auditions and see if any majority opinions emerge. Take some time to workshop the play and give everybody an opportunity to play many different roles from the play. What you may think of at first as your dream role may turn out not to be once you have improvised around it or represented it in a more informal session outside a rehearsal.

Try to play to the strengths of the group and don't be frightened of letting more experienced members take on the more difficult roles. Big parts don't automatically mean big marks. What counts is the success of the whole play and your role within that success. The size of your role is unimportant as long as it contributes to a successful whole. Create an ensemble focus for the play by keeping your cast in full view of the audience at all times, and allow the mechanism of theatre to be in view of the audience. Costume changing, set preparation, playing more than one role – all can be presented to the audience in a way that is just as important as the events, the characters and the words they speak. This is a great way of giving equal importance to all members of the cast.

You might like to consider plays:

➢ Which are **ensemble** pieces, so each actor plays many parts

➢ Which allow actors to **share the lead** role in a coherent way

➢ In which the **story is all-important**, rather than the characters.

**Casting**

66 There are no small parts, only small actors. 99

Motto of Stanislavski's Moscow Art Theatre.

The characters might, for instance, be represented as numbers or job titles rather than names.

If you are confused about where to find such plays, or would like some examples, this section will go on to give you some tangible suggested texts to work with (see pages 157–183).

## Rehearsing

Organisation is a very important key to success in this unit. The two plays that are given as example texts later in this section will give you some clear ideas as to how to approach rehearsals; there are also some general principles to follow when it comes to rehearsing which are outlined below.

**Schedule** Try to create a rehearsal schedule. It should be recognised and understood that, although all your lessons during this unit of study may be given up to rehearsal, you will be expected to rehearse outside lesson time as well. Break the play down into manageable sections or units of action that can be rehearsed within the time limit of your lesson or in the time allocated outside of the lesson.

The exam board gives an excellent pair of equations for the relationship between text and rehearsal, and between rehearsal and performance. They suggest that:

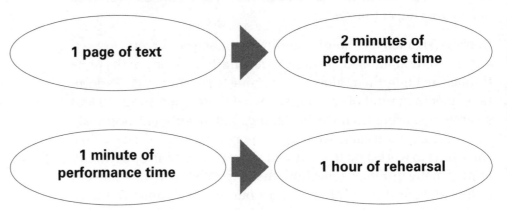

These are good general principles to use when breaking the play down into sections that can be rehearsed in your lessons and sessions.

When creating a rehearsal schedule, put down the day and date of all the slots available to you leading up to the performance date. It is sometimes useful to work backwards in the schedule by placing the performance date, the dress rehearsal, the technical rehearsal and the full run first, in order to ensure that you reserve sufficient time for these rehearsals. Then start from the beginning date and enter in the selected sections of your play, in chronological order. Be sure to leave slots for repetition of rehearsed sections and an opportunity to run sections together as you get closer to the full run. It is also good to have a column indicating the specific characters needed at each rehearsal. Here's an example:

| Day and date | Lesson or time | Scene/section to be rehearsed | Who is needed |
|---|---|---|---|
| Monday 1 March | Periods one and two | Devise the opening sequence | Everyone |

Try to set yourself clear targets for each rehearsal. They may be as simple as 'we must block three pages of text in order to create the staging patterns for those scenes'; they may refer to exploring and understanding a character, a theme or a passage of dialogue; they may even be as practical as working out entrances or exits for people or props. Whatever your target for each rehearsal, declare it at the beginning and, at the end, reflect on whether or not it has been achieved.

Don't launch straight into the text of the play. Use your early lessons and sessions to play games, to help the group bond and to create a good working atmosphere. Then move on to workshopping ideas and wider concepts based on themes, scenes, characters and performance styles. This is not wasted time: it will help you to build a vocabulary of theatrical ideas to use on the text as you rehearse.

Make your rehearsals a positive and pleasant experience with a good working atmosphere by:

**Be positive**

➤ Being on time

➤ Setting clear targets for the rehearsals

➤ Leaving your emotional baggage of the day at the studio/ classroom door

➤ Putting aside personal grievances or relationship problems by focusing on the good of the play

➤ Bringing all the necessary equipment like your script, a pencil, a notebook and the right clothes to rehearse in

➤ Spending time thinking about the rehearsal before you arrive so that you are ready and willing to make creative contributions

➤ Spending a short time at the beginning of each rehearsal doing a warm-up or playing a game to energise and focus

➤ Seeing the rehearsal as work and treating the time as work time

➤ Being positive towards one another and using positive language to praise work

➤ Always being constructive in criticism and avoiding personal comments; try to talk about the work/character and how to improve this rather than the actual actor themselves.

Above all, rehearsals should be great fun and should be enjoyed. Even the darkest and most serious of plays can still have a really enjoyable rehearsal process if everybody feels valued as a participant and is fully aware of what is trying to be achieved. It is important to make the whole process a shared responsibility.

## Performing the play

Obviously the main rationale behind this performance is that it is an exam and part of your AS course, but you need to remember that it is also a piece of theatre designed to entertain and engage an audience. The examiner will want to see a complete piece of theatre that has been well rehearsed, sensibly thought through and well presented.

Try to make the exam an occasion. Give it a sense of completeness and significance. With this in mind, you need to really think about the following areas:

**Where are you going to perform?** Will you be able to rehearse in your performance space? How will you use your performance space to meet the needs of the play best?

**Who will your audience be?** You need an audience to make the play a valid piece of theatre. Will you target a certain age range for your production or will you look for a more general audience? Think carefully about your target audience as you rehearse the play.

**Where will the examiner sit?** They will need a table and a table-lamp to write notes. Plan where they will have maximum access to the play with minimum disruption to the rest of the audience.

**Make sure that the examiner can identify you within the performance.** It is sometimes conceptually appropriate for all the cast to wear black or dress similarly but this will not help the examiner. Think carefully about how you represent the characters within the play and allow time before the performance to meet with the examiner and let yourself be identified.

**The play has to be recorded**, so make sure you set a camera up well in advance and make sure that it has a good sight-line. It does not need to be a professional film of the show, just a simple record of the performance. This will be sent to the examiner.

> You should have provided a photograph of yourself in costume and you need to identify yourself on camera before the performance.

## Example playtexts

Hopefully the advice above will be useful to you, but it is sometimes much easier to get ideas on how to work with a text if you have an actual example in front of you. On the following pages you will find a detailed breakdown of how to work with two very different playtexts for performance. You may choose (or have already chosen) to use one of these texts for your own production, in which case you will find the information below very useful indeed! However, it can be just as helpful if you have decided on another text: the advice below on approaching the material is as generic as possible. This means that it should be easy to adapt to whatever text you are studying. When reading it through, consider how you could use the approaches below to help you when working on your chosen material.

The two plays discussed here, *Find Me* and *The Last Resort*, have been chosen because of their contrasting styles, in order to give you an idea of the different approaches it is possible to take in this unit.

## Find Me

*Find Me* by Olwen Wymark (born 1934) is based on the true story of Verity Taylor whose difficulties in conforming to society's constraints led her to being incarcerated in Broadmoor for an indefinite period of time.

Wymark was born in America but now lives and works in London. She is a successful playwright who has produced award-winning scripts for radio, television and film. Her theatrical work is diverse and she has worked in partnership with the National Theatre, the Royal Court Theatre and Shared Experience.

*Find Me* opens with a cold, factual narration of Verity's fate: she was 'charged by the police with damaging a chair by fire – value six pounds' and admitted to Broadmoor. The play goes back in time, to an excitable image of her with her family, and then charts the events that led to her imprisonment. The text presents these as a series of episodes in a variety of theatrical forms, with all actors playing a multitude of roles. Her mental state gradually deteriorates and her family moves from optimism to despair. We share in her achievements and begin to understand the motivation behind some of her extreme outbursts. The play concludes where it started, with all of the five 'Veritys' asking for someone to 'find me'.

*Find Me* contains many of the necessary elements for creating a successful AS-level performance:

➤ There is a good mixture of small-group and ensemble scenes

➤ The mood of the play varies from humour to pathos

➤ Each of the characters is clearly defined and possesses enough complexity to show a sense of development during the performance

➤ The multiple characterisation means that actors need to define the physicality and vocal delivery of each distinct role

➤ The episodic nature allows for easy editing of the text to suit the needs of the group

➤ Although the protagonist is female, many of the roles can be adapted to reflect the particular gender balance of your group.

### Approaching the play

At the beginning of any rehearsal process, it is important to be clear about the challenges you are going to face. Start by asking yourself the following questions:

➤ How many lessons will we have to work on the script?

➤ Where could the piece be performed?

➤ Are any students doing design for the piece?

➤ How much direction is going to be offered by the teacher?

➤ Who is responsible for casting the play?

### Further study

Use a search engine to look at the history of Broadmoor Hospital, so as to understand the conditions which Verity experienced there.

### Web link

Visit www.royalcourttheatre.com and www.nationaltheatre.org.uk to find out about these two London theatres. Look at www.sharedexperience.org.uk for information about the theatre company Wymark has worked with.

**Why choose this play?**

See the section on Stanislavski and his definition of given circumstances on pages 17–18.

When making these decisions it is important to bear in mind the specific demands of the text. In your first group read-through, it is vital to make notes on the characters and their given circumstances. This will ensure that all of your discussions remain tightly focused on the information that Wymark conveys through her writing.

In your group, read *Find Me*. Make notes on the individual characters, their age, appearance, behaviour and any references to their life. These given circumstances could also include their emotional reactions to any moments in the play. For example, your notes for the character of Mark may look something like this:

**Mark.** Three years older than his sister Verity. Feels unable to talk about his frustrations. Frequently embarrassed and at times intimidated by her behaviour. Is protective of his mother and tries to put on a brave face in her presence.

This factual information will provide you with the foundations for each rehearsal. Compile everyone's comments and make sure each person in the group has a copy.

## Casting the play

It's important to cast the play carefully in order to ensure a balanced performance. The constant swapping of roles means that there will be an opportunity for each actor to demonstrate their skill in portraying the protagonist. However there are still several casting questions which you will need to consider carefully. The play contains a number of key monologues: which members of your group would be best suited to delivering these? Where is the humour in the piece and who would enjoy communicating these moments to an audience? The characters age as the piece progresses: is anyone particularly suited to playing a role of a certain age? Remember that casting is a complicated balancing act and you need to provide everyone with opportunities to succeed. It is not as simple as giving your best performers the most interesting scenes – you must consider the demands of the characters and the physicality of the group.

Take time over deciding who plays what. Ask other people for their opinions. You may want to play a character that is similar to yourself or you may want to act against type. It may be useful to ask members of your group to read scenes from the script so that you can hear how different voices work alongside each other.

## Exploring the characters

Before beginning work on the text, it can be useful to experiment with the given circumstances. Now the play is cast, you can use the character information to improvise scenes, which will allow each individual to develop their role.

---

**Status cards.** Take a pack of cards and remove the jacks, queens, kings and jokers. The 40 cards that remain are going to be used to indicate the status of characters. Ten is extremely powerful, scared of no one. Ace is timid and unsure, unable to hold eye contact with others. Randomly distribute a card to each member of the group. Keeping their number secret, each person should now walk around the space with that status level, imagining that they are walking around your school or college. How would they react to the others? Avoid using any words and instead focus on the physical work. After two minutes of walking and meeting the other people, come out of character and try to order yourself based on what you have learnt from how other people have reacted to you. Create a line along one wall from highest to lowest status. Remember, up to four people could have the same numerical value; if someone feels they have the same value as another character then they should stand in front of them. Once everyone has decided on their position, reveal your cards.

Look at how successful you were as a group in conveying your status. Who should have had the most power in the room? Was this communicated?

In addition to showing levels of status, cards can be used to focus on the intensity of emotion. For example, ask two members of your group to improvise the following scenario as children. Before they begin, they will need to choose a card randomly. A is building a structure out of Lego. B approaches A and watches what is happening. The numerical value of A's card indicates how intimidated they are by B's presence. B's card indicates how much they want to disrupt B's play. Repeat the scene with different actors and new numbers. Experiment with changing the age of B.

---

**Family improvisation.** Imagine the family have decided to spend the night camping in the wood. Nicky is five, Verity 15 and Mark 18. The family have just unpacked their tent and now need to work together to erect it. Using the given circumstances, consider how the family would react. While the script often focuses on the negative aspects of the family's relationship, imagine they are sitting round a campfire, talking. What would make them laugh? Improvise this scene and discuss what it reveals about the characters.

Now choose a character at random to collect some wood for the fire. How does the dynamic of the family change when they are not there? Fast forward the scene to ten minutes later. How does the rest of the family feel about the other family member taking so long?

What games might the characters play? Think about both intellectual and physical activities. How might the different characters react? Which games might Verity like? Try to explain the rules of the game in role. How do you feel when others ask questions?

Exercises like these are vital throughout the rehearsal process. The play relies on high energy levels, both physically and mentally. As a group of actors, you need to be actively engaged in the rehearsal, and warm-up activities will help to ensure you remain focused during the lessons.

## Staging the production

**Set design**

Wymark's stage directions imply quite a sparse stage. She states that there is a raised platform upstage which the Veritys inhabit. In addition to this, there is a range of locations implied by the text which include a school, swimming pool and a psychiatric hospital. The nature of the play suggests that these locations should not be presented in a realistic manner. Wymark's style is more influenced by Brecht than Stanislavski and as a consequence the actors should look to create the environment through their movement. When writing the play, Wymark didn't want the audience to become lost in the realism of the piece; it was important to her that the audience reflected on Verity's actions and the reaction of society to them. This needs to be remembered when creating your set and staging the action.

> The second scene suggests using a video camera. If you are completing a modern interpretation of the text, what Edward films could be projected onto a screen, emphasising Verity's attention-seeking behaviour.

Before you begin rehearsing, it is important to discuss the needs of your piece. These are issues that the whole group should consider, even if one or more members are going to be responsible for the design aspects. Try focusing on the following points:

How are you going to create a sense of the different **locations**? For example, a cyclorama positioned upstage could have bold images projected onto it to symbolise each setting.

What form will the raised **platform** take? What material will it be made from and how large will it be?

Where are the **audience** going to be positioned? Remember you could choose from performing end-on (audience on one side), traverse (two sides), in the thrust (three sides), round (four sides) or promenade (audience walks to the action).

> For more on these types of staging see pages 43–45.

**Costume**

The multiple characterisations inherent in the text make it impractical to have a detailed costume for each character. However, you could choose to use signers to represent each of the characters. For example, a white knitted cardigan could suggest Edward's homely instinct and his desire to maintain the peace. Alternatively, you could decide against individual costumes entirely and instead create a uniform approach. You could dress all the female characters in black – although this could blur the action and make it very difficult for the examiner to mark the piece. Choosing two or three colours which all the actors have to wear is another way of approaching the dilemma, with each individual given freedom as to which item of their clothing is which colour.

The narrator suggests that the action of the play is set in the early 1970s although Wymark identifies the time as 'present'. Would you want to suggest a sense of period in your costume or do you wish to maintain the timeless quality?

The demands of lighting the play will very much depend on the nature of the performance and the facilities available to you. The Brechtian nature of Wymark's writing means the play could be staged without any changes in lighting at all. The cold and impersonal tone of most scenes might suggest that a steel blue general cover would be sufficient for the action. However, there is also the possibility for a more sophisticated lighting design.

Think about how the burning chair could be conveyed through lighting. A rotating gobo with different shades of red and orange gels could provide a sense of the flickering flames. The magical effect of the swimming pool could be accentuated by a blue wash with occasional shafts of white light. By suggesting the different locations through lighting, different areas of the stage will begin to show your command.

The level of sound you use in the piece will obviously depend on the specialist equipment available to you. However, several cues are suggested in the text in order to complement the action on stage. At the end of Act 1, the pounding of the door and the sound of rushing water produce a soundscape of Verity's chaos during the blackout. You could also look at other noises to suggest location like a school bell or a ticking clock, while Edward is being interviewed.

The numerous scenes could run more smoothly by underscoring some of the movement with music. Look, for instance, at the music of the Doors. Their musical style would give the play a sense of period; yet the fact that their music is often sampled, would also have the effect of giving the production a sense of contemporary relevance. The distorted quality to some of the tracks is well-suited to conveying a sense of Verity's instability. 'Bird of Prey' is a familiar and yet haunting melody which could be repeated at moments of significance.

## Rehearsing

There are approximately 25 scenes in *Find Me* although the division between them is often blurred. Some of these are static passages of text, while others are extremely complex passages of action with all actors on stage at the same time. Begin the process of rehearsing by dividing up your rehearsal time to ensure that all moments are given equal attention. It is useful to look at the possibilities of multiple rehearsals when finalising which actors play who, in which scene. There will be times when two scenes can be rehearsed simultaneously. For example, depending on your casting, you could rehearse the interviewer and Edward at the same time as Mark's monologue and one of the duologues between Edward and Jean. However, if scenes have been worked on independently, then it is useful to share your work with the rest

**Lighting**

**Web link**

The stage electrics website has specific examples of gobos that are available: www.stage-electrics.co.uk. The international theatre design archive has images of lighting designs for various productions that could provide a reference point for your ideas: www.siue.edu/ITDA

**Sound**

See the Doors, *The Very Best of the Doors* CD (Rhino 2007).

**Organising rehearsals**

of the group in order to receive constructive feedback and retain continuity in the characterisation.

It is vital that you are clear about deadlines so that there is no confusion within your group. Make sure everyone knows when lines need to be learnt, when the first run-through will take place, and when designs will be presented. Allow time for a technical rehearsal and a dress rehearsal at the end of the process to ensure that the final performance to the examiner runs as smoothly as possible.

**Rehearsing the text**

Part of the success of your performance will undoubtedly lie in your ability to create truthful portrayals of the different roles. The audience needs to believe in the action and the complex situations that are presented if they are going to reflect on society's treatment of the family. Therefore, one of the initial ways of approaching the text is to use elements of Stanislavski's work (which is described in more detail on pages 15–24). However, this is not the only method: it should be used as a starting point, a way of accessing the text. Here we will look at specific scenes from the play and suggest different approaches influenced by different practitioners. Many of the activities we suggest are generic and can be applied to any scene and, indeed, to any play. The key point to remember is that, as actors, you will need to embody your characters, and this is difficult to achieve if you simply spend each lesson reading the scene and then acting it out.

## Rehearsal methods

**Units and objectives**

During rehearsal Stanislavski broke the play into temporary divisions called units; each new unit began where there was a change in the psychological state of the character. Once each unit had been worked on individually, they were linked back together demonstrating the emotional journey the characters followed during each scene.

Look at the following extract from Act 1:

**Edward:** Hello Verity. What's that you're making?

*Verity is immediately silent and stiff.*

**Verity:** *(sharply)* Be careful. You'll step on it.

**Edward:** I won't. I won't. I'll be careful. What is it?

**Verity:** *(still warily)* It's my village.

**Edward:** Oh, it's very nice. Clever girl.

**Verity:** This is my castle *(she looks at him sideways)*. I'm inside it.

**Edward:** Are you?

**Verity:** Yes. And nobody else can get in.

**Edward:** Well, well!

**Verity:** It's all locked up and safe and they can't get in.

*Jean comes in.*

**Jean:** Hello darling. You're back *(she moves to Edward)*.

**Verity:** Look out!

**Jean:** What?

**Verity:** You're knocking it over!

**Jean:** *(good naturedly)* Well honestly, Verity, you've taken up nearly the whole floor. Look, you'll have to move it now anyway. We're going to have tea in here *(she stoops to pick up a block)*.

**Verity:** *(fiercely)* Don't touch that!

**Edward:** *(with a warning look to Jean)* We won't touch any of it, Verity. You put it away yourself.

**Verity:** I don't want to put it away. I want to play with it.

**Jean:** You can play with it later.

**Verity:** I don't want later. I want now!

**Jean:** We're going to have tea.

**Verity:** I don't care! Now, now, now! I want my village now!

**Jean:** Stop shouting like that and do as you are told.

**Verity:** *(insolently)* What? What? What did you say? I'm deaf. I can't hear you. I'm deaf. I'm deaf.

**Jean:** *(beginning to lose control)* I said to do as I tell you.

**Edward:** Jean – don't.

**Verity:** *(violently knocking over some of the village)* You tell me! You tell me! Mine! It isn't yours. I'll break it *(rising and kicking the blocks)*. I'm smashing it. You can't have it!

**Edward:** Verity – stop!

In this short extract, there is a clear change in the relationship between the characters, but it is important to chart this change in terms of their mental state. Break this section into three separate units of rehearsal, using Jean's entrance and her stooping to pick up the block as natural divisions. Give each character an objective for each unit, remembering that it must be in the form, 'I want …'.

In the first unit Verity could simply want to play, which could be shown through her commitment to the building blocks. Wide eyes and an almost ritualistic approach to building could highlight this. Edward might want to respect his daughter. His movement could be quite cautious, allowing her the space to play. His delivery should be calm, maintaining eye contact with Verity as he speaks. When Jean enters, the atmosphere needs to change. Jean's objective could be 'I want to keep an ordered house', her frustration at Verity's mess could be shown in her expression. Verity might want to be in control; gesturing with her arms to protect her blocks in an exaggerated manner could suggest this. Despite not talking in this short section, Edward may want to support his wife. Look at the final unit and decide on appropriate objectives for each character.

Work on each of these units separately, playing the objectives to the full. Focus on the intention of each character for that moment of the text. If you don't feel the objective works, modify it to something that does.

The level of emotional detail in a scene can be made more complex by adding an adverb before each line. Wymark frequently does this in an attempt to guide the actor's delivery. Try adding your own adverbs to each sentence. Obviously, this addition is only temporary but it allows you to focus on the different shades of emotion that the characters are experiencing. For example:

> **Verity:** (*defensively*) This is my castle *(she looks at him sideways)*. (*forcefully*) I'm inside it.
>
> **Edward:** (*encouragingly*) Are you?
>
> **Verity:** (*boldly*) Yes. (*privately*) And nobody else can get in.
>
> **Edward:** (*admiringly*) Well, well!
>
> **Verity:** (*magically*) It's all locked up and safe and they can't get in.

Read through the units saying the adverb before speaking the line. This will help to reinforce the delivery. Note that some of the adverbs that we have suggested encourage creative interpretation from the actors. This shouldn't be a bland exercise in which you use a string of synonyms – be inventive. Once you have done this, act out the extract, trying to focus on the objective and the adverbs. Experiment with the extent to which the characters' thoughts are revealed on their faces.

## Emotion memory

In the scenes where you are playing a character younger than yourself, you should try to recall your own experiences as a young child and feed them into your portrayal. Stanislavski wanted his actors to convey an emotional truth by using their emotion memory.

Take a moment on your own to think about your memories of playing by yourself as a child. Try to recall where you were, what you did, how it made you feel. Think of the sights, the sounds and the smells. Who used to intimidate you when you were younger? How did you feel when moments of creative play were interrupted by others? How did you react? Do you have memories of interrupting the play of others? Can you remember why?

You may wish to talk within your group about these experiences or keep the thoughts to yourself. Use these memories in your performance to intensify the portrayal of Verity. You may also find the visual images you created useful in communicating a sense of locale to the audience.

The performance of the other roles will also require you to call upon your own experiences. You will probably have observed how adults respond to children in such a situation; you will need to use your imagination to ask yourself the question 'If I was that character, how would I feel?'. By discussing the situation in greater detail in your group you will be able to generate a more complex understanding of the character.

## Off-the-text exercises

The scene between Verity and Tom in Act 2 is one of the few scenes of optimism in the whole piece. It is a scene of relative calm and the pace of the action is slowed right down to provide the audience with a sense of hope. The idealistic image of planting the window boxes is a powerful symbol, showing Verity working with rather than against another character, although Wymark cleverly uses this episode to provide a moment of pause before accelerating the audience to the inevitable denouement.

---

Each member of your group needs to stand in a space. They need to choose one of the people in the room as their enemy. When the game begins, they keep as far from that person as possible. They now choose a second person to be their friend who will protect them from the enemy. They should make sure that the friend is between them and the enemy at all times. The game runs for two minutes. At the end, someone should shout stop and everyone freezes. At this point, the identity of each enemy and friend is revealed. The fun in this game is that someone's enemy may have chosen them as a friend.

Repeat the exercise but this time explain that the game is going to be limited to ten steps. A member of the group will count from 1 to 10, with the group taking a step (not a leap) every time a number is called. This version of the game is a lot more strategic. Individuals need to plan their moves while anticipating the actions of others. Divide the group into pairs and decide who is going to play Tom and Verity. In this exercise, the Veritys will need to be blindfolded and the 'Toms' are going to take them outside. The Toms will need to lead them to different places using as few words as possible. They must make the Veritys feel safe and while doing so they should introduce them to different smells and textures. The aim of the exercise is to build a rapport between the actors, which might emulate the trust experienced by the two characters.

Now look at the text. Stand two metres from your partner and read through the text. Every time Tom says something which increases Verity's confidence, she should step forward. However, if she is feeling uncomfortable she should step backward. Repeat the exercise, but this time add gestures to see if this provides Verity with any more confidence.

Now run the whole scene independent of these exercises, trying to convey both a sense of location and the relationship between the characters.

---

**Status graphs**

Look at the scene in Act 2 where Verity returns home for Christmas. Draw a graph with status marked 1 to 10 on one axis and time on the other. Decide on an initial status level for Edward and Verity. Look at key lines spoken by the characters that will either raise or lower their status. Plot these points in chronological order on your graph, indicating any changes in the characters' status. How does

This is quite a formal way of structuring your scene and in some ways can appear a little forced. However, it does allow you to identify specific moments of dramatic interest and to focus on how vocal delivery and movement might alter during these status changes.

the arrival of Mark change the status of Edward? How does Jean's entrance alter the dynamic? Remember to look at the stage directions as well. Note their final status level at the end of the scene.

## Physicalising the text

The different locations suggested in the texts will need to be well defined if you are going to be successful in your performance. The pressure of rehearsal may lead to a tendency to be lazy and simply position yourself randomly on stage. However, in order to achieve good marks for your performance, you need to show a strong command of movement through gesture, poise and stillness.

### The swimming pool

Although most of us have memories of walking in swimming pools, it would be useful to actually rehearse this scene in a pool, looking closely at how physicality is affected.

The scene in the swimming pool has the potential to be a passage of text, which demands close attention to movement. While the use of monologue in this scene might lead to physicality becoming secondary, in fact it is the sensation of the swimming pool which should dominate. Wymark's stage directions suggest that the Veritys do 'different swimming strokes with their arms'. However, this scene offers far greater dramatic potential than simply a literal interpretation of this direction. Consider, for instance, the action of the Veritys stepping into the water. Perhaps some could lower themselves from the central platform upstage. How do children walk in water? How does the water feel on their hands? How does it drip through their fingers? What physical image could the actors hold while each monologue is delivered?

### At school

Wymark's frequent blurring of time and location helps the audience to judge Verity's behaviour and society's reaction to it. However, despite this blurring, it is extremely important that the actors are precise in their creation of each scene. The scene at school requires the cast to move quickly from external to internal settings without slowing the pace of the performance.

Look at the image of Jean and the mothers talking in the rain. Consider where you might position them to communicate the intimacy of talking under umbrellas. What aspects of their movement might suggest they are adults? Now look at the image of the classroom. How might this change be indicated physically? Where do the other actors appear from? How are they positioned to suggest that they are children? How would you recreate the image of outside the school?

### Image sculpting

In longer scenes it can be difficult to structure the subtle changes in physicality. For example, the restaurant scene might become dominated by Verity's aggressive dialogue. Instead, try to communicate the essence of this scene through five still images which represent the gradual deterioration of the meal. Be clear about the changes in the characters' reactions as the action unfolds. Once you have decided on these, allocate a line of text for each image. Now try to block the rest of the action around these moments. This should encourage greater physical variety.

## Vocalising the text

In order to score highly in your performance, you will need to demonstrate a very strong command of voice through clarity, pause, pace, pitch, tone inflection and projection. It is important that you show a range in your delivery that appears natural to the character. A forced example of each skill for every character in every scene is inappropriate and will not be rewarded by the examiner.

Look at the beginning of Act 2. This scene highlights the difficulties involved in getting Verity admitted into the children's ward. Sitting on chairs with pencils in hand, read the script from the start of the scene to the point where they agree to admit Verity. Do not pause between lines. Any changes in pace should be created by the delivery of the lines themselves. Now read through it again twice. In between readings, do not talk about which moments were most successful; instead, try different ideas while you are reading and hearing the script.

Discuss among the group where you think the pace naturally increases or slows. Mark these areas on your text. Now explore the use of pause in the scene. Stand up and walk to each doctor who is positioned in a different area of the space. Keeping the same decisions about pace, repeat the scene three times, focusing on natural breaks that can be made in the dialogue. Some are indicated by Wymark's use of stage directions, but don't slavishly rely on these: find an interpretation that works for you. Once the group has found moments for pause, discuss how long these could be. Some might be no more than a natural beat between lines to add emphasis; others might be a long moment of silence, adding to the awkwardness of the situation. During the pauses, consider what non-verbal action might take place.

Varying your vocal tone in this scene is vital. The repetitious structure is there to reflect the characters' frustrations but you need to be careful that the action doesn't become tedious and predictable. All of the characters show different shades of emotion and these need to be represented by your inflection.

In Act 2, Edward writes a letter requesting support for their situation. The formality of this scene is brought to life by the anonymous voices that appear 'out of darkness'. Look at each short monologue in turn. As you rehearse as a group, ask everyone except the person delivering the lines to close their eyes. This focuses the attention on the vocal skill of each actor rather than facial expressions. Discuss the intended impact of each section. Does it vary as the scene progresses? Look at how changes in tone could emphasise this.

**Tip**

Even though the actors in this section can't be seen, exaggerated facial expressions will alter the quality of the words. Experiment with this as you rehearse.

## The Last Resort

### Background

**Playwright**

Chris Owen is a freelance playwright, director and lecturer and workshop leader who specialises in creating challenging, entertaining plays for performance by young people. He has a varied catalogue of plays which cover a wide spectrum of ideas and issues; at the heart of all of them is a theatrical storytelling style that gives performers an opportunity to get to grips with the characters and situations.

Chris Owen describes *The Last Resort* as an 'affectionate and amusing portrait of a day in the life of a bustling seaside town'. It begins in the early morning with the dawn milk float and finishes on the cliffs 24 hours later. The story is populated by a wide variety of different characters. It employs a great deal of comedy, yet it also has a darker side.

### Research

A great way to start thinking about the location of the play is to visit the seaside yourself. You could do this individually or get your whole class to organise a trip. It should stimulate excitement about the project, help you to visualise the setting and help you to understand and empathise with the characters that populate the story. Prepare a series of targets and objectives to take with you, such as:

➤ Where could the action of the play happen?

➤ What could the different characters and groups of characters in the play look like?

➤ What props could be used in the play?

**Web link**

Chris Owen has created a very useful and supportive website about his work: www.chrisowenonline.co.uk.

It would be useful before beginning work on *The Last Resort* to do some research on British seaside towns. There is an excellent poem by Roger McGough called *Cento* (the first line reads: 'Point the telescope and insert coin') about the changing face of modern Britain. It would be worth looking at with your group; think about what it says about the way contemporary seaside towns are changing.

Read the poem through as a group and then spilt your group up and share out the verses. Each choose between six and 12 key words and phrases from your section that are important to the poem. Now create a series of freezes that represent the words, either literally or symbolically. Think about what music you could use to accompany the freezes. For instance, *Chasing Cars* by Snow Patrol might work well with the poignant images in the poem, while *In the Summertime* by Mungo Jerry would create a more humorous counterpoint.

**Web link**

Read Roger McGough's poem at: www.poetrysociety.org.uk/content/aboutus/npd/npd03/centos

**Similar texts**

Read some complementary texts, to gain a sense of how *The Last Resort* builds upon other dramatic works.

Read the opening of *Under Milk Wood* (1953) by Dylan Thomas. *Under Milk Wood* was originally written as a radio play, and was later turned into a stage play and film. The storyteller invites the audience to listen in to the dreams of a fictional Welsh village called Llareggub (the name is 'bugger all' spelt backwards, but it appears in print as Llaregyb, so as not to offend anyone). The villagers' innermost thoughts and dreams are laid bare to us as the town wakes, and we see the villagers go about their daily business.

Read some of the scenes from *Road* (1986) by Jim Cartwright. The play has many similarities to *The Last Resort* in terms of its chronology and location. It moves between various locations on a run-down street in Lancashire – from street corner to living room, from bedroom to kitchen  – under the guidance of Scullery, a drunken resident. It details the deprivation and desperation of the inhabitants' lives, yet also contains a streak of bitter humour.

> If you like the style and content of these two plays, you might like to consider selecting a monologue or duologue from them. See pages 128–148 for more guidance on selecting your monologue or duologue.

Some other plays which you could approach in a similar way to *The Last Resort* are:

➤ *The Yarn* by Rob Brannen (Hodder Arnold H&S 2000) – a series of witty, poignant stories about village life and how a sense of community is important but in danger of being lost.

➤ *Canterbury Tales* by Phil Woods and Michael Bogdanov (Iron Press 1995) – a series of interlocking stories that offer similar casting and theatrical opportunities to *The Last Resort*.

➤ *Beauty and the Beast* by Laurence Boswell (Nick Hern Books 2003) – for a flexible ensemble, tells just one story in a series of short scenes.

➤ *The Company of Wolves* by Angela Carter, collected in *The Curious Room* (Vintage 1997) – originally written as a radio play, it combines narration and characterisation. It tells the story of Red Riding Hood, a young woman growing up and rites of passage.

➤ *Arabian Nights* by Dominic Cooke (Nick Hern Books 1999) – a collection of well known stories about characters such as Sinbad and Ali Baba, told in a fresh and physical manner. A framing device is used of a young woman telling the stories to her husband on their wedding night in order to prevent him from killing her.

*The Entertainer* (1957) is a play by John Osborne, which depicts a failing music-hall performer against the backdrop of the declining music-hall tradition and Britain's post-war decline. The film version (1960) stars Laurence Olivier and was shot in the Lancashire seaside town of Morecambe.

*Twin Town* (1997) is a fast-paced black comedy directed by Kevin Allen, filmed and set in Swansea, south Wales. Notice how it draws comedy and pathos from the setting of a seaside town. Its music soundtrack is an example of how to use music to support action and mood.

## Plot summary

*The Last Resort* depicts life in a seaside town. During the course of a single day we encounter a wide array of different individuals

## Similar films

66 Imagine Dylan Thomas's *Under Milkwood* peppered with Alan Ayckbourn characters and set by the seaside and you have still only conjured up half the delights. 99

Barbara Fisher, *Uxbridge Gazette*.

whose lives, relationships and problems are explored, and in some cases resolved, before the day closes.

The action begins in the early morning; we meet Vic, the milkman, who dreams of being a cowboy hero in a film of his own, and Nelly who collects flotsam and jetsam from the beach with Mr Minesweep who uses a metal detector. Visiting the town are two families who are coming to enjoy a day at the beach – the brash Killjoys and the idealistic Brights – and a group of old ladies who are commemorating the death of their husbands in the same town, some years before. We are also introduced to a young pregnant girl who has arranged to meet her boyfriend at the place where they first met.

A Chorus is used to link the disparate episodes together and comment on the action of the play. The donkeys that give rides on the beach and the scavenging seagulls are used to create witty juxtapositions with the main action, and provide a commentary on the events. There are also a variety of teenagers, surfers and boy racers who punctuate the story. The play climaxes at the local night club where the town's young people meet, and where things don't quite go according to plan.

### Why choose The Last Resort?

**Flexible casting**

While *The Last Resort* was originally performed by a cast of 12 actors, the writing and structure of the play allows for a minimum of four actors. A cast-size of eight would allow some of the actors to multi-role. The style of the play also allows for cross-gender casting. In fact, casting boys as girls and vice versa could add to the comic nature of characterisation, particularly in the scenes in which stereotypes are explored.

**A range of acting styles**

The script gives you many opportunities to show the examiner the full range of your acting skills, from character-based performances through to exaggerated caricature, and physical and movement-based work.

The wide variety of characters in *The Last Resort* allows you to play both serious and comic roles, from the caricature portrayals of the Killjoy and Bright families to the more complex portraits of characters such as Jackie. There are old and young characters, as well as representations of animals such as donkeys and seagulls. The play also gives you the opportunity to take on the role of a neutral storyteller and narrator or an ensemble member, using your voice to create a soundtrack or your body to create elements of the set. There are further opportunities to create physical performances; for instance, in the new-age Punch and Judy show, you could play both the puppets and the puppeteers.

**Units of action**

The play could easily be broken down into units of action and contains various narrative strands running through it. You could therefore select the scenes and stories you want to perform so as to meet the time constraints of the exam, and still give a varied and coherent performance.

The text of the play does not necessarily require a set and props; the vivid world drawn by the text itself demands that the actors engage the imagination of the audience and draw them into the story. This type of text is liberating for an actor but also challenging, as there is little to hide behind. It lends itself to mixed styles of performance and therefore it would allow you to explore the work of some of the practitioners you have studied – you could look at the character journeys in Stanislavski's work, for instance, or the notion of demonstrating characters in Brecht's work.

Most importantly, this type of text will challenge you to use the primary and secondary tools of acting, so giving you the opportunity to score highly within the framework of the AS exam, as either a performer or designer.

**Challenges**

Think about how you use your **voice** to tell the story, to create characters and show their emotions. If you are playing a variety of roles and different types of characters, such as this play demands, you will have to use your voice to clearly denote changes in character as well as changes in emotional states. Accent, pitch, volume, intonation, inflection and pace will all play a part in how you use your voice to create characters.

**Facial expressions** are a key component of communicating who you are, what you are like and how you are feeling. *The Last Resort* gives you opportunities to use a wide range of facial expressions, for instance to show youth and age, class and emotion, and representations of animals.

Physical control of your **body** and an understanding of stance, gesture, speed and type of movement are essential in creating an effective performance. Remember that you are never physically neutral while you are performing. Even if you are telling the story as a narrator, your body position is as important as when you are representing a seagull.

The director/actor/practitioner Steven Berkoff does not like to allow chairs into the rehearsal **space**. This means that the actors are not allowed to relax but must constantly be aware of their bodies as tools, to create and communicate the roles they are playing. It forces them to be creative in developing their characters, rather than becoming reliant on props.

**Primary tools**

These primary acting tools correspond well with the criteria that you will be judged against by the examiner in this unit. They will be looking at your: vocal skills; movement skills; characterisation; ability to communicate with other performers and the audience.

Your **costume** helps to create a character and a sense of location and time period. It not only communicates directly to the audience, in terms of details of shape, colour and texture, but also, when used during the rehearsal process, can help you to develop a character, as you can see in some of the later exercises.

**Secondary tools**

For more on costume and props, see pages 178–180.

**Props** not only support the action of the play in a functional way, but can also symbolically represent themes within the play.

## Approaching the play

*The Last Resort* has a straightforward structure built upon a series of chronological episodes. We're introduced to a large number of characters, some of whom reappear later, while others only appear

**Unit breakdown**

once in the play. It is therefore important to gain a thorough overview of the play as a whole; you can achieve this by doing a scene-by-scene or unit breakdown. This will also give you a good working knowledge of all the characters – when they appear and how they relate to one another – and will allow you to make selections from the play, so as to ensure your piece falls within the 60-minute time restraint stipulated by the examination board.

Although the play takes the form of continuous action and is not written in scenes, there are clear units when the action changes between characters and groups of characters. Identify these units. Your scene or unit breakdown might look like this:

1. Chorus introduce us to Ferrytown

2. Milkman mugging

3. DJ and the town wake up

4. Nelly and Mr Minesweep

5. DJ and weather

6. Killjoy family on motorway

7. Bright family in lay-by

8. Chorus again

9. Donkeys

**Group size**

While the play-text was originally written for a cast of 12, your performance group needs to be smaller than this, to meet the exam criteria. Once you have established how big your group is and how many characters you are going to feature, go through the play and identify the narrative strands that you want to feature in your production and the characters you want to include.

**Performance space**

Make sure you are aware of the dimensions of the space that you will be performing in and where the audience will be sitting. This will significantly affect the way you present the piece. Consider exploring one of the following performance spaces:

➢ End-on stage

➢ Theatre in the round

➢ Thrust stage

➢ Promenade performance

➢ Traverse stage.

> If you are uncertain about any of these terms refer to pages 43–45.

## Rehearsals

**Rehearsal phases**

Split your rehearsal sessions into **three** distinct phases:

1. **Early exploration.** Have some general introductory sessions, early in the rehearsal process, in which you explore the style of the play. Think about elements of staging, props and costumes and experiment with voices, bodies and the space. You should also

make your final decisions about casting during this period.

**2. Tackling the units.** Think about the Chorus, the characters and their dialogue, and help each other understand the intent of each scene/unit. Detail blocking and movement.

**3. Polish and performance.** This is when you glue the units together into a coherent piece and gain a firm understanding of their relationship to one another. It is the time to make sure you have a firm grasp of your characters and the story, and that the design elements of the performance are secure.

Always set a clear target and objective for each rehearsal at the beginning of the session. Even if your teacher is taking some, or all, of the responsibility for the direction of rehearsals, it is still important to discuss what you want to have achieved by the end of each session. This helps to keep all group members focused on the task, moving collaboratively towards achieving something.

The best way to begin exploring a script like *The Last Resort* is through practical work. If you start rehearsals by working practically, you will set the tone for all subsequent rehearsals. You need to develop a vocabulary of movement ideas during your early workshop sessions and be willing to try out new ideas. Successful rehearsals can only be achieved if the whole group are really focused.

In the following pages we look at various practical approaches you can take to exploring *The Last Resort* during rehearsals.

## Image-making

The Chorus are central to the story line and to the establishment of mood. While the Chorus' narration could be delivered by a solo narrator, it would be more theatrically exciting if delivered by a number of actors. This would give you the opportunity to vary your vocal delivery by sharing sentences and joining voices; you could also create physical images as a group, supporting the words you are communicating through visual clues.

---

Look at the Chorus' speech which introduces the first entry of Dawson's Donkeys, from 'Now, back to Ferryton prom ...' to 'And by the pier, we pause to observe the arrival of Ferryton's must illustrious attractions ...'

Read through the speech and choose between five and ten images that are spaced out throughout the text and which jump out at you in terms of their physical imagery.

Create these images as abstract physical freezes or as literal interpretations – whichever you feel is more appropriate. Make sure that each freeze is significantly different from the one before (it could be on a different level or perhaps connecting with someone in the group). Now, give each image a title; this could be the single word or phrase the image represents. Say the title, as a group or individually, and hold the image.

**Practical work**

The theatre company Complicite spend a large proportion of their early rehearsal time playing, which allows actors to get used to one another, to experiment with props and to explore the story of the play freely, without being restricted by a script. For further information about Complicite see page 42.

**Chorus**

The images in this speech have real movement and sound quality: create a movement and sound to connect to the next image. For instance, after you have spoken the title 'Joggers and dog walkers' and created this image, use the movement and sound of joggers and dog walkers to move to the next image.

Introduce some music to your freezes as an underscore to assist the movement between images and establish a mood. For instance, you might like to choose some summer music, such as Will Smith's *Summertime*. Choose one particular image in your image-sequence and turn it from a frozen image into a moving one. Keep it short so that it doesn't put the rest of the image-sequence out of balance. After you have said the title of the image, take a few seconds to create a movement and sound which represents that image, and then move on. For instance, think about which image and sound you would use for 'Postcards on whirling carousels' or 'Candyfloss machine whirls'. You must maintain the pace of the speech for the humour and impact of the words to work.

Run through all the images you have developed, including the music, movement, sound and you have developed. Now return to the full text of the Chorus' speech. Share the words out among your group, so you all have some lines. Read the speech; when it comes to the titles and images you have worked on, use them to give physicality to the whole speech. Making selections from the speech and developing them in this way means that you don't overcrowd the speech with images and ideas, while still allowing physical work to complement the words at key moments.

If you have enjoyed working in a visual- and image-based style then you may want to continue this approach in your work on monologues and duologues. An excellent narrative-based piece, which allows you to be both a narrator and a character, and lends itself to physical imagery is *Adult Child/Dead Child* by Claire Dowie.

## Music

Recorded and live music can be used in a number of ways in theatre and are an immensely important part of the way we shape plays, tell stories, create moods and elicit audience responses. We should not underestimate the role that film, pop videos and TV have had in influencing the way we use music, sound and song in contemporary theatre or how theatre has embraced the notion of soundtracks.

Music and movement are an integral part of *The Last Resort*. The character DJ Bobby Brewster and West Coast Radio punctuate the story throughout the day, and the playwright, Chris Owen, gives a detailed and helpful list of possible songs that could be used throughout in a production. Your choices should reflect your own musical tastes, the contemporary setting of the play and what is topical at the time of your performance.

Music in *The Last Resort* is used in **four** distinct ways. You will need to consider these before making any musical choices:

**1. Link between scenes**. The key to successful storytelling in *The Last Resort* is pace; because there are many short episodes and scenes, the pace could easily be lost by the changes in location, time and characters. The use of music between scenes has a number of effects:

> It helps to maintain **continuity** of the action, so that there is no opportunity for the audience to switch off between scenes

> It maintains the **pace** of the piece – there is always something going on

> The lyrics of songs provide **commentary** on the action (for instance, before the arrival of the Killjoy family stuck in a traffic jam on their way to the beach we hear *Road to Nowhere* by Talking Heads).

**2. Underscoring.** Underscoring is an excellent way to give the audience further information about location, time, character and tone. You could use underscoring in various different places:

> **The Chorus' speeches.** This will give the speeches extra depth and richness and keep the audience tuned in to the location and setting. For instance, *Albatross* by Fleetwood Mac during the Chorus' speech, before the entry of the Seagulls, will evoke a real sense of heat and lethargy in the middle of a hot summer's day.

> **Dialogues.** This will quickly give the audience a sense of character and location without having to create a completely different set.

> **The bouncers' speeches** at the end of the play. Use of disco/club music would give the audience a clue as to location and character.

> **Monologues.** For instance, you could use the opening sequence of *Dry Your Eyes Mate* by the Streets to introduce and underscore Jackie's final monologue. This would bring an added emotional depth to her words and help the audience emphathise with her.

**3. Motifs**. Music can be used as a motif to introduce and familiarise the audience with certain groups of characters. It could be used to build anticipation for who is about to appear and create familiarity with the mood and content of a scene. For instance, in order to increase the anticipation of the arrival of the Old Ladies, who appear in a number of scenes, and to provide comment, Chris Owen suggests using *Young at Heart* by the Bluebells or *Justified and Ancient* by KLF. There are many other character groups in *The Last Resort* who would benefit from such a motif.

**4. To drive the action.** There are a number of movement and action sequences in the play that should be choreographed to music, to drive and support the action. Chris Owen gives an excellent example of this when he introduces the surfer characters. In order to create a sense of the fun and energy of these characters and to signal that they are surfers, he suggests using the surf song classic, *Wipe Out* by the Surfaris, while the three surfers create a surfing routine in shopping trolleys pushed around by other members of the cast. You might also like to use music to drive the action of the Boy Racers.

Do not underestimate your own musical expertise and the way in which it can be used to communicate with and engage an audience.

## Monologues

There are a number of monologues which communicate directly to the audience in *The Last Resort*.

One of the central characters in the plot is Jackie who has run away from home to meet her boyfriend at Ferryton but he has yet to turn up. Her monologues punctuate the story and end with an aborted suicide attempt. If you are taking on the role of Jackie, or any of the other monologues in the play, try the following exercises to prepare your role.

Sit in front of the rest of your group in the hot seat or get the group to sit in a circle around you. Read or act your chosen speech to them. Now invite your group to ask you questions about your character. You must answer in role and make up the information that you give back to them. For instance, if you are playing Jackie, you might be asked how you and your boyfriend met, what he was like, what they did together, why she thinks he is coming to meet her again. This exercise is a great way of fleshing out your character and giving them a sense of truth and authenticity.

In role as your character, do some creative writing to get yourself thinking as if you were them. For example, Jackie could write a letter home to her mother or father explaining why she has run away and what she hopes to do in Ferryton.

Bring in a piece of music or a song which you think could be the favourite track of your character. Share it with the rest of your group and explain in role why you have chosen it and why it means something to you. This piece of music could then be used in the production as the character's motif before they appear, or as an underscore.

**Context** It can be difficult to deliver a monologue because you have no other actor to interact with on stage. It sometimes helps to imagine you are speaking to a particular person, in order to put the words in a wider context.

Look at Jackie's first monologue. Try the following performance approaches:

➢ Imagine you are being interviewed by the police. You are sat in a room with the officers facing you (this will help you to think about the emotion of the words)

> You will need to tackle a monologue or duologue during your course. Understanding how they work in *The Last Resort* will contribute to your understanding of the course as a whole.

➤ Imagine you are on the telephone to your best friend (you will need to make sure the words work in themselves)

➤ Imagine you are telling the story to a group of young children and you have to act out the actions of the words (this will help you to examine the physicality of the words).

## Character development

*The Last Resort* is not written as a naturalistic piece of theatre and within the piece there are groups of characters which represent particular character types. They range from truthful, poignant portraits, such as Jackie, through to the eccentric and quirky Old Ladies. However, Chris Owen is keen that your portrayal of such character types does not become simply a caricature; your interpretation should not be judgmental, instead you should encourage the audience to empathise with the characters.

There are a number of character groups in *The Last Resort*:

➤ The Brew Up Posse on the radio

➤ The Killjoy family

➤ The Bright family

➤ The Old Ladies

➤ The Surfers

➤ The Lads

➤ The Ladettes.

It is likely that you will have to play a number of roles in your production, as well as contribute to the Chorus and the animals. Multi-roleing is an excellent way of showing a range of acting skills and techniques. However, it must be done with great clarity if the audience are to be able to distinguish between different characters.

Consider the differences between the Brights and the Killjoys, who are always at loggerheads with one another. In many ways, the Brights seem like a family straight out of a *Famous Five* novel, while the Killjoys are like a dysfunctional family from *EastEnders*.

Create a family picture of the Brights on holiday for their family album. Think about how they relate to each other, how they feel about each other and the holiday they are on. How could you show the physically of the scene? Now create a similar family picture of the Killjoys on holiday.

Improvise the Bright family having a picnic on the beach or going to the funfair. Use your voice, facial expressions, gestures and interaction to show how they feel. Now improvise the same situations with the Killjoy family. Think about how you could show the differences between the two families.

**Further study**

If you have enjoyed the monologues in *The Last Resort*, particularly those of Jackie and the bouncer Psycho, look at the work of John Godber (*Bouncers*, 1977) and Jane Thornton (*Shakers*, 1985, cowritten with John Godber), which also contain some excellent monologues in a similar style.

**Character groups**

**Further study**

If you have enjoyed the character interaction in *The Last Resort*, you may wish to look at some other plays in this style for the monologues and duologues section of the exam. Explore plays by Alan Ayckbourn and Mike Leigh, and *Stags and Hens* (1978) by Willy Russell which is set in the toilets of a club during the course of a night when a stag and hen night are happening concurrently.

## Costume

While the primary acting tools of voice, face, body and space are necessary to differentiate between the characters that you are playing, you might also like to support your performance by using the secondary tool of costume design.

For the Chorus, you might choose to wear a basic group costume. However, if you are playing multiple roles, you should generally not remain in one costume throughout the performance, as the audience may become confused about who you are and struggle to follow the narrative.

Bearing all this in mind, your costume selection should allow for a basic outfit to which additional costumes can be added to clearly indicate characters. Each costume becomes an **emblem** to describe the individual character and it needs to be chosen carefully. It doesn't have to be too complex; the emblematic costume might just be one article of clothing – a shirt, jacket or hat – that is added to the basic costume.

Carefully consider the setting of the play, when choosing costume. Think about:

➤ **When** the play is set (during the summer, in the present)

➤ **Where** the play is set (the seaside)

➤ **Who** the characters are (surfers, old ladies, the perfect family, and so on).

---

If you have chosen a costume design skill, there are specific demands from the exam board that must be fulfilled. You must create: a portfolio of research and sketches showing the development of ideas; a final design for all the characters in the production (a minimum of three); a costume plot with a list of costumes/accessories worn by the actors and an indication of when they change; a justification for the final design decisions; a demonstration of the costumes within the performance. You must also *supervise* the construction, buying, dyeing, altering, hiring and/or finding of any of the designed costumes; however, you only need to *carry out* one of these tasks yourself.

---

Collect together any t-shirts, jackets, waistcoats, coats and hats that you are able to find at home, school or from charity shops, which you think could represent the characters in the play. Place them around your space. Write the groups of characters in the play on pieces of paper and place them in a container in the centre of the room. On some other pieces of paper write some activities that occur in the play, such as sunbathing, waiting in a traffic jam, doing a voiceover on the radio, dancing at the disco, surfing and so on. Place these in a separate container. Get individuals or pairs to pick out one piece of paper from each container. Without telling the rest of the group what is written on their pieces of paper, they must choose an item of clothing and physicalise the action, in role as their particular character type, to the rest of the group.

On the instruction 'change' they should select two new pieces of paper, take off the item of clothing and choose a new one to physicalise the new action, in role as the new character.

Clearly represent characters through action and costume but also enjoy the humour of quick changes, showing the mechanisms of theatrical representation. The task could be made even more dynamic by introducing music (if you have already chosen motif music for your groups of characters, use this as a cue to change), so making it a game of musical costume change.

## Staging and props

Your starting point when considering your staging and the props you are going to use must be the demands of the playtext and the group of actors you are working with. Think about the following questions:

➤ What is my **performance space** like and where will the audience be sitting?

➤ What have I got at my disposal to make the **set**?

➤ How much **time** do I have?

These basic logistical questions must run in tandem with the needs of the text and the actors working on the text. If the actors are working in a simple, character-driven, story-telling style, then you need to think about what must be provided for them. Think about the following questions:

➤ Where are the **locations** demanded by the text?

➤ What is the **action** of the play?

➤ What elements of **set** are specified by the text?

Once you have analysed the functional requirements of the text, you can begin to make artistic decisions about how you are going to interpret these demands. You may decide that you would like a performance space which is largely neutral, so that it can become many places quickly and aid the pace of the piece. You could then identify key pieces of staging to add to the set; they could be used in sophisticated and imaginative ways, representing different things in various scenes.

There is a witty episode in the middle of *The Last Resort* in which you are required to create a new-age Punch and Judy show on stage. The puppeteers are the characters Roberta and Shirley. The challenge here is to create a puppet show which links with the rest of your design concept for the play. You could take two approaches, among many others, to designing the Punch and Judy show, as outlined below:

**Approach 1.** You could decide to have fun with this part of the play and use hand puppets and voice them as in a traditional Punch and Judy show. This would require a Punch and Judy puppet theatre; however, by designing such a detailed item of staging you would have to serve the rest of the play in a similar fashion. Suddenly you are faced with creating a radio studio, a helicopter, a motorway, a beach, a promenade, a funfair, a disco, a cliff top and more! While you could attempt to create such a sophisticated set, you might not have the space, resources and time to do so.

**Approach 2.** Alternatively, you could choose to create a neutral space in which to show a variety of locations and the passing of time. By keeping the space uncluttered and working in a simple and minimalist staging style, you allow the words, characters and music to conjure the mood and atmosphere of the episodes. By

If you have chosen a set-design skill, there are specific demands from the exam board that must be fulfilled. You must create: a portfolio of research and sketches showing the development of your ideas; a 1:25 scale model of the final design; a 1:25 scale ground plan and scale drawing of any designed props; a justification for your final design decisions; the design as realised in the performance. You must also take a lead role in the supervision, construction, painting, hiring and/or finding of any of the scenic elements.

**Puppets**

**Tip**

It is a good idea to choose key elements of your staging and props early on in the rehearsal process. If you are working with these from the beginning then they quickly become an integral part of the physical representation of the story.

The original production of *The Last Resort* used a large, uncluttered performance area that was raised at the back to represent the prom and pier.

solving these staging problems using only the resources of the actor – voice, body and use of space – you will not only meet the demands of the different episodes, but it will also help you to maximise your scoring potential.

Introduce deck chairs and windbreaks as key pieces of staging. These could be used not only to decorate the edges of the set but also to create and support the locations within the production, such as the cars, the beach and the pier. They could also be used to create the puppet show, allowing the actors themselves to become the puppets.

Try to find some windbreaks and experiment with using them on stage. Use two or three to create a barrier representing a puppet theatre. The actors could hide behind them and then pop up when delivering their lines. They could speak their lines themselves or mouth them to Roberta and Shirley's voices. This presentation of the puppets will give the actors an opportunity to find humour in humanising the wooden toys and display their physical skills. This simple design decision ensures that the props become integral to the telling of the story and function as symbols of the seaside.

## Dramatising animals

There are two inventive sections in *The Last Resort* which require you to humanise groups of animals. **Dawson's Donkeys** provide a refreshing and funny view of the activities on the beach, as seen through the eyes of some old, experienced donkeys who have been giving rides to children for as long as they can remember. They also link other elements of the story and appear twice. The **seagulls** only appear once; they provide a segue between two character-driven elements of the story and an opportunity for some vocal and physical caricatures of aggressive and yob-like behaviour.

They should therefore be represented as animals, but with some human facets, such as opinions and attitudes about what is happening around them and the ability to give voice to these views. Your challenge here is to physically represent animals in a recognisable way using the primary acting tools of voice, face, movement and space. You may also want to support your representation though the use of a simple costume or prop.

Before tackling the actual scene try the following exercises to get you thinking about how best to represent the donkeys and seagulls. They will give you a vocabulary of ideas and theatre forms that you can dip into.

Imagine that you are all guests at a rather pompous and decadent dinner party. Choose a student to be the host of the party. Imagine you are all dressed in rather formal clothes and are gathered around a dining table heaped with food. There is champagne to be opened and you all have glasses ready to be filled. Create an exaggerated character. Decide on an animal that best represents your character. If your character is gossipy and nasty to others behind their backs you may wish to represent them with a hen or if they are loud and boisterous, perhaps a hyena. Be as imaginative as you can.

Create loud and pompous small talk between the guests, discussing the weather, the cars you drive and gossip about other guests. You could even make the exercise more difficult by not using any words at all, but just making the sort of sounds that your characters would use. Gradually, over a period of two to three minutes your characters should slowly transform into your chosen animals. The transformation should be complete in terms of physical representation and noises (if you choose to be a cat you should go on all fours and make appropriate movements and noises). Interact with the other transformed animals and then slowly return to your human state, as if nothing had happened.

In *The Last Resort*, both the animal scenes contain groups of animals, rather than individual ones; it would therefore be useful to explore the idea of animal groups.

Think about which group of animals would best represent a crowd of football supporters. Choose a series of chants directed at rival supporters, players or even the referee. Slowly transform over a period of two to three minutes into your chosen animal group and then slowly change back again. Consider the difficulty of this exercise physically, vocally and spatially as an actor. What does your choice of animals tell you about the caricatured football supporters? Think about the aggressive and greedy nature of the seagulls in *The Last Resort* and how you could apply the ideas you have explored here in that scene.

The donkeys act as sardonic commentators on the action, therefore movement may not be the most important aspect of their characterisation. You may want to concentrate more on their voices and faces.

**Dawson's Donkeys**

Think about some simple props to help you develop a caricature of a donkey. Chris Owen suggests in his production notes that the actors playing the donkeys could simply turn some chairs round, so that the chairs become the donkey's bodies and the actors become the donkey's necks and heads, thereby emphasising upper-body and vocal skills. This idea might be even more effective if you were to use deck chairs to construct the donkeys.

**Further study**

An interesting theatre company based in Scotland and working primarily for a children's audience is Wee Stories. They have developed a unique way of working on texts, focusing on the importance of using key props. You can find more information about Wee Stories at: www.weestoriestheatre.org

**Seagulls**

**Further study**

If you have enjoyed using the metaphor of animals to make comments on human behaviour you may want to develop this further in the monologue or duologue element of the unit. Here are some suitable plays to look at: *Dog* (1993) by Steven Berkoff is a funny monologue which requires the actor to play both the thuggish owner of a ferocious dog and the dog itself; *Rhinoceros* (1959) by Eugène Ionesco follows the inhabitants of a small, provincial French town as they turn into rhinoceroses; *The Cagebirds* (1971) by David Campton is a story about a group of birds who are locked in a room until a wild bird arrives to show them the way to freedom; *Insect Play* (1922) by Karel and Joseph Capek concerns a tramp who finds himself among a world of insects.

If you have chosen a lighting design skill, there are specific demands from the exam board that must be fulfilled. You must create: a portfolio of research and sketches showing the development of ideas; the final lighting design with grid plan and lantern schedule that shows the use of at least two different kinds of lantern and uses a minimum of 16 lanterns; a lighting plot or cue sheet showing at least six different lighting states; a justification for the final lighting design; a demonstration of the lighting plot within the context of the performance. You must also supervise the rigging, focusing and operating of the design; you only need to carry out one of these tasks yourself.

Look at the seagull scene and note how aggressive their language is and how short the sentences are, forcing you to keep the interaction fast and to fill the words with a great deal of action and movement. Draw upon the work you have done on football supporters and aggressive shoppers, and bring these vocal and physical qualities to the scene.

Think about some simple costumes to develop a seagull caricature. Find some Doc Marten boots and braces. Read through the dialogue, allowing your costume to dictate your movements: the boots should make you move in a particular way and by hooking your thumbs into your braces you could mimic wings. The image of boots and braces also suggests an archetypal yob or skinhead – does this fit with the image of the seagulls?

## Lighting

The beauty of a text such as *The Last Resort* is that the power of the play lies in its action and characters, and is not reliant on any additional staging elements. It could easily be performed in a room or studio under normal lighting. However, if you do have access to theatre lighting, then the play gives you plenty of potential to use lighting in imaginative and interesting ways.

As with set and costumes, the lighting should support the action and clarify details such as location and time. Your primary concern when designing lighting for a piece such is this is to create one good general state which lights evenly and well. The majority of the scenes will be seen in this light. It should represent the neutrality of the story and allow the actors to create mood through their words and action.

However, when looking at how you can enhance scenes with lighting, think about the following questions:

➢ Where is the scene **located** – on the beach, in a night club?

➢ What **time** of day is it – morning, midday, night?

➢ Is a particular **mood** being created, such as the loneliness and isolation of Jackie displayed in her monologues.

➢ Are there any **effects** within the scene that need supporting by lighting? – for instance, the boy racers on the prom or the girls and boys at the disco.

By the use of a spotlight, the volume of light, the colour gel chosen and the angle used, a whole array of subtleties of meaning can be created.

Set up three single spot lights, each with a different colour gel: white, red and blue. The white gel will represent day, the red will represent stylised locations and the blue will represent night or an indoor location. Now, improvise with your group a number of different scenes, such as the Killjoys in their car, one of Jackie's monologues, Psycho the bouncer's monologue, the boy racers or the romantic liaison at the end of the play.

Think about which lighting works and enhances an event or mood and which lighting is too intrusive.

## Exam criteria

Remember that the examiner will be looking for some specific areas of your performance.

**Physicalising the text**

➤ As a character actor, you need to clearly depict the range of characters you play with appropriate movement and **mannerisms**

➤ As a Chorus member, you need to communicate the story and the mood clearly with **gesture** and body language

➤ As a member of the ensemble, you need to use your **body** and the bodies of the rest of the company and space to support the movement sequences.

**Vocalising the text**

➤ As a character actor, you need to depict the range of characters you play using an appropriate, clear and sustained **accent** or characterisation

➤ As a Chorus member, you need to communicate the story and the mood clearly, exhibiting a wide range of **vocal qualities** (for instance, lyrical, harsh, staccato, flexible, mannered and so on)

➤ As a member of the ensemble, you will need to use your voice and the voices of the rest of the company to support the location, staging and mood of the play through the creation of soundscapes, soundtracks and sound effects.

**Communication**

You must be clear about the intent of your piece and your characters and their journeys, and be able to communicate this to the audience. This will be visible in your interpretation, and conveyed through your performance space, staging, costumes, lighting and props as well as your actual performance.

If you have enjoyed the AS Drama and Theatre Studies course, there will be much to interest and challenge you at A2 level. You will be required to tackle devising and directing, and apply the analytical and performance skills developed throughout your AS course to playtexts from different periods. Rhinegold's *Edexcel A2 Drama Study Guide* (due 2009) will provide you with help in all aspects of your A2 course.